GREAT CAMPAIGNS

The Shiloh Campaign

Grant at the height of his career.

GREAT CAMPAIGNS

THE SHILOH CAMPAIGN

March - April 1862

David G. Martin

DA CAPO PRESS
A MEMBER OF THE PERSEUS BOOKS GROUP

Cataloging-in-Publication data for this book is available from the Library of Congress.

ISBN 0-306-81259-2

First Da Capo Press edition 2003
Maps by Kevin Wilkins

Published by Da Capo Press
A Member of the Perseus Books Group
http://www.dacapopress.com

Da Capo Press books are available at special discounts for bulk purchases in the U.S. by corporations, institutions, and other organizations. For more information, please contact the Special Markets Department at the Perseus Books Group, 11 Cambridge Center, Cambridge, MA 02142, or call (800) 255-1514 or (617) 252-5298, or e-mail j.mccrary@perseusbooks.com.

1 2 3 4 5 6 7 8 9—07 06 05 04 03

Contents

Sidebars

Maps

Preface to the Series

*J*onathan Swift termed war "that mad game the world so loves to play." He had a point. Universally condemned, it has nevertheless been almost as universally practiced. For good or ill, war has played a significant role in the shaping of history. Indeed, there is hardly a human institution which has not in some fashion been influenced and molded by war, even as it helped shape and mold war in turn. Yet the study of war had been as remarkably neglected as its practice commonplace. With a few outstanding exceptions, the history of wars and of military operations has until quite recently been largely the province of the inspired patriot or the regimental polemist. Only in our times have serious, detailed and objective accounts come to be considered the norm in the treatment of military history and related matters.

Yet there still remains a gap in the literature, for there are two types of military history. One type is written from a very serious, highly technical, professional perspective and presupposes that the reader is deeply familiar with the background, technology and general situation. The other is perhaps less dry, but merely lightly reviews the events with the intention of informing and entertaining the layperson. The qualitative gap between the last two is vast. Moreover, there are professionals in both the military and academia whose credentials are limited to particular moments in the long, sad history of war, and there are interested readers who have more than a passing understanding of the field; and then there is the concerned citizen, interested in understanding the military phenomena in an age of unusual violence and unprecedented armaments. It is to bridge the gap between the two types of military history, and to reach the professional and the serious amateur and the concerned citizen alike, that this series, **GREAT CAMPAIGNS** is thus not merely an account of a particular military operation, but is a unique reference to the theory and practice of war in the period in question.

The **GREAT CAMPAIGNS** series is a distinctive contribution to the study of war and of military history, which will remain of value for many years to come.

Introduction

The battle of Shiloh showed all of America how bloody and serious the Civil War really was. When the Southern states first left the Union, patriotic volunteers and militiamen on both sides flocked to the colors amidst much loud music and many long-winded speeches. Some of these citizen soldiers clashed at Bull Run in Virginia in July of 1861, but this was only a preliminary bout. That fall huge armies were raised on both sides in preparation for the main event, a fight that would continue without time limit until one side or the other collapsed from exhaustion.

In the war's western theater both sides marshalled their troops on the borders of Kentucky, a no man's land that at first tried to maintain neutrality. In this war of brother against brother, neutrality was impossible, and the Blue Grass State was soon occupied by the two opposing armies. Rebel strategy was clear: to defend the South's borders against the invading Yankee hordes. That is why most Southerners enlisted, to defend their states and their homes and their way of life. Northern strategy was also clear: to invade the South and force the rebellious states back into the Union. The war at first was not fought over slavery, but was a struggle over the limits of states' rights and the powers of the government in Washington. The Southerners, to be certain, were fighting to defend slavery as part of their way of life, but it was not until later in the war that Lincoln turned the conflict into a crusade against slavery.

The soldiers on both sides were young mostly, under 20, single, and valiant, the cream of their societies. In the spring of

1862 they were still becoming acclimated to the routines of army life and constant drill, and their enthusiasm was high. Their generals were optimistic, even though none of them, not even the veterans of the Mexican War, had ever led bodies of troops as large as those involved in the Shiloh campaign. Indeed, the battle of Shiloh would be the largest battle of the war—and all American history—up to that time.

As the Northern armies began their campaign in the spring of 1862, the Confederates realized that they had a hard task ahead of them, to defend a line 300 miles long from the Mississippi to the Appalachians. They simply did not have the manpower or the mobility to defend such a long line against superior Union forces. Soon the Confederacy's defensive perimeter was dented and then broken, and Southern troops were forced to abandon Kentucky and the industrial areas of central Tennessee. In a desperate attempt to regain what had been lost, Confederate commander Albert S. Johnston gathered all the forces he could to stop the Northern invaders. New units were raised, church bells were melted down to make cannon, and the defenses from Missouri to Florida were stripped of guns and men to reinforce Johnston's army.

At Shiloh Johnston made a bold gamble, trying to overwhelm Grant's Union *Army of the Tennessee* in one of the most successful surprise attacks of the war. The closely fought battle was long and intense, and made a deep and lasting impression on the inexperienced men who fought it on both sides. The war was definitely for real. Death had no regard for the soldiers' convictions or cause. When the battle was over, its long casualty lists impressed both North and South that the war was indeed a bloody and serious affair that would not be decided quickly.

CHAPTER I

The War in the West Begins

At dawn on 6 April 1862, Confederate troops under Gen. Albert Sidney Johnston came pouring out of the woods near Pittsburg Landing, Tennessee, to assault the sleepy camps of Maj. Gen. Ulysses S. Grant's Union *Army of the Tennessee* in one of the greatest surprise attacks in all of military history. In the previous months, Grant had maneuvered Johnston out of Tennessee, severely damaging the Confederate cause and Johnston's reputation. The Confederate commander was determined to redeem both by making a bold strike against his nemesis before Grant could be reinforced by additional forces under Maj. Gen. Don Carlos Buell. For two days, over 100,000 Northern and Southern soldiers attacked and counterattacked in what was the greatest and most fiercely fought battle in the Western Hemisphere up to that time. When the smoke cleared, Johnston's gamble had failed and over 24,000 men, one in four of those who fought, lay casualty. Buell's army had arrived in the proverbial nick of time to save Grant, and Johnston himself lay dead. As the Confederate army limped back into Mississippi, Grant reorganized his forces and prepared to continue his drive into the heartland of the Confederacy. From Shiloh, Grant would march on the next year to victory at Vicksburg and Chattanooga, and then to even greater successes.

The Civil War was won and lost in the western theater; in the East, the war in Virginia was a stalemate for four years as Robert E. Lee and his generals parried and turned back successive Union blows but could not deliver a knockout punch for the Confederacy. Meanwhile, the outcome of the war was being

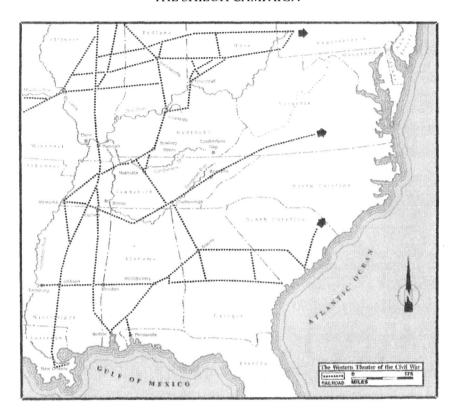

decided in the South's heartland, where the Confederacy lacked enough troops and good generals to defend her lengthy borders against superior Union strength. The Shiloh campaign was the opening and perhaps most critical stage of the Union conquest of the South's interior. At Shiloh the North confirmed its conquest of Tennessee, and from Shiloh began the road to Vicksburg and the strangulation of the Confederacy.

The Early Days

The key to winning the war in the West was control of the critical border states of Missouri, Kentucky, and Tennessee. These states, which were divided in sentiments, were the first line of defense for both the North and the South. Here were located the large and wealthy cities of St. Louis, Louisville, Nashville, and Memphis, with their potential for providing

U.S. Grant as a Brigadier General in 1861, before he began his rise to fame at Fort Donelson and Shiloh.

troops and supplies. In addition, whoever controlled this border area would be able to use it as a springboard against the enemy. This was particularly so in Kentucky and Tennessee, where the Mississippi, Cumberland, and Tennessee Rivers were navigable for some distance into the interior of the Confederacy. If the Confederacy lost control of these rivers, the entire Deep South would be open to invasion. On the other hand, if the North lost control of Kentucky and Tennessee, Cincinnati and southern Ohio, Indiana, and Illinois would lie open to invasion and capture.

To command this critical sector, Confederate President Jefferson Davis appointed his good friend Leonidas Polk. Polk, a relative of former President James K. Polk, was one of the war's more interesting figures. While attending West Point his interests changed, and soon after graduation he resigned from the army to enter divinity school. He rose to the post of Bishop in the Episcopal Church, and in 1860 helped found the University of the South in Sewanee. In June of 1861 he was persuaded by his former classmate Jefferson Davis to accept a commission as a Confederate major general. Polk accepted out of respect for his friend, even though he had no experience at field command. His assignment was to defend the northern frontier of the Confederacy at its most vulnerable point, northwestern Tennessee, between the Mississippi and Tennessee rivers.

Facing Polk was a relatively unknown Union officer, Ulysses S. Grant. Grant had not done particularly well at West Point, where he graduated 21st in the 39-man class of 1843. He rose to captain during the Mexican War, but afterwards took to drinking and had to resign in 1854 to avoid a court martial. His several attempts at private business then failed, and there is no telling what direction his life might have taken if the Civil War had not come along. Soon after the war began, he became commander of the *21st Illinois Infantry*; political connections then brought him an appointment as a brigadier general. On 1 September 1861 Grant was assigned to command the District of Southeast Missouri, an area that also included southern Illinois and western Kentucky and Tennessee. Grant's superior was Maj. Gen. John C. Fremont, "The Old Pathfinder," who had held command of the Union's Western District since 9 July 1861.

Between the small armies which Grant and Polk initially commanded stood the neutral state of Kentucky. The citizens of the Blue Grass State were painfully aware that war would pit neighbor against neighbor and brother against brother, so they optimistically declared the state to be neutral and hoped that the war would go away. But tensions were too deep to disappear. Pro-Union and pro-Southern sympathizers formed military units and began drilling openly. Only a spark was needed to ignite the two opposing sentiments.

The long dreaded spark was finally struck on 4 September 1861, when Polk led his Confederate troops into the southeastern corner of Kentucky, to seize the city of Columbus, situated on the high bluffs that dominated the Mississippi River. Columbus was a key position, and whoever held it would have a great advantage. However, whatever advantage Polk gained by grabbing Columbus was lost by the fact that he was the aggressor, the first to break Kentucky's fragile neutrality. His action angered Kentuckians of all persuasions, and drove many neutralists into the camp of the Unionists. The Kentucky legislature at once ordered the Confederate and Tennessee troops to be withdrawn from her soil unconditionally. Polk remained. Three

General Albert Sidney Johnston's surprise attack on 6 April at Shiloh came very close to success. He was killed at the height of the fighting at about 1430.

days after Polk seized Columbus, Grant retaliated by invading Kentucky and occupying the town of Paducah on the Ohio River. Soon over two-thirds of the state was occupied by Union forces, and the Confederates found themselves scrambling to build a viable defensive line.

This sudden change of events in no way pleased Gen. Albert Sidney Johnston, the overall commander in the Confederacy's Department of the West. Johnston was then at the height of his career and was considered to be the South's best military officer. At age 59, he was tall and impressive in appearance, every inch a soldier. He had graduated from West Point in 1826 and then served in the Texan revolution and the war with Mexico. After being promoted to colonel of the U.S. 2nd Cavalry, he advanced to brevet brigadier general and commanded the Utah expedition of 1858-1860. The outbreak of the war in 1861 found him in California as commander of the Department of the Pacific. Johnston resigned from the United States Army after Fort Sumter, but on his return East he was reportedly offered a position as second in command to Winfield Scott, commander of all Northern armies. Johnston turned this offer down, as did Robert E. Lee when he was offered a similar position. Instead,

Johnston accepted a commission as a full general in the Confederate army. His rapid advancement and appointment to command of the crucial Western department had been due in no small part to his close personal friendship with Confederate President Jefferson Davis. The two had been friends ever since they attended Transylvania College together in the early 1820s.

Johnston tried to take advantage of the confusion in Kentucky by advancing to occupy Bowling Green, which dominated the south central portion of the state. The town was located at the spot where the Louisville and Nashville Road crossed the Big Barren River, and it stood astride the Louisville and Nashville R.R., the only railroad that traversed Kentucky from north to south. Johnston's plan was to form a defensive line across the southern portion of the state stretching 300 miles from Polk's fortress at Columbus through Bowling Green to Cumberland Gap in the southeast corner of the state. To hold this long line, he had at his disposal only 30,000 men against Union forces at least twice that number. Therefore Johnston directed all Confederate forces in the state to solidify their positions and recruit as many Kentuckians as possible.

An uneasy stalemate dominated Kentucky throughout the late fall of 1861 and into the following winter. At Bowling Green, Johnston, who had the largest Confederate force in the state, had little difficulty holding his position. He succeeded at this partly because of the nervousness of his Union counterpart, Brig. Gen. William Tecumseh Sherman. Sherman, who commanded the Union forces around Louisville, overestimated Johnston's strength and aggressiveness and was in constant fear that the Rebels would swoop down on him and destroy his little army. An 1840 West Point graduate, Sherman should have been less apprehensive. He had missed combat service during the Mexican War, when he was stationed in California, but he had commanded a brigade that was actively engaged at First Bull Run in July of 1861. A month later he had been sent west to Kentucky as second in command to Robert Anderson, the aged "Hero of Fort Sumter," who had received a command in Kentucky largely because he was a native of that state. On 8 October 1861 Sherman succeeded Anderson as commander of the *Department of the Cumberland*. During this period, Sherman spent a

Confederate defenses at Columbus, Kentucky, the "Gibraltar of the West."

great deal of time dreading the enemy, arguing with the press, and criticizing the strategy of his superiors. It appears that the pressures of Sherman's position caused him to have what would today be termed a nervous breakdown. His condition was not helped by the fact that the press found out about his problem and labeled him "insane." Bad feelings between Sherman and the newspapers would continue for the rest of the war.

The Confederates were most sensitive about their position in western Kentucky. Here, Polk's forces controlled the Mississippi from their fortifications at Columbus, called the "Gibraltar of the West." To prevent Union navigation of the Mississippi, the Southerners ran a huge iron chain across the river from Columbus to Belmont in Missouri. The chain worked well, but required a Confederate force in Belmont to protect and maintain its western terminus. This detachment also served as a "corps of observation" and a link to the Confederate forces in Missouri, then led by Sterling Price.

The Battle of Belmont

In early November of 1861, the Union high command decided to test the Confederate line in western Kentucky, a movement that resulted in the first major battle in this theater of war. One Union force was directed to march from Cairo, Illinois, to threaten the area near Paducah, Kentucky, while another force, under Grant, was to advance against the Confederate positions at Belmont, Missouri, and Columbus, Kentucky. Grant's movement was also timed to support another Union advance from Missouri into northeastern Arkansas.

Grant's plan was to advance his force in three columns. One would march along the eastern shore of the Mississippi to menace Columbus, while a second advanced by land toward New Madrid, on the western bank of the Mississippi. Grant himself would lead a force of 3000 men on river steamers under the protection of the gunboats *Lexington* and *Tyler*. Using the river, he would be able to threaten Columbus, Belmont, and New Madrid. His real purpose, however, was to eliminate the Confederate position at Belmont, which was usually garrisoned only by a reinforced infantry regiment.

On 6 November Grant loaded his command—five infantry regiments, two cavalry companies, and six cannons—onto four transports at Cairo. Early on the 7th he landed three miles north of Belmont and began to approach the Confederate positions. Polk had feared such an attack, and had sent four regiments to reinforce Belmont as soon as he heard of Grant's movements. These reinforcements did not prove to be enough. Grant's troops drove the Rebels off and triumphantly began to pillage their camps. This Union success, though, was not to be long lived. While Grant's men were in action, Polk sent another 10,000 men across the river from Columbus in an attempt to cut the Yankees off from their transports. As soon as Grant realized what Polk was doing, he raced his men back to the river. It was a close contest, but Grant's men got there first, in time to escape Polk's trap. Thus the battle of Belmont ended in a draw, with each side losing about 600 men. Nevertheless, both sides afterwards claimed victory: Grant because he had sacked the Confederate camp and Polk because he had made the Yankees run for their lives in order to reach their boats. The battle actually had won no strategic advantage for either side.

Johnston's Line Is Unhinged

The next Federal attempt to break Johnston's Kentucky line took place at its other extremity, at the Cumberland Gap, and was far more successful than Grant's raid on Belmont. Throughout the last months of 1861, the opposing sides in eastern Kentucky skirmished with each other and urged the local populace to help drive out the "enemy invaders." In November, the Confederate commander at Cumberland Gap, Brig. Gen. Felix Zollicoffer, advanced his defensive perimeter 70 miles to the northeast, to a line north of the Cumberland River near Mill Springs. While Zollicoffer's superior, Maj. Gen. George Crittenden, heard of this move, he ordered Zollicoffer to withdraw south of the Cumberland River for fear that he would be trapped north of the river. Zollicoffer was slow to obey the order, and Crittenden's fears were soon fulfilled.

At the end of December, Union Brig. Gen. George H. Thomas was ordered to drive Zollicoffer's force away from the Cumberland River. After a hard march over extremely muddy roads, Thomas camped on 17 January 1862 at Logan's Cross Roads, near Somerset. Crittenden, who had arrived at Zollicoffer's camp, boldly decided to advance against Thomas' force before the Yankees reached his position. The Confederate attack struck Thomas' camp soon after dawn on 19 January. The ensuing battle was closely fought between opposing forces that each numbered about 4000 men. The troops on both sides were still green, but fought with much more determination than had the equally raw troops at Belmont or First Bull Run. As often happens in closely fought battles like this, a chance event determined the outcome of the fight. At Logan's Cross Roads, Zollicoffer, believing some of his men were firing on friendly troops, rode forward to order them to stop, only to discover that the men he was addressing were Federals. He was shot dead, and his troops were immediately demoralized. The whole Confederate army broke and barely escaped across the swollen Cumberland River. The Rebels had to abandon most of their equipment during their hasty flight, and the road to the Cumberland Gap lay open to the Yankees. Thomas, however, was not able to follow up his victory immediately because of supply problems. While Thomas was preparing to move against Cumberland Gap, Maj. Gen. Don Carlos Buell's *Union Army of the Ohio* was preparing to try to maneuver Maj. Gen. William Hardee's large Confederate army out of Bowling Green. Meanwhile, in western Kentucky, Grant was much more decisive in his plans.

What's in a Name

Shiloh is one of several major Civil War battles that were known by more than one name. Even today many are known by two different names. For a time after the war the battle of 6-7 April 1862 was called Pittsburg Landing in the North but Shiloh in the South. Today the Southern name has become more predominant. Quite often Southern writers preferred to call a battle by the name of the nearest town (Sharpsburg, Murfreesboro, Manassas, Olustee, Winchester) while Northern writers preferred the name of the nearest river or stream (Antietam, Stones River, Bull Run, Ocean Pond, Opequan). The names for other battles simply never became standardized. Hence we have Pea Ridge/Elkhorn Tavern, Perryville/Chaplin Hills, and Fair Oaks/Seven Pines, among others.

The North and the South also differed in the manner they named their armies. Union armies were regularly named after rivers—*Army of the Tennessee, Army of the Ohio, Army of the Potomac*. The Confederates usually preferred to name their armies after states or districts—Army of Tennessee, Army of Mississippi, Army of Northern Virginia. This was not the case, however, at Shiloh, where the Southern army was entitled Army of the Mississippi. In later usage "the" would have been omitted.

The problem of names in the Civil War extends even to the name of the struggle itself. The name of the war even now varies in different parts of the country, with "Civil War" finding favor in the North and "War Between the States" dominant in the South. Actually, neither name is particularly accurate. "Civil War" implies a dispute over control of the federal state, which was not at all the issue, since the South did not wish to take control of the United States but merely to secede from its control. "War Between the States," aside from being gramatically incorrect, makes equally little sense unless one subscribes to the Southern political view of the conflict; the same can be said for the North's term, "War for the Union." Other names have been offered for the war from time to time, notably the "War of the Rebellion" and "War of Southern Arrogance" favored by Unionists in the last century, and the equally silly "War of Yankee Aggression" favored by Southerners. More accurate than any of these are the "War for Southern Independence," a term popular in the South in the last century and "War of the Slaveholders Rebellion," a term that once held favor in the North. None of these names is entirely satisfactory to all parties concerned. There is, of course, a perfectly accurate and politically neutral name that has never found much following—the "War of Secession."

Brother Against Brother

The Civil War tore many families apart, especially in the border states. The divisions extended even to the highest circles. Mary Todd Lincoln, the wife of the President, was but one native of Kentucky who had relatives fighting on both sides. Her eldest son Robert served in the Union army, while a brother, three half-brothers, and three brothers-in-law were in the Confederate Army. For this reason, her loyalty was held in suspicion by many Northerners, particularly after her half-sister, Emilie Helm, widow of a Confederate general killed at Chickamauga, visited her in the winter of 1863-1864.

The noted Crittenden family of Kentucky was also deeply divided by the war. John J. Crittenden (1787-1863) was a powerful politician and former governor who was a member of the United States Senate when the war broke out. He was a staunch Unionist who played a key role in keeping his state in the Union. One of his sons, Thomas L. Crittenden (1815-1893) became a Union general and commanded the *5th Division* of the *Army of the Ohio* at Shiloh. Later in the war he rose to the rank of major general and commanded a corps. Another of John J. Crittenden's sons, George B. (1812-1880), gave his service to the Confederacy. His career was not as successful as his brother's. He too held the rank of major general, but he was defeated badly at the battle of Logan's Cross Roads on 19 January 1862. His conduct at this battle was still being investigated when he was appointed head of the newly created Reserve Corps of the Army of Mississippi on 29 March 1863. On 31 March Bragg heard that Crittenden was drinking to excess (a vice for which the Kentuckian was famous) and sent Hardee to investigate. Hardee found Crittenden drunk with one of his subordinates, William H. Carroll. Both were immediately relieved of duty. Crittenden did not return to command and eventually resigned from the army seven months later. Another Crittenden, Thomas T. (1832-1909), was a cousin of George and Thomas. He rose to the rank of brigadier general in the Union *Army of the Cumberland.*

The war also divided the Breckinridges, another noted Kentucky family. Maj. Gen. John C. Breckinridge (1821-1875), leader of the clan, fought for the South along with his three sons. Two of his cousins fought for the Union, and a female cousin, Margaret E. Breckinridge, served as a nurse and Sanitary Commission agent in Grant's army from 1862 to 1864. One of John's cousins, Dr. Robert J. Breckinridge, had two sons in the Confederate army and two in the Union army. One son, Col. J.C. Breckinridge, had the peculiar honor of capturing his gray-clad brother W.C.P. Breckinridge at the battle of Atlanta on 22 July 1864.

A fourth leading Kentucky family divided by the war was the Clay clan. Three of Henry Clay's grandsons fought for the Union and four fought for the South. Cassius Marcellus Clay (1810-1903), one of Henry's cousins and Minister to Russia, was a Union major general.

There are numerous recorded cases of troops from the same states fighting each other in battle. Two of the most famous such incidents occurred at Gettysburg in July of 1863. Here the Confederate 1st Maryland Battalion fought against a Union *1st Maryland Regiment*, and the Union *7th West Virginia* regiment clashed with the Confederate *7th Virginia*. During this fighting Lt. Col. Jonathon Lockwood of the *7th West Virginia* captured his own nephew, a lieutenant in the Rebel army.

The only recorded instance of a brother killing a brother during the Civil War occurred in a naval engagement at Hampton Roads, Virginia, on 8 March 1862. On that day Franklin Buchanan (1800-1874), commander of the Confederate ironclad *Merrimac*, sank several Union war-ships including the U.S.S. *Congress*. One of those killed aboard *Congress* was Buchanan's brother McLean Buchanan. Franklin Buchanan was himself wounded the next day while his ship was engaging the Federal ironclad *Monitor*.

There were, however, numerous cases in which brothers on opposite sides were killed in the same or different battles. One case involving generals severely affected the Terrill family of Virgina. Brig. Gen. William R. Terrill (1834-1862) fought for the Union and was killed at the battle of Perryville. His brother Brig. Gen. James B. Terrill (1838-1864) was killed at Bethesda Church in Virginia in Confederate service.

It was a truly "civil" struggle.

Armament Problems

There were no standardized shoulder weapons for the troops of either side at Shiloh. Unlike modern armies, where most infantrymen are equipped with identical weapons, Civil War soldiers at first often entered battle with whatever arms were at hand. This was especially true for Southern units, whose men sometimes carried only Bowie knives and shotguns. Other Confederate units carried obsolete muzzle loaders that had been rusting in state armories for years. Some Northern units had the same problem. New and more efficient weapons were available in large quantities in the North, but cost-conscious bureaucrats insisted on using up their supplies of antiquated weapons before purchasing new ones. Moreover, many of the newer weapons were no prizes. This was especially true of the foreign-made Belgian and Austrian muskets carried by numerous Northern units.

The best shoulder weapons in the field were the .58 caliber Springfield rifled-muskets. These were carried by many Union regiments, particularly those from Iowa. The reliable English .577 caliber Enfield rifled-musket was also carried in large quantities by troops of both sides. During the ammunition shortage that developed in the course of the battle of Shiloh, troops came to realize that Enfield and Springfield ammunition were not interchangeable. Enfield ammunition did not fit tightly enough into a Springfield rifle and would lose velocity more quickly when fired. Springfield ammunition could be squeezed into an Enfield rifle for a few rounds but would then jam up in the barrel. Ammunition supply and resupply was a major problem in the battle. One historian estimated that Union troops carried over 200 types of weapons, and that Sherman's division in particular had six major types of rifles. After the fighting ended, Grant issued a special order for his troops to trade weapons with each other so that each regiment would have only one type of musket.

Obtaining adequate armament was a particular problem for the Confederate army before Shiloh. Many of the troops that joined the Confederate army in March of 1862 were state militia or green troops armed only with shotguns, pistols, or just knives. Even the South's veteran troops were inadequately armed. For example, the men of the famous Orphan Brigade from Kentucky were carrying inferior Belgian muskets, old-fashioned flintlocks, squirrel guns, and converted smoothbores. This variety of weapons presented more than just a reduction in efficient fire power. It also posed a nightmare for the supply department, since each type of gun used different ammunition. Through strenuous effort, Johnston managed to rearm many of his men with superb Enfield rifles brought through the blockade from England. Over 3,000 of these rifles had arrived in February, and 15,000 were aboard one blockade runner that ar-

rived in New Orleans later in the month. Most of these were being shipped to Johnston's army at Corinth, but they did not all arrive in time for the battle.

The Confederates also had difficulty obtaining enough artillery to arm their batteries. Unlike the North, which had several foundries working around the clock to produce cannons, the South had only a few sources for cannon. Many of the pieces which its own foundries did produce were physically inferior to those produced in the North. Excellent artillery pieces were available from England, but most of the pieces that came through the blockade did not make it to the West. To help remedy this situation, Beauregard on 8 March called for the gathering of all available bells and other large brass items to be melted down for cannons. Donations poured in, and the foundry at Natchez, Mississippi, was kept busy casting new guns. This was a slow process, however, and ony helped partially to fill the South's artillery shortage at Shiloh. One result of this was that most Confederate pieces were much lighter than Union ones. In addition, while only 13 Rebel guns were rifled (11.3%), fully 64 Yankee ones were (48.9%).

Another problem with artillery was ammunition supply. Many of the cannon the Confederates used at Shiloh were obsolete or were of nonstandard calibers. This hodge-podge of artillery types posed ammunition supply problems almost as complicated as those presented by the muskets and small arms.

CHAPTER II

Grant Moves South

*E*ver since Belmont Grant had been thinking about how to deal with the Confederate fortress at Columbus, which anchored the western end of Johnston's Kentucky line. Situated on high bluffs above the Mississippi, Columbus' 140 artillery pieces completely dominated the river. Their effectiveness had already been demonstrated during the battle of Belmont, when guns with nicknames such as "Lady Polk" and "Long Tom" had given the Union gunboats *Lexington* and *Tyler* all the blasting they could handle. After this engagement, the fort's position had been strengthened by heavy entrenchments on its landward side and by the placing of "torpedoes" (as mines were then called) in the river. Garrisoning the fort was a large force of over 19,000 men.

Grant was well aware of Columbus' strength and how costly an attack against it would be. Instead of an attack, Grant reasoned that it would be much easier to bypass the fortress and force its evacuation without a fight. Much to Grant's pleasure, an excellent bypass route lay immediately at hand. The land between Columbus and Bowling Green was drained by the Tennessee and Cumberland Rivers, which flowed in a general south-to-north direction on their way to the Ohio. These rivers were navigable and offered a ready invasion route into Tennessee.

The Confederates were aware of their vulnerable position along the Tennessee and Cumberland Rivers, and built several forts to block any Federal advance in this sector. The most notable of these were Forts Henry and Donelson, which were located just south of the Kentucky-Tennessee border. Fort Henry was by far the smaller and weaker of the two places. It was located on low ground just east of the Tennessee River and contained only 17 guns. It and nearby Fort Heiman, which was on the opposite (western) bank of the Tennessee, were still under construction when the campaign began. Fort Donelson, located on the south bank of the Cumberland River about 12 miles east of Fort Henry, was much larger and stronger. Its garrison included 10,000 men and 15 heavy caliber guns.

Grant's plan of attack was worked out after close consultation with Flag Officer (later Rear Admiral) Andrew Foote, commander of the Mississippi naval squadron based at Cairo, Illinois. Foote had helped develop a small fleet of shallow-draft ironclad river gunboats designed for combat on inland waterways. Shepherded by these gunboats, Grant's troops would be able to move quickly and decisively aboard a flotilla of river transports to threaten Forts Henry and Donelson before the Confederates could summon help from either Columbus or Bowling Green.

Grant's campaign began on 2 February 1862, when Foote secretly gathered his squadron of seven gunboats at Paducah, Kentucky, at the mouth of the Tennessee River. The next day Brig. Gen. John McClernand's *1st Division* was loaded on transports. In less than twenty-four hours, McClernand's men were disembarking near Fort Henry, some fifty miles up the Tennessee from Paducah. As Grant awaited the arrival of his *2nd Division*, commanded by Brig. Gen. C.F. Smith, he made his plans for a combined army and navy attack against Fort Henry.

Brig. Gen. Lloyd Tilghman, the Confederate commander at Fort Henry, viewed Grant's approach with alarm. He had only a few unarmed steamboats to face Foote's fleet, and only 3000 raw and poorly armed troops to pit against Grant's 15,000 men. In addition, he was aware that the site of the fort had been poorly chosen: it was located on low ground, dominated by higher ground on both sides of the Tennessee River. Tilghman saw no way to resist Grant's force successfully with only 1100 men in Fort Heiman and 1900 in Fort Henry. On 4 February he decided to abandon Fort Heiman, which had already been subjected to a brief enemy naval bombardment, and concentrate all his troops

Fort Henry was not as strongly built or heavily defended as nearby Fort Donelson, and surrendered after a brief fight on 6 February.

at Fort Henry. There, his main line of defense would be Henry's 17 large bore, but antiquated, pieces of artillery.

Grant's attack on Fort Henry did not come off as planned. Due to muddy roads, his troops were late reaching their assault positions. When they finally reached Fort Henry, they were disappointed to learn that the fort had already surrendered to Foote's squadron. Without waiting for infantry support, Foote had advanced his gunboats alone against the enemy fort. Tilghman moved his infantry out of range and prepared to slug it out with his artillery against the Union boats. His guns at first scored quite a few hits, causing over 40 Union casualties and disabling *Essex* by a shot through her boilers. However, Henry's fate was sealed when its biggest gun burst and another malfunctioned. Superior Union firepower began taking its toll on the defenders. Tilghman had no choice but to surrender. Before he did so, however, he sent most of his command overland to Fort Donelson. Thus he actually surrendered only about 80 men, after suffering about 20 battle casualties. The entire battle lasted only an hour and a half and had been over for almost an hour when the first Union land forces arrived on the scene. The bulk of Grant's command did not reach the fort until late in the afternoon.

After the surprisingly easy capture of Fort Henry, Grant was eager to move immediately on Fort Donelson. Foote, however, needed time to repair his badly battered boats. Consequently,

Admiral Andrew H. Foote commanded the gunboat fleet that cooperated with Grant to help capture Forts Henry and Donelson.

Grant delayed his advance on Fort Donelson until 12 February. In the intervening days, Foote repaired some of his boats and sent the rest to destroy some Confederate ships at Florence, Alabama. He then sailed his whole fleet back to the Ohio River, and then turned up the Cumberland to Fort Donelson, a trip totaling over 100 miles.

Unconditional Surrender

It was clear to everyone that after the capture of Fort Henry Grant's next objective would be to move against Fort Donelson. Donelson was located in a much stronger position than was Fort Henry. It was not situated at river level, but was on bluffs 100 feet above the left bank of the Cumberland. Because of a bend in the river, the fort's guns were able to sweep the river for as far as they could shoot. On the landward side, Fort Donelson's flanks were well guarded by two creeks and their tributaries. In addition, the nearby town of Dover furnished a ready supply

Map of Fort Donelson

base. The fort's armament included fourteen heavy guns and a few additional field pieces.

Donelson's major weakness was the small size of its garrison. Even with the addition of most of the Fort Henry garrison, Brig. Gen. Bushrod R. Johnson had only 6000 men at his call. To reinforce him, Johnston sent two of his divisions from Bowling Green. These divisions, commanded by Brig. Gen. John B. Floyd and Simon B. Buckner, numbered some 8000 men. Other nearby detachments were also ordered to concentrate at the fort, including 2000 men from Polk's command at Columbus. Altogether, the fort held some 20,000 men and 57 cannons when Grant's blue-clad troops began arriving on 12 February.

This number was greater than the force Grant could muster,

and should have been enough to hold the fort. However, during the upcoming battle, the Confederates were hampered by two major problems. One was the presence of too many generals. Johnson, Pillow, Floyd, and Buckner all had their own opinions about how to conduct the fort's defense, but none could exercise enough authority to persuade the others to follow him. To make matters worse, Pillow, the senior general in rank, was by far the most indecisive of the lot. As a result, the old adage that "Too many cooks spoil the soup," is exactly what happened at Fort Donelson.

The other Confederate weakness at Fort Donelson was one of position. To the north, Hickman Creek was broad enough to form an excellent shield for the fort. However, the creek's breadth would also protect any besieging forces from counterattack. To the south, Indian Creek could have protected the fort well enough, but with the arrival of the numerous reinforcements, the Confederates decided to extend their southern defenses farther to the south, to include the town of Dover. This meant that Indian Creek and its marshy tributaries would bisect the Confederate defensive line and be a hindrance to movement and communications, which negated any advantage the Confederates might have enjoyed from holding interior lines.

Legend has it that Grant was uncertain whether or not his superior, Maj. Gen. Henry ("Old Brains") Halleck, would approve of an immediate attack on Fort Donelson. For this reason, Grant told Halleck that he was marching on Donelson and then allegedly cut the telegraph wires leading to his commander's headquarters. This act would have prevented Halleck from ordering Grant to turn back from Donelson. The story, appropriate as it seems, appears to be untrue. Records published in the official war reports show that the telegraph lines between Grant and Halleck were open throughout the campaign, and that Halleck was supporting Grant's movements in every way that he could.

Grant had at first entertained hopes of making a swift and decisive attack on Fort Donelson, which was only twelve miles from Fort Henry. Had he been able to do so, he would have reached the fort before it was heavily reinforced. However, road and weather conditions were not in his favor. Local roads were so bad that he had to double team his artillery pieces. Even then, he could not advance very quickly because rising creek waters flooded the roads. Some of his cavalry managed to reach the Confederate positions on 7 February, but most of his infantry did not arrive until the 12th. Grant's advance was led by McClernand's division, which then formed on the Union right facing Pillow's troops. Grant's other division, led by C.F. Smith, formed on the left, facing Buckner. The weather than turned so mild that many of the Yankees cast off their heavy overcoats during their march, an act they would soon sincerely regret.

Thus did Grant and his 15,000 Union troops settle down to besiege 20,000 Confederates in Fort Donelson. As the two armies jockeyed for tactical advantages, the Confederates never realized their temporary numerical superiority. By 14 February, Grant was being heavily reinforced by troops from Buell's army and other nearby commands. These were formed into a third division, under Brig. Gen. Lew Wallace. Wallace's division was then moved into position at the center of Grant's besieging line.

The siege at first did not go well for the Union forces. When the *17th* and *49th Illinois Regiments* of McClernand's division were attacking the Confederate left on 13 February, the dead leaves that covered the ground caught fire and many helpless wounded were burned to death. Later that day, the weather changed, becoming abruptly colder. The temperature dropped to 10 degrees Fahrenheit and a blizzard set in. This severely affected the men of both armies, but especially those improvident Yankees who had discarded their overcoats and blankets a few days earlier. To make matters worse, the wind blew so strongly that fires could not be started for warmth.

Grant's first serious attempt to capture the fort took place on 14 February. On that day he ordered Foote's fleet, which had arrived the night before, to make a naval attack. No doubt, Grant was hoping that Foote would be able to make Fort Donelson surrender as easily as Fort Henry. Unfortunately for Foote, Donelson was much better fortified and manned than its weaker neighbor. At about 1500 hours Foote steamed his six gunboats up the river towards the fort. In the ensuing 90-minute battle, the boats worked their way to within 400 yards of the fort, but were not able to crack its defenses. In return, the fleet

McAllister's **Battery D, 1st Illinois Artillery,** *in action at Fort Donelson on 13 February 1862.*

The water battery at Fort Donelson played a key role in repulsing the Union gunboats on 14 February. Admiral Foote was badly wounded during this fight.

suffered terribly, particularly from the well placed Confederate water battery. Foote's flagship, the ironclad *Louisville*, suffered 59 hits, including one that disabled its steering; as a result, the warship drifted helplessly down river and out of the battle. In addition, one gun burst on *Carondelet*. Personnel losses totaled 54, including Foote, who was badly wounded. At the end of the day it was all too clear that the naval forces would not be able to take the fort. Everything now rested in the hands of Grant's infantrymen.

Despite their success against Foote's flotilla, the Confederate commanders had little confidence in their ability to hold the fort. Many of their troops were green and poorly armed, and not enough food or ammunition was on hand to withstand a siege. (It should be noted, though, that many of Grant's troops were also green, and the Yankees did not have stockpiles of supplies, either.) Consequently, the Confederate generals decided that it would be best for their army to break through Grant's lines and escape to the southeast. The breakout was scheduled for the afternoon of 14 February. Pillow was to lead the way, with Buckner covering the withdrawal. Buckner made all his preparations as ordered, but Pillow had second thoughts after he formed his men for the attack. He persuaded Floyd that it was too late in the day to accomplish anything, and Floyd canceled the attack.

That night, the Confederate generals decided to attempt their breakout early the next morning. All the brigade commanders were briefed as to their military objectives, but no one was told how much food or supplies to carry.

The Confederate attack began as scheduled shortly after dawn on 15 February. Baldwin's brigade led the advance and achieved success until it ran into Oglesby's Union brigade. The Confederates were relying on the element of surprise to catch the Yankees in their camps. Oglesby's men, however, had been so cold all night that they had not slept. As a result, they were already awake when the attack began and were able to form into battle line much more quickly than the Confederates had anticipated.

Though they had lost much of the advantage of surprise, the Confederates began to succeed in their attack because they were

The Confederate surprise attack on 15 February opened an escape route for the Fort Donelson garrison, but indecision of the Confederate commanders bungled the opportunity.

able to bring superior numbers to the point of contact. The Yankees defended valiantly, but were outflanked near the river and began to run out of ammunition. The turning point came when the Union *25th Kentucky*, sent in as reinforcements, mistakenly fired into the *8th* and *29th Illinois Regiments*. These unfortunate regiments broke and fled, forcing the whole Union line to peel back in order to protect itself. At this point, as planned, Buckner's men advanced to assault Wallace's *3rd Division*, in the center of Grant's line. This movement kept Wallace from reinforcing McClernand, whose weary division was soon swept from the field by the victorious Confederates.

At this point the Confederates had what they wanted. Grant's right wing had been smashed, and the road to Nashville and safety lay open. Better yet, it was then possible for Buckner and Pillow to roll up the remainder of Grant's line and so win a smashing victory. Through some fluke, the Confederate generals chose neither of these two attractive alternatives. Instead, they picked a third option that led straight to disaster.

The Confederate battle plan called for Buckner to strip his trenches in front of Fort Donelson and commit most of his men to the attack on the Union center. This plan was working perfectly, as the Union leaders were too busy defending their own right flank to notice how weak the Confederate right was. It was at this point that the Confederate command suffered a failure of nerve. Just as the Confederate army was on the verge of marching for Nashville, Pillow had second thoughts about the safety of Buckner's original line. For some inexplicable reason, he ordered Buckner to stop his attack and return to his trenches. As Buckner was retiring, he ran into the surprised Floyd, who preferred to continue the day's battle plan. Floyd told Buckner to hold his position while he consulted with Pillow. By the time he found Pillow, the Confederates had lost their momentum, and Grant had recovered from his initial disadvantage. Grant sent one of Smith's fresh brigades to the right, where Pillow's confused Confederates were filing back into their trenches. On the other flank, Buckner's men had to fight hard to reestablish the original Confederate right. Smith's *2nd Division* had advanced into Buckner's entrenchments, and could not be completely driven out. Thus the Confederates literally snatched defeat from the jaws of victory. After effectively winning the battle at the cost of some 2000 casualties, they ended the day in a worse position than that in which they had started.

When the Confederate generals met for a conference that night, there was a great deal of bitterness, particularly between Pillow and Buckner. After passions had cooled somewhat, it was decided to evacuate the post as soon as possible before the situation worsened. Scouts were sent out to determine if the escape routes opened earlier in the day were still open. When the scouts returned they reported that all the Union works had been reoccupied. The generals refused to believe them and sent out still more scouts. These also reported that all escape routes were blocked by the enemy. The Confederate generals finally realized the seriousness of their situation: if their army could not escape, it would have to surrender. During the day's confusion, some Union troops had occupied part of Buckner's entrenchments, rendering the whole Confederate line untenable.

Each Confederate general revealed his true character in his reaction to this predicament. Floyd, the senior officer present,

Confederate prisoners captured at Fort Donelson, wearing old blankets and pieces of carpet to keep warm. The battle was fought in bitterly cold weather.

feared that the Northerners might execute him on charges of treason; he had been accused of betraying large quantities of weapons to the South when he was serving as Buchanan's Secretary of War in the last days of 1860. For this reason, Floyd decided to make his own escape. He ignobly turned command of the post over to Pillow, and went to his room to pack. However, Pillow also had no interest in surrendering with his men. As quickly as he received command of the Confederate army at Fort Donelson, he passed it on to Buckner. Buckner, the most manly of the lot, accepted the command and began preparations to contact Grant about surrendering.

While Buckner was preparing white flags for his troops, Floyd and Pillow were searching for a means to escape. The easiest route was by water, but no steamboats were on hand, Floyd having previously sent them upriver with prisoners and wounded. Finally a small boat was found and Pillow and his staff crossed the river to freedom. Floyd had to wait until dawn to escape. At that time two steamboats, unaware of the fort's imminent surrender, arrived at Dover carrying 400 new recruits. Floyd immediately commandeered the boats and unloaded their cargo. When the first boat was empty, Floyd ordered aboard his two favorite Virginia regiments. As his Virginians were being ferried to safety, a crowd began to gather at the docks clamoring for room on the remaining boat. Floyd persuaded the 20th Mississippi Regiment to hold the throng back by promising to save room on the last boat for the Mississippians. As the Mississippians were carrying out their part of the bargain, Floyd loaded two other regiments on the boat and then boarded himself. He then gallantly steamed off, leaving his angry guardians behind.

Only one other organized body of Confederate troops escaped the fort before its surrender. Fiery Nathan Bedford Forrest, commander of a Tennessee cavalry regiment, was determined not to surrender to the dread Yankees. He sought and obtained permission from Buckner to attempt an escape along an unguarded route he had discovered near the river. Taking with him almost all the army's cavalry and about 200 infantrymen mounted on artillery horses, Forrest waded to safety through deep mud and water.

The departure of Floyd's brigade and Forrest's command left Buckner with around 13,000 men, half the number commanded by Grant. Soon after dawn on the next day, Sunday, 16 February 1862, a bugle call sounded from the Confederate entrenchments and an officer rode out toward the Union lines with a proposal to have a cease-fire until noon so that surrender terms could be discussed. Grant's reply is now famous: "No terms except an unconditional and immediate surrender can be accepted." Buckner's wordy response is not so famous: "The distribution of the forces under my command, incident to an unexpected change of commanders, and the overwhelming force under your command, compel me, notwithstanding the brilliant success of the Confederate army yesterday, to accept the ungenerous and unchivalrous terms which you propose."

Most of the Confederate troops were astounded to see white flags pop up along their works and enemy troops moving unmolested into their lines. Grant directed the Rebels to surrender their arms in Dover and await transportation to Cairo,

When Brigadier Generals John Floyd and Gideon Pillow fled in order to avoid capture, the task of surrendering Fort Donelson fell to Brigadier General Simon B. Bucker, who had been a close friend of Union victor U.S. Grant before the war.

Illinois. Hundreds chose to sneak off into the swamps and darkness rather than surrender. Among these was Brig. Gen. Bushrod Johnson. About noon on the 16th, the very day of the surrender, he and another officer began walking out of the Confederate camp. They made it through the Union camps without being challenged, and so escaped. Altogether, over 7000 Confederates escaped capture at Donelson in one way or another. Of the fort's original garrison of about 21,000, some 500 were killed and about 13,000 captured; most of the wounded were numbered among the prisoners. Total Union losses from the battle were less than 3000.

The scale of Grant's victory was much greater than would be suggested by the capture of two Confederate forts and most of a small Rebel army. The loss of Forts Henry and Donelson shattered what was left of Johnston's defensive line in Kentucky. Johnston evacuated his strong position at Bowling Green on the 14th and had to move quickly so as not to be trapped between Grant's army and Buell's command. Thus Grant's victories won control of the state of Kentucky, which would remain in Union hands for the rest of the war. They also opened Tennessee to invasion. As a reward for his victory, Grant was immediately appointed to the rank of major general. A month later, his chief assistants, Smith, McClernand, and Lew Wallace, received the same promotion. Halleck, who supposedly masterminded the entire campaign, was given a larger command, the *Department of the Mississippi*, and Grant received command of the newly created *Military District of Western Tennessee*.

The Invasion of Tennessee

Union momentum after the fall of Fort Donelson carried the Northern troops deep into Tennessee. Johnston had constructed no defenses at Nashville, and so was forced to evacuate it without a fight when pressed by Buell's *Army of the Ohio*. The dejected Confederate army left Nashville on 23 February, only hours before Buell's men began entering the city. Johnston then established a new base at Murfreesboro, poised to block any advance by Buell, who settled in at Nashville, some 30 miles to the northwest. The Confederate loss of Nashville and central Tennessee was more than a severe psychological blow. Nashville was the first Confederate capital to be lost, and was also a key supply center. In addition, the Nashville area was the largest producer of iron ore in the Confederacy. The South could ill afford such losses.

The North's deepest penetration of Tennessee was made by Grant's army. By early March, Grant had advanced up the Tennessee as far as Savannah, near the southern border of the state. Here Halleck wanted to concentrate a large force in preparation for an attack on Corinth, the chief railroad center of northern Mississippi. Corinth was located at the junction of the Mobile and Ohio Railroad, a major north-south line, and the Memphis and Charleston Railroad, a key east-west line that was called "the vertebrae of the Confederacy" by the Confederate Secretary of War.

New Madrid and Island No. 10

The main Union objective in western Tennessee was the control of the Mississippi River and the capture of Memphis, which was a key financial center and a conduit for trade from the Trans-Mississippi. On 18 February, two days after the fall of

Fort Donelson, Halleck directed Brig. Gen. John Pope, commander of the *District of Central Missouri*, to organize his troops for an advance up the Mississippi. Pope was a 40-year-old graduate of West Point (Class of 1842) who had won fame as an explorer in the West in the days following the Mexican War. His service in the war so far had been rather uninspiring, and certainly was not as controversial as his later deeds. Quite appropriately, Pope named his new command the *Army of the Mississippi*. By the end of the month, he was leading an advance towards New Madrid, a small Confederate outpost on the Missouri side of the Mississippi River, some 30-odd miles downstream from Columbus, Kentucky.

Pope's advance spelled the end of Polk's occupation of the bastion of Columbus. Ever since the fall of Henry and Donelson, Polk's position had been precariously exposed and was vulnerable to encirclement and capture. Polk was well aware that Union capture of New Madrid would open up the Mississippi well below Columbus, making useless his further occupation of the "Gibraltar of the West." For this reason, he began evacuating Columbus on 25 February. It took almost a week to remove most of the 140 pieces of artillery from Columbus and transfer them to forts at or near Island No. 10, which was located a few miles upstream from New Madrid. Island No. 10 was so named because it was the tenth island downstream from the junction of the Ohio and Mississippi Rivers. The fortifications there could easily control the Mississippi, but they were very vulnerable to enemy attack. A huge swamp to the east of Island No. 10 prevented the movement of men or supplies in that direction. For this reason, all supplies and reinforcements had to be brought in by river. If the Yankees seized control of the river above and below Island No. 10, they could easily starve its Confederate garrison into surrender.

Pope reached New Madrid on 3 March and immediately realized the fort was too strong to attack; its garrison comprised 50 heavy guns and over 7000 men. Consequently, he brought up his own heavy guns and prepared for a siege, which started ten days later. For fear of being cut off, the Confederate commander at New Madrid abandoned his position and most of his guns and fled to Island No. 10, an act for which he was immediately

Pope used nine specially constructed mortar boats to help capture Island No. 10.

relieved of command. His abandonment of New Madrid permitted Pope to advance freely to the south of Island No. 10 and begin operations against the Confederate supply line. It also enabled Pope to clear up his own supply line, which was dependent on river boats. These had been unable to reach Pope's men operating near New Madrid because the river route was blocked by the Confederate fort at Island No. 10. For this reason, Pope cut a canal linking the bends in the Mississippi between Island No. 9 and New Madrid, both north of Island No. 10. This enabled his supply boats to reach his men without running the gauntlet of Confederate cannons.

Following the completion of the canal on 4 April, Pope turned his full attention to completely severing Island No. 10's supply lines. His plan was to cross his infantry to the east side of the

Major General John Pope's victory at Island No. 10 on 7 April vaulted him to national attention and an unsuccessful stint as Commander of the **Army of Virginia** *during the Second Bull Run Campaign.*

Mississippi at Tiptonville, and from there advance north against the weakest point in the Confederate lines. To support the river crossing, Admiral Foote on 6 April ordered the ironclads *Carondelet* and *Pittsburgh* to run past the Confederate batteries to New Madrid.

Pope then sent four regiments across the river on the 7th. They easily occupied Tiptonville, cutting off the Confederate supply line to Island No. 10. They also cut off the Confederate line of retreat. The Confederates were well aware of their predicament and attempted to evacuate, but only about 500 men managed to make their way through the swamps. The rest, including a large number of sick, had no choice but to surrender. In his usual bombastic manner, Pope listed his captives in detail in his official battle report: "Three generals, two hundred and seventy-three field and company officers, six thousand seven hundred privates, one hundred and twenty-three pieces of heavy artillery, thirty-five pieces of field artillery, all of the very best character and of the latest patterns, seven thousand stand of small arms, tents for twelve thousand men, several wharfboats loaded with provisions, an immense quantity of ammunition of all kinds, many hundred horses and mules, with wagons and harness etc., are among the spoils."

Pope's well earned victory thrust him into the national limelight, eventually leading to a disastrous period in command in Virginia. The capture of New Madrid and Island No. 10 cleared the Mississippi River as far as Fort Pillow, which was the last major riverine obstacle to the capture of Memphis. Pope and his army left for Fort Pillow on 12 April, and arrived there on the 14th. He was preparing to besiege it when he received orders from General Halleck to march to Pittsburg Landing to reinforce Grant's and Buell's battle-scarred armies. As a result, Fort Pillow, and Memphis, received a short-lived reprieve from capture.

While Pope was reducing Island No. 10 and Buell was jockeying against Johnston's army south of Nashville, Grant was fighting to keep command of his army. His major opponent was not any Confederate general, but rather his superior, Maj. Gen. Henry "Old Brains" Halleck. In his mid-fifties, Halleck possessed a cautious nature. He had graduated from West Point in 1839, and was noted as an author, strategist, and organizer. However, he was personally quite disagreeable in appearance and temperament, characteristics that made it difficult for anyone to get along well with him. He especially had no patience for restless and independent subordinates such as U.S. Grant. It seemed almost inevitable that the two would clash at some point during the campaign.

Grant and Halleck came at loggerheads less than a month after the fall of Fort Donelson. Halleck had laid plans for the next campaign, but did not send precise orders to Grant until 1 March. His overall strategy was to have Grant advance south along the Mobile and Ohio Railroad and destroy its junctions with other lines at Humboldt and Jackson, in Tennessee, and Corinth, in Mississippi. Grant had already anticipated such a move and had sent troops ahead to occupy Paris on the Louisville and Nashville Railroad, about twenty miles southwest of Fort Henry. However, he was reluctant to proceed further than that without precise orders. Chafing under the inactivity, Grant made a two-day trip to Nashville on 27-28 February in order to observe Buell's troops entering the town.

Unfortunately for him, his bored troops at Fort Donelson got a bit rowdy while he was gone.

Halleck was not at all pleased to hear that Grant had left his army without permission, and that his troops had been ill behaved in his absence. Worse yet, Grant had dared to leave his assigned department and enter the department commanded by Don Carlos Buell, Halleck's chief rival in the west. Grant's actions so aggravated Halleck that "Old Brains" sent a telegram to Washington on 2 March: "I have had no communication with General Grant for more than a week. He left his command without my authority, and went to Nashville. His army seems to be as much demoralized by the victory of Fort Donelson as was that of the Potomac by the defeat of Bull Run. It is hard to censure a successful general immediately after a victory, but I think he richly deserves it. I can get no reports, no returns, no information of any kind from him. Satisfied with his victory, he sits down and enjoys it without any regard to the future. I am worn out and tired by his neglect and inefficiency. C.F. Smith is almost the only officer equal to the emergency."

The next day Halleck reported to Washington that he had heard rumors from Fort Donelson that Grant "has resumed his former bad habits" and was drinking again. This report prompted an immediate reply from Maj. Gen. George B. McClellan, then Commander-in-Chief of the Union armies: "The future success of our cause demands that proceedings such as General Grant's should at once be checked. Generals must observe discipline as well as private soldiers. Do not hesitate to arrest him at once if the good of the service requires it, and place C.F. Smith in command. You are at liberty to regard this as a positive order, if it will smooth your way." Accordingly, Halleck relieved Grant of command on 4 March and placed Maj. Gen. C.F. Smith in charge of his army.

Thus, U.S. Grant, the future commander of all the United States' armies and future President of the United States, was relieved of command while he was in the field. For the next ten days, telegrams flew madly back and forth between Halleck and Grant and between Halleck and Washington. At one point Grant was ready to demand a court of inquiry, but Halleck was tiring of the game. On the 13th he suggested that Grant resume command and lead the army to victory! Grant accepted the olive branch, and rejoined his army on the 17th.

Earlier that week, Halleck's rivalry with Buell had also been resolved. On 11 March, Halleck's and Buell's departments were joined into a new department, the *Department of the Mississippi*, under Halleck's overall command. Finally, the Union's western armies had the unity of command necessary for success.

Grant

Before the war, U.S. Grant (1822-1885) showed little promise of the great success he would later attain. He had to fight for an appointment to West Point, where his best subjects were math, engineering, and horsemanship; he graduated in 1843 ranking 21st in a class of 39. In the Mexican War, he won notice for his bravery, but could not endure the boredom of post-war garrison duty on the west coast. He became depressed about being separated from his family, and took to drinking, a vice that forced his resignation in 1854. He then tried his hand at several business ventures—farming, shopkeeping, and real estate—but was a success at none.

The Civil War came as a welcome opportunity for Grant. He quickly volunteered his services, and received command of the *21st Illinois Infantry*. When a political connection won him an appointment as a brigadier general, Grant was on his road to fame. His first battle, at Belmont, was indecisive, but his capture of Forts Henry and Donelson won him enough fame to overcome the accusations of incompetence and drunkenness that were brought against him for being so badly surprised at Shiloh. After Shiloh he was temporarily shelved when he was "promoted" to being Halleck's second-in-command. Once he was permitted to resume army command, Grant showed his pertinacity and skill by capturing Vicksburg and rescuing Chattanooga. He was then promoted to command all the Union armies, and finished the war by capturing Richmond and Lee's army.

Grant is much better remembered for his generalship than for his political ability. The fame he earned during the war made him an obvious candidate to succeed Andrew Johnson as president. After a narrow victory over Democrat Horatio Seymour in the 1868 presidential election, he began a two-term tenure that was rocked by scandals. He had been fortunate during the war to find trustworthy, honest and responsible subordinates such as Sherman and Sheridan. As president, his inexperience at politics and his trust in friends and poltical cronies brought on one crisis after another in an era when politics and corruption went hand-in-hand. Affairs such as the Credit Mobilier scandal, the Whisky Ring, and the impeachment of Secretary of War Belknap caused Grant to go into seclusion in 1877.

Grant's closing years were far from happy. In 1879 he failed in a bid for a third term as president. He soon went bankrupt after a series of bad investments. To support his family, he began writing his memoirs, a task made difficult by a painful case of throat cancer he developed from his habit of smoking cigars. He finished his book only a few days before he died. The memoirs were then published by Grant's friend Mark Twain (Samuel Clemens), and were an instant critical and financial success.

"Unconditional Surrender" Grant

"No terms except an unconditional and immediate surrender will be accepted. I propose to move immediately upon your works." This demand for the unconditional surrender of Fort Donelson was to win Grant great fame. The newspapers of the day quickly noted that "Unconditional Surrender" had the same abbreviation ("U.S.") as the name of the country and also of General Ulysses Simpson Grant himself. Ironically, Grant's real name did not happen to be "Ulysses Simpson." He had been christened "Hiram Ulysses," but changed his name to "Ulysses Simpson" through some confusion on his application to West Point. ("Simpson" was his mother's maiden name.)

Admiral Foote

Admiral Andrew Hull Foote (1806-1863) had his promising career cut short by a wound he received while commanding the Union flotilla that attacked Fort Donelson on 14 February 1862. Foote had been a pioneer in the use of warships on inland waters. One of his most successful actions was when he used four ironclads mounting only twelve guns to reduce and capture Fort Henry on 6 February 1862. After Fort Donelson fell, Foote helped Pope in the New Madrid campaign, but he had to retire to the sick list because his wound was not healing well. For his role at Forts Henry and Donelson, Foote was given the official thanks of Congress on 16 June 1862. He then spent a year in charge of a naval bureau in Washington. In early June of 1863 he requested a return to active duty and was given command of the fleet blockading Charleston, South Carolina. But he died on the way to Charleston at the age of 57.

The Confederate Commanders at Donelson

It is reassuring to learn that John B. Floyd and Gideon Pillow, the Confederate generals who gave up their command and ran away rather then surrender to Grant at Fort Donelson, were never again allowed to hold field commands. On the other hand, Simon Buckner, the general who nobly stayed to surrender to Grant, had a distinguished service record for the rest of the war.

Brig. Gen. John B. Floyd (1806-1863) had received his generalship solely because of his experience as President James Buchanan's Secretary of War from 1857 through 1860—a post he had earned through his political connections. For his actions at Fort Donelson, he was relieved of command by Confederate President Jefferson Davis on 11 March 1862. Two months later he was given a desk job as a major general of militia in Virginia. He died of exhaustion in 1863, at the age of 57.

Brig. Gen. Gideon Pillow (1806-1878), who was the same age as Floyd, had achieved national power in the Democratic Party because he had once been the law partner of President James K. Polk and had used this connection to win an appointment as a major general of volunteers during the Mexican War. At the start of the Civil War, he was commanding officer of the Tennessee militia. Following his escape from Fort Donelson, Pillow was censured and suspended from command.

Brig. Gen. Simon Bolivar Buckner (1823-1914) was a West Point graduate (1844) and fought well in the Mexican War and on the frontier. He prospered in the Chicago real estate market, and at the start of the Civil War was a senior militia commander in his native Kentucky. He was offered a senior commission by both the Union and Confederate governments. He finally sided with the South after Polk broke Kentucky's neutrality. After surrendering Fort Donelson, he was held prisoner until he was exchanged in August of 1862, when he was promoted to major general. He later fought well at Perryville and Chickamauga. At the close of the war, he reached the rank of lieutenant general in commmand of the District of Louisiana. After the war, Buckner served as governor of Kentucky (1887-1892), and was nominated for vice-president by the National Democratic Party in 1896. He died in 1914 at the age of 90.

One reason why Simon B. Buckner accepted command of Fort Donelson from Floyd and Pillow may have been the hope of receiving lenient surrender terms from his old friend "Sam" Grant. Buckner and Grant had been close friends at West Point, and Buckner had loaned Grant money to get home when the latter resigned from the army in 1854 while under suspicion of excessive drinking. If these were Buckner's hopes, they were totally dashed by Grant's "unconditional surrender" demand. Their adversary relationship during the war did not destroy their old friendship, which continued until Grant's last painful days. When Grant was poverty stricken in 1884, Buckner offered him another loan, which Grant proudly refused. When Grant died a year later, Buckner was one of his pallbearers.

Hindquarters in the Saddle: John Pope

Maj. Gen. John Pope (1822-1892), the victor at New Madrid and Island No. 10 in early April of 1862, had a checkered career. An 1842 West Point graduate, he served well in Mexico and as an explorer in the west, before being named to command on the Mississippi. After his success there in April of 1862, he went on to play a significant role in the ensuing capture of Corinth, Mississippi. Pope's successes brought him to the attention of President Lincoln, who was looking for a fresh face to lead Maj. Gen. John C. Fremont's demoralized *Army of Virginia*, which had just been severely embarrassed by Thomas "Stonewall" Jackson's famous Valley Campaign. Pope was summoned east in June and placed in command of the *Army of Virginia* on 26 June.

It did not take Pope long to earn the hatred of both his own troops and the enemy. Pope's treatment of Southern sympathizers caught within his lines angered Rebel Gen. Robert E. Lee so much that Lee, who was usually a complete gentleman, came to dislike Pope more than any other opponent. Pope then earned the animosity of his own troops by openly declaring that they were inferior to the Western troops he had formerly commanded. The following quote is from his first official address to his troops in Virginia:

"Let us understand each other. I have come to you from the West, where we have always seen the backs of our enemies; from an army whose business it has been to seek the adversary, and to beat him when he was found; whose policy has been attack and not defense. In but one instance has the enemy been able to place our Western armies in defensive attitude. I presume that I have been called here to pursue the same system and to lead you against the enemy. It is my purpose to do so, and that speedily. I am sure that you long for an opportunity to win the distinction you are capable of achieving. Meantime I desire you to dismiss from your minds certain

phrases, which I am sorry to find so much in vogue amongst you. I hear constantly of 'taking strong positions and holding them,' of 'lines of retreat,' and of 'bases of supplies.' Let us discard such ideas. The strongest position a soldier should desire to occupy is one from which he can most easily advance against the enemy. Let us study the probable lines of retreat of our opponents, and leave our own to take care of themselves. Let us look before us and not behind. Success and glory are in advance, disaster and shame lurk in the rear. Let us act on this understanding, and it is safe to predict that your banners shall be inscribed with many a glorious deed and that your names will be dear to your countrymen forever."

Pope's haughty attitude earned instant dislike from his soldiers and from the press. When one reporter asked him where his headquarters would be, Pope responded that they would be "in the saddle" as he pursued the enemy. This led a wag to observe that Pope's headquarters would be where his hindquarters ought to be. Pope also managed to earn the dislike of many of the old line Eastern commanders in Maj. Gen. George B. McClellan's *Army of the Potomac*. This had disastrous repercussions when Pope was badly outmaneuvered by Lee in the Second Bull Run campaign, and critically needed the cooperation of McClellan's generals. Several of them advanced so slowly that Pope's army met with disaster. Pope took all the blame for this defeat and was relieved on 5 Sept. 1862. He was then sent to the Civil War equivalent of Siberia, the *Depart-*

ment of the Northwest, and he went to Minnesota to fight Indians. After the war he had a successful peacetime military career, rising to major general in the regular Army.

Artillery at Shiloh

Artillery used a great variety of ammunition, each designed for a special purpose.

Smoothbores, although technically obsolete, were actually quite effective. They used five types of ammunition.

Solid shot was just that, solid cannon balls. It was fired low to knock over soldiers and other targets like a bowling ball hitting pins, except that it would smash the targets to pieces. It could be richocheted off hard ground to cause even greater damage.

Shell was a round hollow ball filled with gunpowder. It was exploded by a timed fuse that would break the shell into several devastating metal fragments.

Case Shot was a round hollow ball with thinner walls than a shell. It contained lead balls that were released by a timed fuse. It had the same effect as canister except at much longer range.

Grape Shot was not used much in the Civil War, but was favored at Shiloh by the Confederate batteries. It contained three tiers of large iron balls that were bigger than those used in case shot or canister. The whole projectile broke apart at fir-ing and traveled in a straight line like a deadly hailstorm.

Canister consisted of 28 small iron or lead balls in a container that burst open upon firing. The balls then spread in a cone-shaped pattern. Canister was the war's most deadly killer at close range (200-600 yards) since it worked like a giant shot gun. It could be loaded in double and even triple charges in some cannons.

Rifled Guns had greater range and accuracy than smoothbores, but often had less effect in action.

Solid Shot was a cylindrical bolt of metal. It was not too effective because the shape of the projectile caused it to become buried in the ground upon impact.

Shell worked the same as smoothbore shell, except that it was cylindrical in shape.

Case Shot also worked the same as smoothbore shot, except that it was cylindrical. But it did not work well because the spin on the shot imparted by the rifling made the small balls disperse in irregular patterns.

Grape Shot in rifled guns had the same problems as smoothbore case shot.

Canister functioned the same as canister in smoothbores.

Artillery Used at Shiloh

Gun	Model	Bore (in.)	Barrel Weight (lbs.)	Proj.	Charge (lbs.)	Range (yds.)
Smoothbores						
6-pounder	1857	3.67	884	shot	1.25	1523
12-pd. Howitzer	1841	4.62	788	shell	.75	1072
12-pd. Napoleon	1857	4.62	1277	shot	2.5	1680
				shell	2.5	1300
				case	2.5	1135
24-pd. Howitzer	1844	5.82	1476	shell	2.00	1322
Rifled Guns						
6-pounder	1841	3.67	884	shell	1.25	1700
6-pd. Wiard	—	2.60	725	shell	.12	1200
12-pd. Wiard	—	3.40	783			
14-pd. James	—	3.80	915			
3-inch U.S.	1861	3.0	820	shell	1.00	2788
10-pd. Parrott	1861	2.9	890	shell	1.00	3200
				shell	1.00	5000
20-pd. Parrott	1861	3.67	1750	shell	2.00	4400

ARTILLERY ARMAMENTS								
	6-pd. SB	12-pd. How	24-pd. How	James Rifle	6-pd. Wiard	12-pd. Wiard	10-pd. Par.	20-pd. Par.	24-pd. siege
1st Div./ A Tenn.									
Bat. D, 1st Ill. (McAllister)			4						
Bat. D, 2nd Ill. (Timony)				6					
Bat. E, 2nd Ill. (Nispel)	2	2							
14th Ohio Bat. (Burrows)					4	2			
2nd Div./ A Tenn.									
Bat. A, 1st Ill., (Wood)	4	2							
Bat. D, 1st Mo. (Richardson)								4	
Bat. H, 1st Mo. (Walker)							2	2	
Bat. K, 1st Mo. (Stone)							4		
3rd Div./ A Tenn.									
9th Ind. Bat. (Thompson)	4	2							
Bat. I, 1st Mo. (Thurber)	4	2							
4th Div./ A Tenn.									
2nd Mich. Bat. (Ross)	1						2	2	
Bat. C, 1st Mo. (Brotzman)	2	2							
13th Ohio Bat. (Myers)	2			4					
5th Div/A Tenn.									
Bat. B, 1st Ill. (Barrett)	4	2							
Bat. E, 1st Ill. (Waterhouse)				6					
6th Ind. Bat. (Behr)	4	2							

	6-pd. SB	12-pd. How.	24-pd. How.	James Rifle	6-pd. Wiard	12-pd. Wiard	10-pd. Par.	20-pd. Par.	24-pd. siege	12-pd. Nap.	3 in Rod
6th Div./A Tenn.											
1st Minn. Bat. (Munch)		2		4							
5th Ohio Bat. (Hickenlooper)	2			4							
Unattached/ A Tenn.											
8th Ohio Bat. (Margraf)								2			
Bat. H, 1st Ill. (Silfersparre)								4			
Bat. I, 1st Ill. (Bouton)				6							
Bat. B, 2nd Ill. (Madison)											
Bat. F, 2nd Ill. (Powell)	6										
TOTAL A TENN	35	16	4	30	4	2	8	14	5		
2nd Div./ A Ohio											
Bat. H, 5th U.S. (Terrill)							2			4	
5th Div./ A Ohio											
Bat. G, 1st Ohio (Bartlett)					4	2					
Bat. HM, 4th U.S. (Mendenhall)										2	2
Unassigned: A Ohio											
Bat.A, 1st Ohio (Goodspeed)		2			4						
TOTAL A OHIO		2			8	2	2			6	2
TOTAL UNION 142 guns	35	20	4	30	12	4	10	14	5	6	2

U.S.S. *Tyler* had one 32-pdr. SB, six 8-inch SB, one 12-pdr. Dahlgren boat How.

U.S.S. *Lexington* had two 32-pdr. SB, four 8-inch SB, one 12-pdr. Dahlgren boat How.

	6pd-Rifle	6-pd. SB.	12-pd. How.	12-pd. Nap.	3-in. Rif.	3.3-in. Rif.	UNK
Clark's Div./ Polk's Corps							
Bankhead's Tenn. Bat.		4	2				
Stanford's Mmiss. Bat.		3	2		1		
Cheatham's Div./ Polk's Corps							
Polk's Tenn. Bat		4	2				
Smith's Miss. Bat.		2		4			
Ruggles' Div./ Bragg's Corps							
Hodgson's La. Bat.		2	2			2	
Ketchum's Ala. Bat.		4	2				
Withers' Div/ Bragg's Corps							
Robertson's Fla. Bat.				4			
Gage's Ala. Bat.			2		2		
Girardey's Ga. Bat.		4	2				
Hardee's Corps							
Swett's Miss. Bat.		4	2				
Miller's Tenn. Bat.							6
Trigg's Ark. Bat.		2	2				
Calvert's Ark. Bat.		2	2				
Hubbard's Ark. Bat.		2			2		
Harper's Miss. Bat.		2	2				
Breckinridge's Corps							
Cobb's Ky. Bat.		4	2				
Byrne's Ky. Bat		5	2				
Hudson's Miss. Bat.		2	2		2		
Beltzhoover's La. Bat.	4		2				
Rutledge's Tenn. Bat.		4	2				
Unassigned							
McClung's Tenn. Bat.		2	2				
Roberts' Ark. Bat.		2	2				
TOTAL 115 guns	4	52	36	8	7	2	6

Abbreviations Used on Artillery Charts: A=Army, Bat.=battery, Div.=Division, How.=Howitzer, Nap.=Napoleon, Par.=Parrott Rifle, Pd.=pounder, Rif.=Rifled, Rod.=Rodman rifle, SB=Smoothbore, UNK=unknown

"That Devil Forrest"

Col. Nathan Bedford Forrest (1821-1877), commander of an unnumbered Tennessee cavalry regiment during the Shiloh campaign, was one of the few Confederate leaders to really shine in those dark days for the South. Forrest was present with his men at Fort Donelson when Grant sent his "unconditional surrender" message on 15 February 1862. Rather than surrender, he got permission to try to escape with whatever troops he could. He found an unguarded path near the river and boldly led to safety all the army's cavalry and about 200 infantrymen mounted on artillery horses.

Forrest continued his good work during the confusion that attended the Confederate evacuation of Nashville. When the Yankee forces advanced much more quickly than expected after the fall of Fort Donelson, Gen. A.S. Johnston had to evacuate Nashville so quickly that he did not have time to remove all the military supplies stockpiled there. It fell to Forrest, who commanded the army's rear guard, to try to arrange for at least part of the remaining provisions to be brought off to safety.

At Shiloh, Forrest's regiment was attached to Statham's 3rd Brigade of Breckinridge's Reserve Corps. It would seem that the forests and heavy terrain at Shiloh would have given Forrest little opportunity for action. Quite the contrary. The fiery leader grew impatient while he waited in reserve almost in sight of the enemy. Finally, he could stand it no longer and led his troops to the front at mid-afternoon. About 1600

he reached the southern edge of the cotton field south of the Union line at the Peach Orchard. When he sought orders from the nearest general, Cheatham, he was only told of the previous bloody repulses the Confederates had suffered on this front. Forrest nevertheless ordered an assault on his own. He formed his men into columns of fours and charged at Prentiss' line. By artful dodging, his cavalry avoided most of the Union fire directed against them; they then struck the *23rd Missouri* just as that Federal unit was beginning to pull back. Forrest, though, was unable to follow up his temporary success because the heavy underbrush slowed down his horses too much.

Forrest saw no more activity until late that night. After the fighting died down, he took it on his own initiative to send a few scouts to investigate the Union lines. The scouts, cleverly dressed in captured blue overcoats, saw Buell's troops landing and reported this to Forrest. Forrest rushed to report this important news to Beauregard, but nobody knew where the commander was, since he had retired for the night in Sherman's tent without telling anyone of his whereabouts. Forrest did find Breckinridge and Hardee, and reported his news to them. They simply ordered him to maintain outposts and continue to report enemy activity.

Forrest's final contribution to the battle came on 8 April, the day after Beauregard retreated from the battlefield. Forrest was serving with the army's rear guard when it was attacked by Sherman's pursuing force about noon near Mickey's Crossroads. Forrest decided that the best defense was a good offense, and ordered his men to charge the Union skirmish line. In the ensuing melee, Forrest was isolated from his men and nearly killed. A Yankee shot him in the side, but he managed to pull free and rush away. Supposedly he then grabbed a Union infantryman, pulled him onto his horse, and used him as a shield against enemy bullets. When he got out of range, he threw down the surprised and scared bluecoat.

Forrest's successful showing in the Shiloh campaign earned him an appointment as a brigadier general. He then began a series of raids that earned him a position as one of the best cavalry commanders of the war. In his first raid he captured an entire Union brigade plus a million dollars worth of supplies at Murfreesboro, Tennessee, on 13 July 1862. Another raid into Tennessee and Kentucky six months later wrecked the supply lines that were needed for Grant's first drive on Vicksburg. Other successes followed rapidly. One of Forrest's most famous victories occurred on 10 June 1864 at Brice's Crossroads, Mississippi. Here he tangled with a force twice the size of his own, which had been sent to destroy his command, and emerged victorious after capturing over 1500 prisoners, sixteen cannon, and 250 wagons. Because of this action, Sherman said during the

Atlanta campaign, "That devil Forrest must be hunted down and killed if it costs 10,000 lives and bankrupts the Federal Treasury." Despite Sherman's efforts, Forrest was never totally defeated. He ended the war as a lieutenant general and was one of the last Confederate generals to surrender their forces. This was quite an accomplishment for someone who had begun the war as an overaged private.

Forrest's successes were all due to instinct and natural ability; his motto "Get there first with the most men" is still famous today. Forrest had little formal schooling, but had already become a rich planter before the war. He was a stalwart man and bold in battle. Less praiseworthy was his attitude towards blacks, extreme even for those racist times. He was the Confederate commander when Fort Pillow, Tennessee, was captured by the Rebels on 12 April 1864. The fort was defended largely by black troops who apparently were shot down while they tried to surrender. The victorious Confederates may have been trying to set an example to deter other blacks from enlisting in the Union army. While the controversy over what actually happened to the black defenders of Fort Pillow is still raging today, there seems little reason to doubt that an atrocity took place. After the war, Forrest was one of the founders of the Ku Klux Klan, and may have been its first Grand Wizard.

CHAPTER III

The Armies Converge

Grant's army had covered a great deal of ground in his absence. He had been ready to lead his men south towards Corinth on 2 March, but his quarrel with Halleck and subsequent removal from command delayed the expedition. Finally, on 4 March General Smith, Grant's replacement, ordered Brig. Gen. W.T. Sherman to advance elements of his *5th Division* to Savannah, Tennessee, and secure the area for the arrival of the rest of the army.

The Union Advance to Pittsburg Landing

This was the opening move of a new major campaign. Savannah was located on the right (eastern) bank of the Tennessee about 30 miles northeast of Corinth, which was Smith's principal objective. Savannah was chosen as a base for the next stage of the campaign because of its accessibility to Buell's army, which Halleck was planning to order south from Nashville before he confronted the Confederate army at Corinth.

The first troops that Sherman sent to Savannah were the men of the *4th Illinois Infantry*, which arrived on 4 March. It was reinforced the next day by the *4th Ohio*. Five days later, the bulk of Smith's army began to arrive after a trip of about 100 miles up the Tennessee River in some 60 steamboats. The size of the expedition amazed many of the Union soldiers. One officer wrote, "We tied up to the west shore where the boats are crowded for a mile, sometimes four and five deep."

Smith wasted little time moving against his assigned objec-

Brigadier General William Tecumseh Sherman was responsible for selecting the Union camp sites at Pittsburg Landing. He failed to interpret accurately the numerous signs of the Confederate surprise attack on 6 April.

tive, Corinth. While his troops were still arriving at Savannah, he sent two expeditions against the rail lines leading to Corinth. On 12 March, Lew Wallace was directed to take his division to Crump's Landing, four miles south of Savannah on the western bank of the Tennessee. From there, he was to proceed against the Mobile and Ohio Railroad near Purdy. Some of Wallace's men reached their objective as ordered and tore up a stretch of track, but the damage was not significant. Another expedition, composed of Sherman's *5th Division*, was dispatched on the 14th to strike the Memphis and Charleston Railroad east of Corinth at a point some 30 miles upriver from Savannah. Sherman penetrated northeastern Mississippi but heavy rains prevented him from reaching his objective.

While Sherman's and Wallace's divisions were on their raids, Smith came to the conclusion that he could not keep the entire army stationed at Savannah. Crowded and unsanitary conditions there were already causing much illness and dissatisfaction among the troops; some officers complained of having to use muddy water for drinking and cooking. To help relieve this situation, on the 15th Smith sent Brig. Gen. Stephen Hurlbut's *4th Division* upriver to Pittsburg Landing, located about nine miles upstream from Savannah on the opposite western bank of the Tennessee. Hurlbut was ordered to support Sherman's men on their return from northeastern Mississippi. On his trip downriver after his aborted raid, Sherman dropped his men off at Pittsburg Landing and hurried to report to Smith at Savannah. There he asked for, and received, permission to march overland against the Memphis and Charleston Railroad. He began this new raid on the night of 16 March, but he had to turn back on the 17th because of increasingly heavy enemy opposition.

When Sherman returned from this raid, he asked for, and received, permission to remain at Pittsburg Landing. In fact, Sherman's report on the advantages of that location were so glowing that the bulk of the army was soon being transferred there from Savannah. Sherman noted that good campsites were available on a tableland west of the Landing; this position was well protected by Snake and Owl Creeks on the north and Lick Creek on the south. The bottoms along these creeks were marshy, but the ground was more open towards the southwest, the direction the army would proceed on the way to Corinth. Hundred foot high bluffs gave ample protection to the "landing," which was actually only a dilapidated warehouse at the foot of the road to Corinth. Named after one Pitts Tucker, the landing was situated about 26 miles north of the junction of the Tennessee and Alabama Rivers, about nine miles upriver from Savannah, and about 100 miles east of Memphis.

The position Sherman chose for his *5th Division* was astride the main Corinth Road, some four miles southeast of Pittsburg Landing. Near the center of Sherman's camp was an old Methodist frame church named Shiloh. Shiloh means "Place of Peace." Ironically, the small chapel would become the center of heavy fighting and would loan its name to one of the war's bloodiest battles. Sherman deliberately posted his division far from the landing in order to leave plenty of room for the rest of the army to encamp. His position also had the advantage of controlling the main road to Corinth as well as another road that led west to a town named Purdy on the Mobile and Southern Railroad.

As senior officer in the area, Sherman was given the task of

Pittsburg Landing, as viewed from the eastern shore of the Mississippi after the war, had only one dilapidated building in 1862.

assigning campsites to the new troops as they arrived. On 17 March, Sherman ordered the men of Hurlbut's *4th Division* to disembark from their transports and pitch camp a mile west of the Landing. From this position, Hurlbut's men would be able to guard the Landing and also watch a secondary Corinth road that branched off from the main road nearby. This eastern Corinth Road ran south at a distance of about two miles from the main road. It then rejoined the main Corinth Road about four miles south of Shiloh Church.

When Grant arrived at Savannah to resume command of his army on the 17th, he approved Sherman's dispositions and began preparations to move additional troops to Pittsburg Landing. The first unit he dispatched was C.F. Smith's *2nd Division*, which was ordered south that same day. However, Smith was indisposed and unable to move out with his troops. On the evening of 12 March he had scraped his lower leg badly when he slipped while boarding a small boat. Though the injury seemed insignificant at the time, it soon became so inflamed that he had to remain in bed: his illness may have persuaded Halleck to hasten Grant's return to the army. Smith became so ill from

Shiloh Meeting House was at the center of the fighting on the morning of the first day's battle. The name Shiloh ironically means "Place of Peace."

the infection (perhaps from tetanus) that he was not able to take the field again; he died from it on 25 April.

Grant appointed Brig. Gen. W.H.L. Wallace of Ohio to take Smith's place as commander of the *2nd Division*. Perhaps because of Wallace's inexperience in command, his division upon arrival at Pittsburg Landing was placed along the Corinth Road, directly west of the Landing. A few days later, McClernand's *1st Division* was sent to the Landing. McClernand was then posted on the main Corinth Road about a mile to the rear of Sherman's camp. His camp was formed facing west, so as to be able to watch the Hamburg-Purdy Road while still giving support to Sherman's advanced position.

Towards the end of March several new regiments arrived at Pittsburg Landing that had not yet been assigned to brigades. About 25 March Grant organized them into a new *6th Division*, commanded by Brig. Gen. Benjamin Prentiss. Prentiss' men were ordered to camp astride the eastern Corinth Road, about a mile southeast of Shiloh Church. This was the best position then available, since all campsites closer to the Landing were already occupied by other troops. Prentiss' camp, however, was more exposed than it had to be because it did not connect with either of the adjoining divisions, Sherman's to the west or Hurlbut's to the north. In fact, none of Grant's divisions were posted so as to meet an attack. No defenses or breastworks of any kind had been constructed, and the only business at hand seemed to be routine patrols and drilling. Drill was more essential for Prentiss' men than most others, since several regiments in the *6th Division* did not receive their weapons until the first week of April.

Grant had posted five of his six divisions near Pittsburg Landing in preparation for the anticipated movement against Corinth. His remaining unit, Lew Wallace's *3rd Division*, was left behind at Crump's Landing near Savannah, some four miles north of Pittsburg Landing. One reason for leaving Lew Wallace behind may have been the scarcity of good campgrounds at Pittsburgh Landing, where almost 40,000 men were encamped by the end of March. Another reason for posting Lew Wallace at Crump's Landing was to guard the direct route between the Tennessee River and Bethel Station on the Mobile and Ohio Railroad. Control of this road, which linked up near Purdy with a back road to Shiloh Church, would help guard Grant's rear. It was also the most direct route from the river to the railroad, which would have to be occupied and cut before the anticipated advance against Corinth.

Grant himself chose to remain at Savannah while most of his troops massed at Pittsburg Landing. His purpose in remaining behind was to be able to meet more quickly with Buell's army and other reinforcements coming upriver. He made daily inspection tours of his army's camps at Pittsburg Landing, nine miles to the south. Nevertheless, it must have been awkward for the army commander to be spending his nights so far away from his troops. Grant was simply too engrossed in making his campaign plans to imagine that events might develop in any way other than what he anticipated.

Buell's 37,000-man strong *Army of the Ohio*, which Grant was intently waiting for, had begun leaving Nashville on March 15. Buell's orders were to join with Grant's army and then await Halleck's arrival before beginning the advance on Corinth. Buell was in no special hurry to reach Grant, and had his five divisions leave Nashville at the rate of one per day so that they would not clog up the roads. Their pace was not forced for fear of wearing out the many new recruits. At night each division was ordered to encamp six miles behind the division ahead of it so as to keep the road relatively secure and ensure adequate supplies of wood and water. Though these procedures produced a slow rate of march, they did serve to keep the troops rested and in relatively good order. Altogether Buell took some 23 days to cover the 123 miles between Nashville and Grant's army. His progress was hindered by muddy roads and two swollen rivers that required bridging; the Duck River alone held up the army for twelve days. His ultimate goal was to reach Hamburg, which was located on the west bank of the Tennessee River about two miles south of Pittsburg Landing.

The Confederates Prepare for Battle

While Grant's army was concentrating at Pittsburg Landing in late March, the Confederates under General Johnston were gathering an army only 23 miles away at Corinth, Mississippi. When Fort Donelson fell on 16 February, Johnston was all too painfully aware that he would be unable to defend Nashville and most of western Tennessee. He had only about 16,000 men, and was faced with the prospect of being overwhelmed by Grant's and Buell's armies. Since Nashville had no fortifications, Johnston had no choice but to abandon the town without a fight. He first evacuated the wounded who could be moved, and then started shipping out all the supplies he could. Unfortunately for the Confederates, Nashville had become so big a supply depot that there was not enough transport available to empty all its warehouses. What could not be carried off was given to soldiers and civilians to pillage, and the rest was burned.

Thus it was a sad sight when Johnston began moving his troops out of Nashville two days after the surrender of Fort Donelson. The war that had begun with so much optimism and such high hopes of conquering Kentucky was now being brought into the heart of Tennessee. Public outcry demanded that Johnston be fired for his failures, but President Jefferson

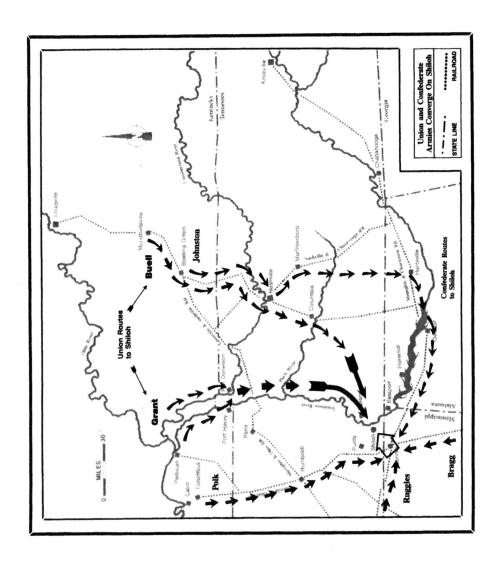

Confederate General Pierre Gustave Toutant Beauregard was an able administrator but was too cranky to get along with his fellow officers. He was Johnston's second-in-command at Shiloh, where his handling of the troops contributed significantly to the Confederate defeat.

Davis stood by his old friend. "I know Johnston well," said Davis, "If he is not a general, we had better give up the war, for we have no general."

After leaving Nashville, Johnston's options were few. His force was too small to counterattack, so he began to gather what strength he could to defend the approaches to Chattanooga. First he led his small command to Murfreesboro, some 40 miles southeast of Nashville along the Nashville and Chattanooga Railroad. There he was reinforced by a few thousand escapees from Fort Donelson. Another reinforcement came in the form of George Crittenden's small command from Kentucky, which had recently failed in its task of defending Cumberland Gap. These and other available units brought Johnston's strength to a little over 20,000, not enough to deal with either Buell or Grant, but still sufficiently large that the Yankees could not afford to ignore them. While at Murfreesboro, Johnston even felt strong enough to detach a brigade of 2500 men to garrison Chattanooga.

While Johnston was gathering troops at Murfreesboro, Beauregard was gathering what forces he could to defend Memphis and the Mississippi River line. The bulk of Beauregard's command consisted of the remains of Polk's army, which was being reinforced with various state units and railroad guards. After Polk evacuated Columbus, Kentucky, on 2 March, about 6000 of his men were sent to reinforce the garrison holding Island No. 10 and New Madrid on the Mississippi River. Polk gathered most of the rest of his force at Humboldt, Tennessee, which was located on the Memphis and Clarksville Railroad halfway between Fort Donelson and Memphis.

Though Beauregard was complaining of ill health (he seems to have been a hypochondriac except when battles were near), he tried to make the best of the situation. He realized that Johnston's army in eastern Tennessee was out of supporting range, so he pressed Tennessee Governor Isham G. Harris to call out all the state troops he could and gather them at Jackson, Tennessee, and Corinth, Mississippi. Beauregard also appealed to the governors of Mississippi, Louisiana and Alabama for troops, pointing out that the safety of the South's heartland was at stake. Beauregard claimed that he would be able to retake Paducah and seize Cairo or even St. Louis if he received an additional 5,000 or 10,000 reinforcements. Response to Beauregard's plea was gratifying, though many of the troops who were enlisted and forwarded to him had signed up for only twelve months' or even 90 days' service.

The Confederate War Department in Richmond also appreciated the precariousness of Beauregard's situation. Taking a calculated risk, the Richmond generals decided to pare coastal and other defenses in the Deep South in order to try to stave off disaster in Tennessee. Beauregard himself had already urged Richmond: "We must give up some minor points and concentrate our forces to save the most important ones, or else we will lose all of them in succession."

The first of these reinforcements to reach Beauregard was Brig. Gen. Daniel Ruggles' Louisiana brigade from New Orleans, which reached Corinth on 17 February, the day after Fort Donelson surrendered. Another reinforcement was Brig. Gen. James R. Chalmers' brigade, which was stationed at Iuka, 20

Major General Braxton Bragg, Commander of the District of Alabama and West Florida, was so eager to help Beauregard after Fort Donelson fell that he reached Corinth ahead of his troops. He succeeded Beauregard as commander of the Army of Tennessee, and lost many more battles than he won.

miles east of Corinth on the Memphis and Charleston Railroad. These new troops gave Beauregard a total of about 21,000 men.

While most regional commanders were reluctant to send troops to Beauregard, Maj. Gen. Braxton Bragg, commander of the Department of Alabama and West Florida, was actually eager to do so. Bragg was well aware that the Confederacy could not hope to win by attempting to defend all its frontiers at the same time. Instead, Bragg felt that large mobile armies should be created to strike the enemy where the South was most threatened, even at the possible risk of losing most of the coastline. During the initial stages of Grant's campaign, Bragg sensed the pressure coming from the north and began to sift his troops towards Tennessee. When he heard of the loss of Fort Donelson, Bragg immediately urged the Confederate War Department to send him and all his available force to join Johnston or Beauregard. When his request was granted, Bragg rushed north ahead of his troops. Beauregard at once placed him in charge of Corinth. A few days later, Bragg's regiments from

Mobile and Pensacola began arriving. By 16 March they had added 10,000 good men to Beauregard's growing army.

While Beauregard was gathering in all the reinforcements he could, he began a dialogue with Johnston that would change the whole nature of the campaign. Beauregard was concerned that Johnston might withdraw towards Chattanooga, away from his own position in western Tennessee. On 22 February he urged Johnston to withdraw instead towards Decatur in north-central Alabama. Once Johnston reached Decatur, some 100 miles east of Corinth on the Memphis and Charleston Railroad, their two armies would be better able to cooperate against the common enemy.

It happened that Johnston was already thinking along the same lines as Beauregard. For this reason, he quickly agreed to Beauregard's request. On 24 February he wrote President Davis that he would soon be marching to Decatur. In order to disguise his movement, he sent a brigade and numerous wagons and trains to Chattanooga. His deception worked masterfully. For the next week, the Union high command was convinced that Johnston was marching to Chattanooga. Meanwhile, Johnston advanced to Shelbyville, Tennessee, on his way to Decatur. During this movement his march was well screened from Union eyes by Col. John Hunt Morgan's Kentucky cavalry.

Johnston's force began reaching Decatur on 10 March, and was concentrated there by the 15th. Fortunately for the Confederates, Buell's army at Nashville had shown no inclination to pursue Johnston or press on to Chattanooga. For a time Johnston even cherished thoughts of being reinforced by Beauregard's force at Corinth and then advancing to attack Nashville. His dreams, however, were shattered by Beauregard's frantic reactions to Union advances against his command. Beauregard had six brigades at Corinth, but appealed to Johnston on the 14th for an additional brigade to repel a reported Union raid on Eastport, Mississippi. This news of Grant's advance in force up the Tennessee convinced Johnston that Grant's army posed much more of a threat than Buell's. Consequently, he began plans to shift his whole force from Decatur to Iuka and Corinth. Johnston's movements were at first delayed by bad weather and then by transportation shortages. He had direct access to

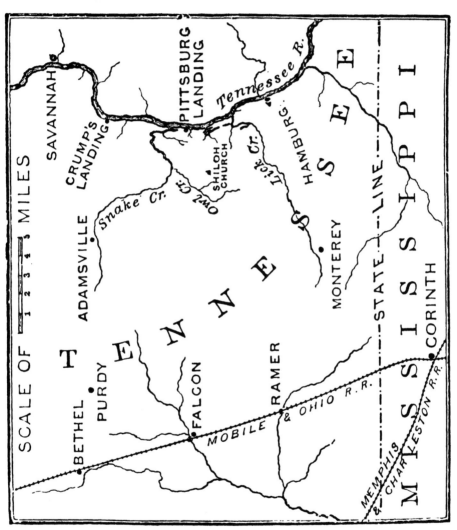

Outline Map of Shiloh Campaign

Corinth along the lines of the Memphis and Charleston Railroad, but 400 railway cars were needed to carry his men. Since only 160 could be located, Johnston's advance was much slower than he wished. In the end, it took him almost a week to transport his 19,000 men 100 miles by rail from Decatur to Corinth.

The week that Johnston was moving his command to Corinth was the same week that Grant was taking firm control of Savannah and Pittsburg Landing on the Tennessee River. Beauregard's immediate reaction to this threat was to move Polk's command from Humboldt to Bethel Station, some 20 miles west of Savannah on the Mobile and Ohio Railroad. Beauregard was anxious about further Union advances, and ordered his patrols to keep a close watch on any Union movements. As a result, there were constant small scale clashes in the no man's land between the Union camp at Pittsburg Landing and the Confederate camps at Bethel and Corinth.

With the arrival of Johnston's army in the Corinth area, the Confederates had gathered all their available western field armies except one, Earl Van Dorn's Trans-Mississippi army. Van Dorn was charged with defending Arkansas and Missouri. A few days after the fall of Fort Donelson he had received from Beauregard a request to cooperate with the armies east of the Mississippi. Van Dorn refused, and chose instead to conduct his own campaign in Arkansas. When this movement ended with a defeat at Pea Ridge on 7-8 March, Beauregard again requested Van Dorn's cooperation against Grant and Pope. Once again Van Dorn refused, preferring to conduct his own campaign to relieve New Madrid and Island No. 10. It was not until New Madrid was evacuated on 13 March that Van Dorn began to be receptive to Beauregard's plea. He did not begin to move east until 27 March, after he bad received definitive orders from Johnston to do so.

Van Dorn rushed to confer with Johnston and Beauregard at Corinth on 1 April, but his troops were not able to move that fast. By 11 April most of his command was at Memphis, but they were to be of no help to Johnston since the battle of Shiloh was over on the 7th. Had Van Dorn reached Tennessee sooner, there is no doubt that his 20,000-man army would have made a significant difference in the outcome of the campaign. To make matters worse, Van Dorn's absence from his department freed over 50,000 Union troops for transfer to Tennessee, where they greatly pressured the battered Confederates after Shiloh.

Johnston Plans an Offensive

Johnston arrived at Corinth on 23 March. He at once had a conference with Beauregard, Bragg, and Hardee over what course of action should be taken. For over a week Bragg had been very interested in attacking the Union forces that had been gathering at Pittsburg Landing, but he had been held back by muddy roads and the disorganized condition of the army. Now that Johnston's arrival had brought Confederate strength to about 40,000, there was a much greater probability of conducting a successful attack. However, several uncertainties had to be dealt with first. There was no way of knowing Grant's plans: would his army sit still in their camp, or would it advance against Corinth or some other objective? Secondly, the Confederate army badly needed reorganization and more equipment. Yet, each day that the Confederates delayed gave Grant more time to reinforce his army and strengthen his position.

The most important result of the Confederate generals' meeting on 23 March was a reorganization of the Confederate army. Each of the four top generals had a body of troops present near Corinth, but no "pecking order" or chain of command existed. In addition, during his recurring "illnesses" Beauregard had recently relinquished his authority at Corinth to Bragg.

This situation was resolved on 29 March with the merging of all the Confederate forces at Corinth into a new Army of Mississippi, to be commanded by Johnston, the senior general present, with Beauregard as second-in-command. Bragg, who was noted for his organizational abilities and strict disciplines, was made chief-of-staff. When it came time for battle, Bragg would change hats and lead an infantry corps. These arrangements appear to have been made almost entirely by Beauregard.

The Army of Mississippi was divided into four corps. The I Corps, under Polk, consisted of four brigades in two divisions (Clark's and Cheatham's). Most of the troops in the corps, which had a strength of about 9000, where from Tennessee. The II Corps had six brigades in two divisions (Ruggles' and Withers'). It had 16,000 men coming mostly from Alabama, Mississippi, and Louisiana. Since it was the largest of the four corps, it would be led in battle by Bragg. The III Corps, under Hardee, had a strength of 7000 in three brigades. About half of its men came from Tennessee, with the rest being from Arkansas, Mississippi, and Alabama. The Reserve Corps, which had a strength of about 7000, consisted of three brigades, one from Kentucky, one from Arkansas, and one from Tennessee and Mississippi. It was first assigned to Maj. Gen. George B. Crittenden. Crittenden, however, was removed for drunkenness on 31 March and was replaced by Brig. Gen. John C. Breckinridge, who had served as Vice-President of the United States in 1857-1861. At least one artillery battery was attached to each brigade in the army. The cavalry was divided up between the various brigades and divisions, with a few left over units being assigned to an army reserve.

The Confederates Close

After making the decision to strike at Grant, Johnston kept in regular contact with President Davis about his plans. The two were close friends, and Davis continued to support Johnston despite the rising clamor to have him removed. Both Davis and his military adviser, Robert E. Lee, supported Johnston's proposed offensive, provided that he moved before Grant's army was reinforced by Buell's army. Davis, who had been Secretary of War in Franklin Pierce's cabinet, wrote Johnston, "If you can meet the division of the enemy moving from the Tennessee before it can make a junction with that advancing from Nashville the future will be brighter. If this cannot be done, our only hope is that the people of the Southwest will rally en masse ... to oppose the vast army which will threaten the country. ... My confidence in you has never wavered, and I hope the public will soon give me credit for judgment rather than continue to arraign me for obstinacy. ...I feel that it would be worse than useless to point out to you how much depends on you."

Johnston shared Davis' belief that something had to be done

to prevent the Yankees from forming a single great army that could travel at will into the heartland of the South. He also felt keenly all the criticism being heaped on him for the loss of Kentucky and most of Tennessee. Davis' trust in him, and his own belief in his role as chief of the Confederacy's largest military department, were leading Johnston to make a calculated gamble.

Johnston had been hoping to wait for the arrival of Van Dorn's army before beginning any offensive. However, circumstances in the last few days of March were developing so fast that they forced his hand. On the 29th he learned that elements of Buell's army were beginning to cross the Duck River. This meant that Buell was marching to join Grant, with only about 80 miles separating their two armies. Johnston thus had less than a week to deal with Grant before Buell arrived. If the two Union armies linked up without interference, they would be much more difficult to defeat, since their combined strength would be greater than Johnston's army even after it was reinforced by Van Dorn.

Johnston was also concerned by Grant's increasing activity at the end of the month. Probes by enemy infantry and gunboats along the Tennessee suggested that Grant intended to advance soon against Eastport, 30 miles to the east of Corinth. Then, on the 31st, came news of a large Union movement towards Purdy, 20 miles to the north of Corinth.

The news of Buell's approach and Grant's pending movements convinced Johnston that it was time to begin preparations to take the field. On 1 April he ordered the I and III Corps to be ready to advance in twenty-four hours; Hardee's II Corps would remain behind to keep an eye on Eastport. In preparation for the coming battle, Johnston held a review of his men on 2 April. He then made plans for his troops to march at 0600 hours on 3 April, each man carrying three days' cooked rations and 100 rounds of ammunition.

This order to advance did not surprise Beauregard, who had been formulating his own plans to attack Grant's camps at Pittsburg Landing. On the morning of 3 April Beauregard met with Johnston, Bragg, Polk, and Hardee to explain his plan of attack. Beauregard's plans were soon adopted without change,

Major General William J. Hardee, author of the famous manual "Hardee's Tactics," commanded the first Confederate attack wave on 6 April.

but the generals' meeting and the drafting of final orders had consumed most of the morning. As a result, most Confederate troops did not begin marching until 1500 hours, after standing around all day ready to go since 0600. An unanticipated problem soon arose when a great traffic jam was created at Corinth because all the troops were trying to reach their assigned march routes.

Beauregard's battle plan gave a set timetable for the army's advance, and prescribed the exact battle lines to be formed. As often happens with such movements, the advance did not proceed as ordered. The first difficulty was the traffic jam in Corinth. Other complications soon began to snowball. Hardee's I Corps, which led the army's advance along the main Corinth Road, ran into difficulty that evening when a portion of the corps left the main road to encamp near a spring located on a parallel road. This movement confused Polk's corps, which was supposed to follow Hardee. Polk's men stayed on the main road until it was time to bivouac. They became confused when they did not run into Hardee's rear guard as they expected. When Hardee's stray troops returned to the main road to resume their march the next morning, they found the road occupied by Polk's men. By the time Polk cleared the road for Hardee, the army's entire timetable for 4 April had been ruined.

Bragg's corps also had difficulty keeping to schedule. Maj. Gen. Daniel Ruggles, commander of Bragg's 1st Division, was the victim of a classic error. Ruggles had been ordered to be ready to march at 0600, "early tomorrow morning." Since the order was dated 3 April, Ruggles naturally assumed that he was supposed to be ready to move out on the 4th. He was actually supposed to begin moving on the 3rd; the error was made by the staff officer who penned Beauregard's marching orders. These were planned and dictated on the 2nd, but were not written out—and dated—until early on the 3rd. By the time the error was corrected, Ruggles was already hours late.

Once Ruggles got under way, his advance was slowed by his wagons and the poor condition of the road he was following. By evening he was running six hours behind schedule. In an effort to speed his march, Bragg ordered him to change roads on the morning of the 4th and follow Withers' division on the Monterey-Savannah Road. Ruggles proceeded as ordered, and ended up blocking an important intersection that Polk needed to march through. As a result, Polk's corps covered less than seven miles on the 4th.

A light rain that began falling on the afternoon of the 4th delayed all the Confederate units, especially the wagons and artillery. As a result, almost everyone was a full 24 hours behind schedule by the night of the 4th. The advance troops, Hardee's corps, had reached a position on the Corinth-Pittsburg Landing Road only three miles from Shiloh Church and the Union lines. Behind Hardee, Polk's corps was strung out along the road for several miles north of the intersection called Mickeys. Bragg's troops were along the Monterey Road south of Mickeys, and the Reserve Corps was at Monterey after a long march of 23 miles.

Despite the rain and the muddy roads it caused, Johnston ordered an attack on Grant's camps to be made early on 5 April. Polk was to begin moving at 0300 hours, and all the troops were to be in position at 0700, for a attack at 0800. To stir the hearts of his men, Johnston sent an inspiring message to be read to each regiment before entering battle:

Soldiers of the Army of the Mississippi: I have put you in motion to offer battle to the invaders of your country. With the resolution and discipline and valor becoming men fighting, as you are, for all worth living or dying for, you can but march to a decisive victory over the agrarian mercenaries sent to subjugate you and to despoil you of your liberties, your property, and your honor. Remember the precious stake involved; remember the dependence of your mothers, your wives, your sisters, and your children, on the result; remember the fair, broad, abounding land, and the happy homes that would be desolated by your defeat.

The eyes and hopes of eight millions of people rest upon you; you are expected to show yourselves worthy of your lineage, worthy of the women of the South, whose noble devotion in this war has never been exceeded in any time. With such incentives to brave deeds, and with the trust that God is with us, your generals will lead you confidently to the combat—assured of success.

The Armies at Shiloh

All three of the armies at Shiloh—Grant's, Buell's and Johnston's—were composed mostly of green troops. A major part of only one, Grant's, had previously seen significant combat. Shiloh was the first major battle in the West and neither side used an organization of the kind employed later for the rest of the war.

The most significant fact about all the armies at Shiloh is that their regiments were big. Averaging well over 500 men, they were simply too large for the inexperienced commanders of the day to lead effectively. Later in the war most regiments averaged around 400 men in battle, due to losses in battle and from disease. This number seems to have worked much more efficently than the 1,000 men a regiment was supposed to have.

Another point to note is that batteries were not centralized into reserves or large battalions, but were dispersed among all the brigades (in the accompanying roster, the Union batteries are listed together by division, but they actually did not serve together, for they were assigned to individual infantry brigades). This practice was in line with period doctrine, and greatly limited the effectiveness of the artillery by making it harder to concentrate fire. Many batteries fought well defensively in their separate positions during the battle, but the advantages of massed fire power were gained only twice: by Ruggles' Confederate line facing the Hornets' Nest, and by Grant's last line. Cavalry on both sides suffered similarly from a lack of central-ized organization. These shortcomings in artillery and cavalry organization, however, were not as deleterious at Shiloh as they might have been because of the way that the woods and heavy terrain of the battlefield limited cavalry and artillery activity.

Above the regimental level, all the armies at Shiloh were organized into brigades and divisions. These were numbered, but were usually called more often by the names of their commanders. Note that in Buell's army, the brigades were numbered sequentially, but bore numbers reflecting a brigade structure that existed before the divisions were formed. Thus Buell's *4th Division* contained the army's *10th, 19th,* and *22nd Brigades.*

The organization of the Confederate army was a bit more efficient than the Northern organization because most of their divisions were assigned to corps. Polk's I Corps had two divisions of two brigades each, as did Bragg's II Corps, but Hardee's III Corps and Breckinridge's Reserve Corps each had three brigades with no division structure. Grant's army, with six divisions and no corps, proved a bit unwieldy to command since there were no intermediate commanders to organize and sort out the divisions. The Confederate army thus had a distinct organizational advantage by having the four corps commanders to organize the divisions and brigades, plus an assistant army commander, Beauregard. This structure worked well enough when the army suffered the loss of it commander, A.S. Johnston; it is interesting to speculate what might have happened to the Union command structure if Grant had fallen casualty.

The Union brigades tended to be more equal in size than the Confederate brigades. Most Union brigades had four regiments and a battery for an average of 2,000 to 2,500 men. Some of the newer brigades had only three regiments, while one of the older ones had six. Union brigade strengths overall ranged from 1,300 to 3,600 (ironically, the weakest brigade in Grant's army, Stuart's was assigned the most critical part of the battle line, the far left near the Mississippi River). The divisions in Grant's army averaged 7,600 men each. Four of the six divisions had three brigades; Sherman's had four and Prentiss' had two. In Buell's army, which did not bring its full strength to the field, two divisions had three brigades and two had two brigades.

Confederate brigades generally contained more regiments than Union brigades, but the typical Confederate brigade had the same strength as its Union counterpart due to the fact that the Confederate regiments were slightly smaller, running about 500 men, while the average Union regiment had over 560.

The Union side had a distinct advantage in both numbers and quality in artillery. Grant and Buell fielded 131 guns in 26 batteries, while Johnston had only 115 guns in 23 batteries. More significant is the fact that almost 50% of the Union guns—64 pieces—were rifled cannons, which had a longer range than

smoothbores. The Confederates had ony 13 rifled guns. In fact, over half of the Confederate guns—58 pieces—were six-pound smoothbores, the weakest type on the field, and also the most common, since the North had 36 of them.

It should be noted that while most of the batteries on both sides had six guns, some had four and a few had five. Standard practice was for a battery to fight in two or three two-gun sections. Very seldom did a battery have all its guns of the same type (only eight Union batteries and one Confederate one did), due mostly to a belief that it was advantageous to have different types of firepower in the same battery. However, this practice also caused supply problems, since ammunition could not be freely interchanged within a battery. There were also supply problems at the army level, with the North having to furnish ammunition to ten different gun types and the South having five different gun types.

Thus, the Confederates in the battle had two major advantages—superior army structure and the advantage of surprise attack. The Union armies had three advantages—more veteran troops, better artillery, and more men. Because of the way the battle was fought, each side lost some of its advantages— Beauregard's battle plans and Johnston's death hurt Confederate organization, and the element of surprise wore off; on the Union side, the heavy terrain restricted artillery use, and many of the more veteran Union troops were overrun by the

Confederate surprise attack. All these factors point to a close battle, with the Confederates having their best chance to win before superior Union strength arrived to turn the battle against them.

Confederate Corps Commanders

Johnston's four corps commanders were all very capable, experienced officers who would serve the South well at Shiloh and in the rest of the war. Though they all had strong personalities, they cooperated as well as could be expected during the campaign.

The Fighting Bishop: Leonidas Polk (I Corps)

Lt. Gen. Leonidas Polk (1806-1864), victor over Grant at Belmont and commander of the Confederate right wing at Shiloh, was noted more for his military bearing than for his military ability. He graduated from West Point in 1827, but his true love was for the Church—he was ordained Episcopal Bishop of Louisiana in 1840. Polk came out of military retirement in 1861 at the insistence of his good friend Jefferson Davis. He proved to be a better organizer than fighter, though he showed great personal courage by leading four charges at Shiloh. His decision to return his troops to their previous night's camp after the first day of fighting at Shiloh left his wing badly out of position for the renewal of combat the next day. Polk later fought at Perryville, Stones River, and Chickamauga. Following Chickamauga, he quarreled with his army commander, Braxton Bragg.

Bragg wanted him court-martialed, but President Davis intervened on Polk's behalf to settle the quarrel. Polk was killled on 14 June 1864 by an artillery shell at the battle of Pine Mountain in Sherman's Atlanta campaign. He was a distant relative to U.S President James K. Polk.

Braxton Bragg (II Corps)

The pre-war credentials of Braxton Bragg (1817-1876) seemed to portend an illustrious Civil War career. He had graduated fifth in the West Point Class of 1837, and had fought well in the Seminole and Mexican Wars. During the battle of Buena Vista in 1847, Bragg's name was immortalized when General Zachary Taylor gave the famous command, "Double shot your guns and give 'em hell, Bragg."

After the Civil War began, Bragg, who had resigned from the U.S. Army and been appointed a brigadier general in the Confederate army, was placed in command of the coastline from Mobile to Pensacola. When the crisis arose in Tennessee in the spring of 1862, Bragg requested transfer to Johnston's army and received command of the II Corps of the Army of the Mississippi. He fought well at Shiloh, and soon afterward was promoted to full general. Bragg was Beauregard's successor as commander of the Army of Tennessee, but proved to be too indecisive to win any victories. His invasion that fall of Kentucky failed, and he suffered defeats at Perryville and Stones River. Nine months of indecisive maneuvering against Rosecrans in Tennessee culminated in Bragg's victory at Chickamauga—a victory that came more by accident and his opponent's errors than by his own plan. When Bragg failed to follow up his victory by capturing Chattanooga, he was relieved and reassigned as President Davis' personal military adviser.

Bragg was respected as an organizer, but was not able to inspire his generals or his men. He also was indecisive much too often, and suffered from constant illness, probably migraine headaches. His sternness and instability often earned him the dislike of his associates. Reportedly during the Mexican War someone had tried to blow up his tent while he was asleep. The most enlightening Bragg anecdote concerns an incident that occurred during the Confederate retreat from Shiloh to Corinth. During this march, Bragg gave strict orders that no one was to fire a gun for any reason, lest the army's position be betrayed to enemy scouts. When one hungry soldier fired at a chicken and wounded a black child by accident, Bragg had the man executed. This gave rise to the story that Bragg had a soldier shot for killing a chicken. Recent opinion of him has not altered much; one recent biography is entitled *Braxton Bragg and Confederate Defeat*.

William Hardee
(III Corps)

William J. Hardee (1815-1873) was a stalwart Confederate corps commander in the West for most of the war. He had a distinguished pre-war career that included experience in the Seminole and Mexican Wars, study at West Point and in France, and a stint as commandant at West Point.

When the war broke out, Hardee was appointed a brigadier general and organized a brigade in Arkansas. His talents soon brought him the rank of major general and command of Johnston's III Corps at Shiloh. Hardee soon earned the nickname "Old Reliable" and a promotion to lieutenant general in October of 1862. He led his corps at Perryville, Stones River, Chickamauga, Chattanooga, and Atlanta. Like almost everyone else he did not get along well with his superior, Braxton Bragg, in 1863-1864. He then requested transfer when John B. Hood took over the Army of Tennessee in mid-1864. While Hood was smashing his army to pieces at Franklin and Nashville, Hardee, as commander of the Department of South Carolina, Georgia, and Florida, had the impossible task of trying to stop Sherman's March to the Sea with a ragtag army made up mostly of militia. Hardee lost Savannah and Charleston to Sherman before surrendering with J.E. Johnston's army in North Carolina on 26 April 1865.

Hardee's name today is remembered mostly for his book *Hardee's Rifle and Light Infantry Tactics*, which he wrote in 1854-55. This handbook was a much needed modification of

Napoleonic linear tactics, and as such it served as a "bible" for troops on both sides during the war. Hardee's name is also associated with the Hardee hat, the tall brimmed black formal hat that was worn by many U.S. regular units and a few volunteer units (like the Union *Iron Brigade*) during the Civil War, because he was on the army board that approved it in 1855. (The hat is also known as the Jeff Davis hat, since Davis—the later Confederate President—was Secretary of War when it was first proposed.)

Earl van Dorn

Maj. Gen. Earl van Dorn (1820-1863) is one of the more interesting figures connected with the Shiloh campaign. He ranked only 52 of 56 in the West Point class of 1842. His career saw a great deal of Indian and Mexican War service; he became a major before resigning in January of 1861. After losing the battle of Pea Ridge (7-8 March 1862) and failing to arrive in time for the battle of Shiloh, he sufferred another defeat at Corinth in October of 1862. These losses prompted a transfer to the cavalry. Here he had only a few successes, most notable his famous raid on Grant's supply base at Holly Springs, Mississippi, on 20 December 1862. Van Dorn's vanity and reputation as a ladies' man brought about his early demise. On 3 May 1863 a jealous husband shot the general dead in Spring Hill, Tennessee.

John C. Breckinridge (Reserve Corps)

John C. Breckinridge (1821-1875), commander of the Confederate Reserve Corps at Shiloh, had a varied and distinguished career both in and out of the army. After participating in the Mexican War, he entered politics and rose to be one of the leaders of the Democratic Party. In 1856 he was elected Vice-President of the United States under James Buchanan, and in 1860 he was the presidential nominee of the southern branch of the Democratic Party. When the shooting war broke out, Breckinridge sided with the South even though his native Kentucky never left the Union. He was immediately appointed a brigadier general, and commanded the unit later famous as the "Orphan Brigade." He was promoted to major general a week before Shiloh. In the two years after Shiloh he remained a division commander, fighting at Stones River, Chickamauga, and Chattanooga. His greatest success came when he was transferred to Virginia in early 1864. In Virginia he commanded the small Confederate army that won the battle of New Market on 15 May 1864. He then served in various commands in Virginia for another year until he was made Confederate Secretary of War in February of 1865. He did not surrender when the war ended, but fled south with President Jefferson Davis and then went into exile in Cuba, Europe, and Canada before finally returning to the United States in 1869.

The Napoleon in Gray

Pierre Gustave Toutant Beauregard (1818-1893) was another of the war's disappointing enigmas. His pre-war credentials were quite impressive—he graduated second in the West Point Class of 1838, became a distinguished engineer, and fought well in the Mexican War. He was even superintendent at West Point for a short period in 1861. His soldierly appearance and French blood enhanced his military reputation. When the Civil War began, Beauregard resigned from the U.S. Army and was appointed brigadier general in charge of the Confederate forces at Charleston, South Carolina. After his small army forced Fort Sumter to surrender on 14 April 1861, Beauregard was hailed as the South's greatest hero since George Washington.

Beauregard's career, though, never reached the heights he seemed to promise. His fiery Creole nature made him difficult to work with, and he had long bouts of undefined illness that kept him from active field command. He was second-in-command to Joseph E. Johnston at First Bull Run, and played the same role to Albert Sidney Johnston at Shiloh. Here, his grandiose attack plans and ill-timed attack orders may have cost the Confederates the battle. Beauregard ordered his men to "march to the sound of the guns" and so lost many men unncesssarily in costly frontal charges when flanking maneuvers would have been more advantageous. His decision to recall his men late on the first day stifled the Confederates' last chance to complete their victory at Shiloh. He then made no preparations for renewing the battle on 7 April, and was totally unaware of Buell's arrival to reinforce Grant. Thus he lost all initiative on the second day, and was forced to fight a defensive battle that had little chance of success.

Following the loss of Corinth at the end of May Beauregard went on sick leave and gave command of his army to Braxton Bragg. President Jefferson Davis, who was now no fan of Beauregard, took advantage of the occasion to relieve the Creole of command. Beauregard was later reassigned to the scene of his greatest success, Charleston, South Carolina, where he directed the defense of the Georgia and Carolina coasts.

After spending the mid-war period in relative oblivion, Beauregard returned to more active duty in early 1864. In April of that year he was called to Richmond and played a key role in defending Petersburg against Grant's first attack on the city in early May. His greatest success came when he bottled up the inept Ben ("Beast") Butler at Bermuda Hundred on the James River between Richmond and Petersburg.

Beauregard's testy disposition and critical tongue eventually jeopardized his stay so close to the Confederate capital. In October of 1864 President Davis thought it best for everyone involved to send Beauregard back to the western theater. There his role was to be almost entirely administrative; he had little to say about the direction of Hood's disastrous Nashville campaign even though Hood was technically under his command. In early 1865 Beauregard joined Joseph E.

Johnston's Army of the Tennessee in its unsuccessful opposition to Sherman's advance through the Carolinas. Here he was once again second-in-command of a Confederate army—clear evidence of how the Confederate high command respected his administrative ability but distrusted him as an active field commander. Beauregard surrendered with Johnston in North Carolina on 28 April 1865.

In post-war years, Beauregard refused several offers to command foreign armies (most notably in Romania and Egypt). He lived in New Orleans, and served for awhile as president of a railroad before holding several state offices.

CHAPTER IV

The Eve of Battle

*H*ad all gone well on 5 April, Johnston's grand attack on the Union forces would have gone off more or less on schedule despite a few difficulties. But all did not go well, resulting in further delays. The fortunes of war, however, favored the Confederates and the Union troops remained largely inactive.

Confederate Delays

Johnston's carefully worked out timetable was delayed by a heavy thunderstorm that drenched everything and everyone from 0200 to 0500 on the 5th. Bragg was not able to begin moving until 0700, and Hardee did not get into his attack position until 1000 hours. Because of the muddy terrain, portions of the extreme right of the line were not in position until nearly noon.

At noon, Johnston was making plans to begin his long delayed attack when he found that Ruggles' 6,000-man division was not in its assigned position in the second battle line. Worse yet, no one was quite sure where Ruggles was. With a little scouting around, Johnston found Ruggles' men standing still along the road. Ruggles claimed that the road ahead was blocked by Polk's troops. Most of Polk's troops were actually following Ruggles' command, but apparently a few units had gotten ahead when Ruggles heard firing and formed some of his men into battle line off the road. Ruggles' delay stalled most of Polk's corps on the road behind him, as well as the Reserve Corps, which was behind Polk.

The infuriated Johnston quickly cleared the road for Ruggles and sent him on his way. Ruggles then finally got into his pre-attack position by 1600, nine hours behind schedule. Once Ruggles moved, Polk's Corps began advancing. These troops finally reached their assigned positions at dark. Most were totally exhausted because they had been up and ready to go since before dawn.

By 1600 both Bragg and Beauregard were getting testy because of all the delays. Their troops were running out of provisions, and there was no hope of making an attack that day. Since the Confederate advance would soon be detected by Grant's scouts, if it had not been discovered already, there seemed to be no choice but to withdraw to Corinth. Soon Polk arrived at the conference, and then Johnston, and finally Breckinridge. When everyone had had their say, Johnston in his role as commander-in-chief announced: "Gentlemen, we shall attack at daylight tomorrow." He was perhaps swayed by Polk's belief that his troops were eager to fight. Retreat at that late hour, when the enemy was almost in sight, was probably to Johnston the same as a defeat. He would trust to luck that he would still be able to carry out his surprise attack. As he left the conference, Johnston supposedly told a staff officer that he would still fight the Yankees even "if they were a million."

Johnston and his officers had good reason to fear that they would lose the element of surprise. Hardee's troops had been within two miles of Sherman's lines for two days, and there had been frequent skirmishes between the pickets of both sides. In addition, the Confederate troops seemed little interested in attempting to conceal their position. Many carelessly fired their guns in order to clear the barrels after the recent rains. Numerous regiments ordered bugle and drum calls as they moved into battle lines within earshot of Union positions. At one point on the evening of the 5th, Beauregard heard drumming and sent an aide to put an end to it; the surprised officer returned to report that the noise came from a Yankee camp.

That night the weary and hungry Confederates anxiously awaited the dawn that would usher in what would be the first battle for most of the army. The Confederate generals were as anxious as their men. In the evening they met one last time to go over their battle plans. Johnston's original plan for battle had been for Polk to hold the left, Hardee the center, and Bragg the right, with Breckinridge in reserve. This disposition, however, had not been adhered to by Beauregard when the Creole made up the order of battle presented in General Orders No. 8. Beauregard decided to follow a pseudo-Napoleonic doctrine and attack in three grand waves, each wave being composed basically of one corps. Hardee's III Corps, would lead the way, with Polk's I Corps in the second line and Bragg's II Corps in the third line; Breckinridge's corps would form the reserve. This plan looked neat on paper, but would be a major source of confusion in Shiloh's woods the next day.

Johnston's tactical plan of battle was also a bit unclear. He told his generals that he wanted to drive back the Union left flank "so as to cut off his line of retreat to the Tennessee River, and throw him back on Owl Creek, where he would be forced to surrender." However, no one had thoroughly scouted the dispositions of the Union camps near the river, or the approaches to them. Any reasonable exploration of the area would have revealed the many hills and deep ravines there, terrain so hostile that awareness of it might have persuaded Johnston to change his line of attack. But no one seemed bothered by these matters. The army spent the night quietly.

Federal Failure

It seems today almost unbelievable that Grant's army was encamped in such a sprawled out position with no prepared defenses or assigned battle lines, when the enemy was less than 20 miles away. Even more amazing is the fact that the army's commander, Grant, did not remain constantly with his troops, but went each night to Savannah, nine miles away on the other side of the river. It was a time when the war was still young, and no battle the size of that which was coming had yet been fought in North America. In any similar situation, 24 or even 12 months later, the Union troops would not have hesitated to erect barricades and entrenchments to guard their camps, and their generals would have deployed the army in defensive lines. But at this stage of the war such precautions were not yet understood, and they had to be learned the hard way.

Grant's officers certainly had received plenty of clues that a large Confederate force was close by. Much of the evidence at first came from the area around Lick Creek near the Tennessee River, where a great deal of Confederate reconnoitering was detected on 1 and 2 April. Late on the 2nd, Sherman decided to send the *54th Ohio Infantry* and *5th Ohio Cavalry* to drive back or capture any Confederates that were lurking around his left flank. The raid succeeded in taking several prisoners from the 1st Alabama Cavalry early on the morning of the 3rd. None of these, however, furnished Sherman any definite information as to Confederate movements. If anything, the prisoners seemed to indicate that the Confederate army was still at Corinth.

This incident, and the results of other occasional patrols, led Sherman to the conclusion that there were only casual Confederate cavalry patrols and pickets on his front. For this reason, he did not hesitate to permit the *70th Ohio* of Buckland's brigade to march a few miles out along the Corinth Road for needed drill on 3 April. The men of the regiment marched as if they were on a picnic, and stacked arms before eating. Their reverie was soon interrupted when their pickets ran into a Confederate outpost. The resulting gunfire persuaded the regiment's officers to beat a hasty retreat from their exposed position. The Ohioans never determined the number or identity of the Confederate troops they had faced. When they reported the incident to Sherman, he thought little of it and apparently never reported it to Grant.

Throughout 4 April Sherman continued to receive reports of enemy troops in his front. His reaction was to become more and more annoyed at his skittish officers for bringing in reports of large formations lurking just down the road. For example, that morning a sergeant named C.J. Eagler, of the *77th Ohio*, had seen Confederate troops preparing breakfast on the far side of Seay Field. When he reported this to his superiors, the information was relayed all the way to Sherman's headquarters. Sherman promptly responded by sending back an order to have Eagler arrested for spreading false rumors!

Later in the morning, Sherman unknowingly set off a chain of events that almost caused the battle to erupt prematurely.

Things began innocently enough when Sherman permitted the *72nd Ohio*, of Buckland's brigade, to proceed out along the Corinth Road for a little drill. About 1430 hours their exercises were interrupted by shots from their picket line. It seems that Col. James H. Clanton of the 1st Alabama Cavalry, was making a raid of his own to avenge the troops he had lost to the *54th Ohio* and *5th Ohio Cavalry* the day before. His attack was successful as he carried off an officer and several men of the *72nd Ohio.*

When Maj. Leroy Crockett, commander of the *72nd,* could not find his lost pickets, he sent another detachment to look for them. The Confederates mounted up to bag this force, too. However, during their advance, the Confederates unexpectedly ran into the *5th Ohio Cavalry,* which had been sent to aid Crockett. The surprised Rebels quickly scattered, pursued closely by the Federal cavalry. Then it was the Yankees' turn to be surprised. As they passed over a hill, the Union cavalrymen ran straight into the deployed lines of Cleburne's Confederate infantry brigade, supported by four cannons. Amidst a rattling of musketry and cannon fire, the startled bluecoats turned and ran for their lives.

The tired Ohioans returned to their camps at about dark. There they found Sherman in an especially foul state of mind. The shots fired by Cleburne's cannons had excited many of the Union camps, and numerous regiments had nervously formed into line. News of the fighting had even brought Grant hurrying to the front in a rainstorm; when he heard that everything had calmed down, he returned to the rear. On the way his horse fell and severely bruised Grant's leg. As a result, Grant needed crutches in order to walk for the next several days.

When the commander of the *5th Ohio Cavalry* reported that he had met a large Confederate force, Sherman rebuked him harshly with these words: "You militia officers get scared too easily." Sherman was also concerned that the cavalrymen had almost brought on a general engagement by alarming a large portion of the army; he was aware that Grant had stern orders not to bring on an engagement until Buell and Halleck arrived. To prevent such a disturbance from arising again, Sherman directed that, in case of an alarm, units should not advance to the front, but should form on their camp's parade ground and await further orders.

Several Confederates captured during the day's fighting were "jailed" for the night in Shiloh Meeting House. The next day these prisoners boasted to their captors that the whole Confederate army was nearby and would run the Yankees "into hell or the river by tomorrow night." Their warnings were not heeded.

The brief fight on the 4th made Sherman's skittish colonels even more nervous than usual. On the 5th, Col. Jesse Appler of the *53rd Ohio* saw some suspicious mounted men in his front. When he sent some skirmishers to investigate, they ran into a strong Confederate picket line. Appler rushed a message to Sherman, only to be irately told, "General Sherman says to take your damned regiment back to Ohio. There is no enemy nearer than Corinth." Col. Thomas Worthington of the *46th Ohio* had similar fears of a Confederate advance, but had learned to hold his tongue. In the previous few days he had "cried wolf" so often that Sherman threatened him with arrest if he showed his face around headquarters again.

Sporadic skirmishes, some as close as a mile from the Union lines, continued all day on the 5th as the Confederates completed their preparations to attack. Occasionally the Confederates advanced too boldly. For example, the Georgia Mountain Dragoons were ordered to scout the Union camps, and came within 200 yards of a regiment that was drilling. Fortunately for the Confederates, the Dragoons withdrew quickly when they were fired on by Union pickets, and no Yankees pursued them. At times during the day Confederate artillery pieces were spotted moving into position, but they were not seen by anyone with enough authority to do anything about it.

Despite growing indications to the contrary, Sherman remained convinced that his force was in no jeopardy. Early in the morning of 5 April he wrote Grant that the enemy had a small force "about two miles out," but "all is quiet along my lines now." Later in the day he wrote his commander, "I have no doubt that nothing will occur today, more than some picket firing. The enemy is saucy, but got the worst of it yesterday, and will not press our pickets far. I will not be drawn out unless with certainty of advantage, and I do not apprehend anything like an attack on our position."

Despite Sherman's confidence, enough reports of enemy activity had come in during the day to persuade him to make a movement the next day to drive off whatever enemy forces were pestering his pickets. Orders were sent to Col. Jesse Hildebrand, commanding Sherman's *3rd Brigade*, to send his cavalry and the *77th Ohio* to Seay Field at 0630 on 6 April.

Sherman's lack of information about the enemy forces on his front, and his lack of concern, were inexcusable by any standard. If the upcoming battle had been a Union loss there is little doubt that Sherman's military career would have been severely curtailed. As it was, there was only one general in the whole Union army who was doing an adequate job of gathering intelligence. This was Maj. Gen. Lew Wallace, commander of Grant's *3rd Division*. Wallace was stationed at Crump's Landing, four miles north of the rest of the army, and was worried about being attacked in his isolated position. For this reason he sent scouts and spies to Purdy and Corinth to monitor Confederate movements. Late on the 4th two of these scouts reported the Confederate advance from Corinth. Wallace forwarded the information to Grant, but Grant apparently disregarded it because of Sherman's assertions to the contrary.

Leaders

Since Shiloh was one of the war's first major engagements, the battle served as a training ground for many future great—and not so great—leaders. Most notably, two future presidents of the United States, U.S. Grant and James A. Garfield, fought at Shiloh, along with several future army comanders on both sides: W.T. Sherman, John A. McClernand, James B. McPherson, John C. Breckinridge, and Braxton Bragg. Some of the battle's commanders never lived up to the early promise they showed, most notably Don Carlos Buell, Lew Wallace and P.G.T. Beauregard. Others won glory but met early death in battle: Pat Cleburne, Leonidas Polk, and, of course, Albert Sidney Johnston. Other participants in the battle included two future secretaries of war (John C. Breckinridge and John Rawlins), one former U.S. Vice President (John C. Breckinridge), two college founders (W.T. Sherman and Leonidas Polk), three famous authors (Samuel Clemens, Lew Wallace, and U.S. Grant), and one noted explorer (Henry M. Stanley).

It is interesting to note that only one of Grant's six division commanders rose to fame after the battle: W.T. Sherman of the *5th Division*. Three (Lew Wallace of the *3rd Division*, Stephen Hurlbut of the *4th Division* and John McClernand of the *1st Division*) rose in rank but had checkered careers later in the war. The battle was the career high point for two of Grant's division commanders. Benjamin Prentiss of the *6th Division*, who was captured after his lengthy defense of the Hornets' Nest line, re-signed from the army in 1863, and W.H.L. Wallace of the *2nd Division* was killed during the battle.

Most of the battle's principal leaders are discussed in separate sidebars. Listed below are the battle's secondary figures on both sides, their commands in the battle, and a synopsis of their later achievements.

Maj. Gen Benjamin F. Cheatham (1820-1886), 2nd Division, Confederate I Corps. Wounded at Shiloh, Cheatham ably commanded his division for three more years in the Army of Tennessee. He later led Hardee's Corps.

Brig. Gen. Charles Clark (1811-1877), 1st Division, Confederate I Corps. Clark was wounded at Shiloh and had difficulty walking ever after. He was captured in July 1862 and was not exchanged until October 1863. Clark then resigned from the army in order to become governor of Mississippi.

Brig. Gen. Patrick R. Cleburne (1828-1864), 2nd Brigade, Confederate III Corps. Cleburne was born in Ireland and then came to America to seek his fame and fortune. When the war began, he cast his lot with the South and soon became colonel of the 1st Arkansas. He fought well at Shiloh, and went on to participate in all the major battles of the western theater, rising to the rank of major general in charge of a corps. His skills and reliability earned him the nickname "Stonewall Jackson of the West." Cleburne was the highest ranking of the five Confederate generals killed at the battle of Franklin, Tennessee, on 30 November 1864.

Brig. Gen Thomas L. Crittenden (1815-1893), 5th Division, Union Army of the Ohio. A member of the powerful Crittenden family of Kentucky, he led a corps at Stones River and Chickamauga.

Brig. Gen. James A. Garfield (1831-1881), 20th Brigade, 6th Division, Union Army of the Ohio. Garfield's brigade was the last unit of Buell's army to reach Shiloh, and as a result did not get to fire a shot there. In 1863 Garfield became chief of staff for Rosecrans' *Army of the Cumberland.* He resigned from the army in order to enter the U.S. Congress at the end of 1863, and spent the rest of his life in politics. He was elected president in 1880, only to be assassinated the next year.

Brig. Gen. Stephen A. Hurlbut (1815-1882), 4th Division, Union Army of the Tennessee. Hurlbut later commanded the *XVI Corps* at Vicksburg, but was charged with corruption while commmanding the *Department of the Gulf* in 1864-1865. He was the first commander of the G.A.R. (Grand Army of the Republic, Union veterans organization) from 1869-1872.

Maj. Gen. John A. McClernand (1812-1900), 1st Division, Union Army of the Tennessee. A political general from Illinois, McClernand briefly commanded the Union *Army of the Mississippi* in early 1863 and then the *XIII Corps* in the Vicksburg and Red River campaigns. He resigned because of ill health in November 1864.

Brig. Gen. Alexander McD. McCook (1831-1903), 2nd Division, Union Army of the Ohio. After Shiloh McCook commanded the *XX Corps* at Chickamauga. He became a

major general in the regular army in 1864. McCook's entire clan fought for the Union cause: his father, nine brothers, five sons, and an uncle.

Lt. Col. James B. McPherson (1828-1864), chief of engineers of the Union Army of the Tennessee. McPherson graduated first in the West Point Class of 1853. After Shiloh he was transferred to field command. He rose quickly to the rank of major general, and commanded the *XVII Corps* at Vicksburg. He was then promoted to command the *Army of the Tennessee* at Atlanta, where he was killed on 22 July 1864.

Capt. John H. Morgan (1825-1864), Kentucky Cavalry Squadron, 1st Brigade, Confederate Reserve Corps. After Shiloh he became one of the South's most able and dreaded cavalry commanders. He was killed in action at Greenville, Tennessee, on 4 September 1864.

Brig. Gen. Benjamin M. Prentiss (1819-1901), 6th Division, Union Army of the Tennessee. After being captured at Shiloh, Prentiss was released in October 1862. He held several minor commands in 1862-1863, and then resigned in order to resume his law practice.

Capt. John A. Rawlins (1831-1869), assistant adjutant general on Grant's staff, Army of the Tennessee. Rawlins was a close personal friend of Grant and served as the latter's chief of staff, rising to the rank of major general. He served as Grant's Secretary of War in 1869.

Brig. Gen. Daniel Ruggles (1810-1897), 1st Division, Confederate II Corps. Ruggles later commanded the District of East Louisiana, but could not get along with his superiors. As a result, he held no command during the final year of the war.

Brig. Gen. A.P. Stewart (1821-1908), 2nd Corps, 1st Division, Confederate I Corps. One of the South's best fighters in the West, Stewart was promoted to major general in 1863 and lieutenant general in 1864. He commanded the Army of Tennessee at its surrender.

Maj. Gen. Lewis Wallace (1827-1905), 3rd Division, Union Army of the Tennessee. Wallace's late arrival on the first day of Shiloh is still a source of controversy. His career declined after the battle. He lost the battle of Monocacy in July 1864 while commanding the *VIII Corps*. After the war he wrote the novel *Ben Hur*.

Brig. Gen. W.H.L. Wallace (1821-1862), 2nd Division, Union Army of the Tennessee. He was mortally wounded at Shiloh.

Brig. Gen Jones M. Withers (1814-1890), 2nd Division, Confederate II Corps. Withers was promoted to major general after Shiloh and fought at Stones River, but was relieved of field command in August 1863. He ended the war commanding the Alabama State Reserves.

Brig. Gen. Thomas Wood (1823-1906), 6th Division, Union Army of the Ohio. One of the North's best fighting division commanders in the West, Wood had been Grant's roommate at West Point. He was wounded at Stones River and again at Atlanta.

Sherman

William T. Sherman (1820-1891) was a native of Ohio who graduated sixth in the West Point Class of 1842. During the Mexican War he was stationed in California and so missed seeing active combat duty. He resigned from the army in 1853 to make an unsuccessful attempt at being a banker, followed by equal lack of success as a lawyer. In 1860 he seemed to have found his calling as the head of a new school in Alexandria, Louisiana, called the Louisiana State Seminary of Learning and Military Academy. The school moved to Baton Rouge in 1869, and a year later changed its name to Louisiana State University. Thus, Sherman could be rightfully called a founder of one of the South's leading colleges.

When the Civil War broke out, Sherman cast his lot with the North, even though he had resided in the South for about twelve years. He was given command of a brigade that saw heavy action at First Bull Run. His subsequent clashes with his subordinates—he had a disdain for volunteer soldiers and was a bit high strung to boot—led to his transfer to Kentucky, where he succeeded Robert Anderson as commander of the *Department of the Cumberland.* During the fall of 1861 the pressure of his post caused him to have the equivalent of a nervous breakdown. He managed to keep his job largely through the influence of his friends, the powerful McCook and Ewing families, and his brother John, a Congressman from Ohio after whom the Sherman Anti-Trust Act is named.

In early 1862, Sherman was transferred to Cairo, Illinois. His long and profitable association with U.S. Grant began on 1 March 1862 when he was given command of Grant's *5th Division* of the *Army of the Tennessee*. Grant immediately took a liking to the feisty Sherman, and trusted him to set up the army's camp at Pittsburg Landing in mid-March. In this role, Sherman bore much of the blame for allowing the army to be surprised and defeated by the Confederates on the first day at Shiloh. He made up for his shortcomings, however, by his bravery during the battle, when he was wounded in the hand and had three of his horses killed.

In the gloomy days following Shiloh, Sherman and Grant grew even closer as they fought together to defend their actions at Shiloh. Grant re-warded Sherman for his loyalty by giving him command of the *XV Corps* during the Vicksburg campaign. After Vicksburg fell, Sherman became commander of Grant's *Army of the Tennessee*, and then joined Grant at Chattanooga. When Grant went east to assume command of all the Union armies, Sherman was appointed commander of all Union armies in the West. In this role he organized the successful Atlanta campaign. His "March to the Sea" and Carolina campaign are known for their harshness, as he brought a scorched earth policy to the Deep South in his effort to bring the war to a speedy conclusion. For this reason his name is still deeply hated in the South.

Sherman remained in the army after the war, becoming a full general in 1869. When Grant became President, Sherman succeeded him as commander-in-chief of the United States' armies. He held this important post until 1883, when he was succeeded by Phil Sheridan.

The Orphan Brigade

One of the most illustrious units in the Confederate army at Shiloh was the Orphan Brigade, an all-Kentucky unit whose men were not able to go home after their state fell into Union hands in the early stages of the Shiloh campaign. The brigade originally consisted of four infantry regiments, the 3rd through 6th Kentucky, Provisional Army of the Confederate States, plus two batteries and a company of cavalry under Capt. John Hunt Morgan. When most of Kentucky was captured by the Yankees in late 1861, the brigade had to complete its organization and training in Tennessee. Its first commander was Simon B. Buckner and its second was John C. Breckinridge, former U.S. vice-president. At Shiloh, the brigade was led by Col. Robert Trabue of the 4th Kentucky, and was temporarily reinforced by two units from Alabama, one from Tennessee and one form Mississippi.

The Orphan Brigade fought with distinction at most of the West's major battles—Shiloh, Corinth, Vicksburg, Baton Rouge, Stones River, Jackson, Chickamauga, Missionary Ridge, and Atlanta—and earned a reputation as one of the most reliable units in the Army of Tennessee. This valor and courage, however, brought high battle losses that could not be replaced because Kentucky was behind Union lines. Reduced from over 4000 men to under 500, the brigade was mounted as cavalry in the war's last months. It was one of the last Confederate units in the East to surrender in May of 1865.

Mark Twain in the Army

Famed writer Samuel Clemens (1835-1910, a.k.a. Mark Twain), the author of *Huckleberry Finn* and *Tom Sawyer*, had a brief stint in the Confederate army during the opening stages of the Civil War in the West. When the war broke out, Clemens was a 25-year-old Mississippi riverboat pilot. Being a native of Missouri, Clemens joned an irregular Missouri militia unit called the Rangers. The unit had only 15 members and was too small to be led by a 1st lieutenant, so Clemens was promptly elected 2nd lieutenant and commander.

Clemens' squad was assigned the task of keeping an eye on the Union forces under Brig. Gen. U.S. Grant that were based at Cairo, Illinois, just across the Mississippi from Missouri. Clemens and his men knew nothing of drill, and had no eagerness to learn. Soon the weeks of boredom, rain and bad food began to dampen the enthusiasm of the Rangers. Clemens himself developed saddle sores from riding an old mule, and injured his foot when he jumped out of a hayloft. These experiences convinced Clemens that the war was not for him, so he headed west for the silver fields of Nevada. The Rangers then disbanded before ever being sworn into the regular Confederate army. Clemens loosely described his wartime experiences in his short piece entitled "A Private History of a Campaign that Failed."

Stanley the Explorer

Sir Henry Morton Stanley certainly led one of the most exciting lives of the Victorian age. He was born in Wales in 1841 under the name of John Rowlands. After spending most of his early years in a poorhouse, he left England in 1857 as a cabin boy in a ship bound for New Orleans. In Louisiana he was taken in and adopted by Henry Morton Stanley, a rich merchant, who gave his name to young Rowlands. Unfortunately for the lad, the elder Stanley soon died without a will and left his namesake penniless.

When the Civil War broke out, Stanley joined Company E of the 6th Arkansas Infantry. This regiment saw its first real combat at Shiloh, where it formed part of Shaver's brigade in Johnston's first line of attack. The 6th was among the first Confederate troops to advance at the start of the battle at dawn on 6 April. After engaging in a fire fight for half an hour, Stanley and the 6th charged the Union lines with fixed bayonets and the piercing Rebel yell. The Yankees broke, and Stanley and his friends rushed after them. Ahead was another Yankee line. The men of the 6th formed up and charged again. Stanley's friend, seventeen-year-old Henry Parker, fell with a badly wounded leg. Earlier in the day, Parker and Stanley had put violets in their hats as signs of good luck. The violets did not help Parker, but they did aid Stanley. Soon after Parker fell, Stanley was struck in the belly and fell down breathless. A bullet had dented his belt buckle, but he was unhurt. The time was only 1000 hours; it took Stanley three hours to find his regiment again.

Stanley was totally exhausted, and fought the rest of the day more as a robot than a man. He obtained his dinner from a plundered Union camp, and crawled into an abandoned tent for shelter when a torrential rain began.

The next morning, Stanley's regiment renewed the battle. At one point Stanley was advancing with his company, but found himself without cover. He rushed ahead to a hollow, and continued firing without noticing that no one had advanced with him. Presently the field was covered with Yankees, and Stanley found himself a prisoner.

Stanley and the hundreds of other Confederates captured at the battle were put on a steamer and sent to St. Louis. From there, they were shipped to Camp Douglass, an old stockyard near Chicago. Conditions there were so wretched, filthy, and dirty that Stanley deserted the Confederate cause to become a "galvanized Yankee." Because he was of English birth, he was permitted to change sides and enlisted in a Union battery. He did not stay in the Union army very long. Three days after he left the prison camp, he came down with dysentery. He was then discharged from the army at Harpers Ferry, West Virginia, on 22 June 1862—only three weeks after he had enlisted.

Stanley was nursed back to health by a friendly farmer, and then earned his living by working at odd jobs. After kicking around quite a bit, he ended up enlisting in the Union navy on 19 July 1864. He soon became a petty officer on the U.S.S. *Minnesota*, but he wearied of naval life and deserted at Portsmouth, New Hampshire, in February of 1865. Thus Stanley had the unusual distinction of deserting from both sides in the same war.

He next took up newspaper reporting in several of the world's hot spots. His successes led him to the most famous assignment—in 1869 the *New York Herald* commissioned him to go to Africa to try to find the noted explorer Dr. David Livingstone, who had not been heard from for over two years. It took Stanley two years of searching before he finally found the object of his quest at Ujiji on Lake Tanganyika on 10 November 1871. Stanley's greeting to the explorer, "Dr. Livingstone, I presume," is now legendary.

In the following years, Stanley became a famous explorer in his own right. He is credited with tracing the entire course of the Congo River, and with claiming the Congo region for the unsavory Leopold II, King of Belgium. Stanley capped off his glorious career by serving in the English Parliament from 1895 to 1900. He was knighted in 1899 and died in 1904.

CHAPTER V

Shiloh: 6 April

One of the few Union officers to take seriously the reports of Confederate activity was Col. Everett Peabody, commander of the *1st Brigade* of Prentiss' *6th Division*. Prentiss' division had been formed only two weeks earlier out of troops recently arrived in camp. Because all the good campsites near the Tennessee River landing were already occupied, Prentiss was assigned a forward camp astride the eastern Corinth Road, on the left of Sherman's division and about 2 miles southeast of Shiloh Church. Prentiss' camp was actually the closest one in Grant's army to the Confederate lines. All the Union officers, however, believed that any Confederate advance would come up the main Corinth Road toward Sherman's position. For this reason, Prentiss posted his pickets only 300 yards in advance of their campsites.

Peabody was a large and assertive man. He stood six feet tall, weighed 240 pounds, and was a graduate of Harvard. For this reason he did not sit still on the afternoon of 5 April when he received reports from two of his reliable subordinates that enemy troops were nearby. When he forwarded this information to Prentiss, the general replied that "it was merely a reconnaissance of the enemy in force." Prentiss' reaction was simply to draw his pickets back so as to avoid capture. This response did not suit Peabody, especially after he had been urging all day that his front be strengthened. Finally, about midnight, Peabody decided to take matters into his own hands. He ordered Maj. James E. Powell to take three companies of the *25th Missouri* and two of the *12th Michigan* on a reconnaissance of Prentiss' front at

0300. The troops were to carry full cartridge boxes, and were ordered to "drive in the guard and open up on the reserve, develop the force, hold the ground as long as possible, then fall back."

As ordered, Powell formed his men at 0300 on 6 April and moved out south through the woods east of Fraley Field. At one point his nervous troops mistakenly fired at their own comrades. Shortly before 0500 Powell's men ran into the advance skirmishers of Maj. A.B. Hardcastle's 3rd Mississippi Battalion, part of Wood's brigade in Hardee's corps. The surprised Confederates fired three shots as a warning to their main skirmish line. The battle of Shiloh had begun.

Skirmishing

Powell's force deployed in skirmish formation and continued advancing until it entered Fraley Field. There they saw a whole enemy battle line crouching in the fog. Powell's men let loose a full volley at 200 yards, but most of their shots went too high. The Confederates' return volley was more accurate and brought down the first casualty of the battle, 2nd Lt. Frederick Klinger of *Company B, 25th Missouri*.

Powell's men found what cover they could, and held their position in the center of Fraley Field, but Hardcastle's had more of an advantage in the woods at the field's edge. Both sides refused to yield, and the noise of their firing drew attention from both opposing armies. Johnston, the Confederate commander-in-chief, noted the firing at 0514 hours and began moving his front line forces to the attack. It took nearly an hour for Wood's brigade of Hardee's corps to move up and relieve Hardcastle's now exhausted line on the south edge of Fraley Field. To Wood's right, across the Corinth Road, Shaver's Arkansas brigade advanced towards Seay Field. Farther to the right, Cleburne's and Gladden's brigades completed the force of 9000 that formed Johnston's first line of attack.

As the sun rose at 0538 hours, several educated Confederate officers noted how red it was, as red as the sun had been on the day of Napoleon's great victory at Austerlitz in 1805. This led

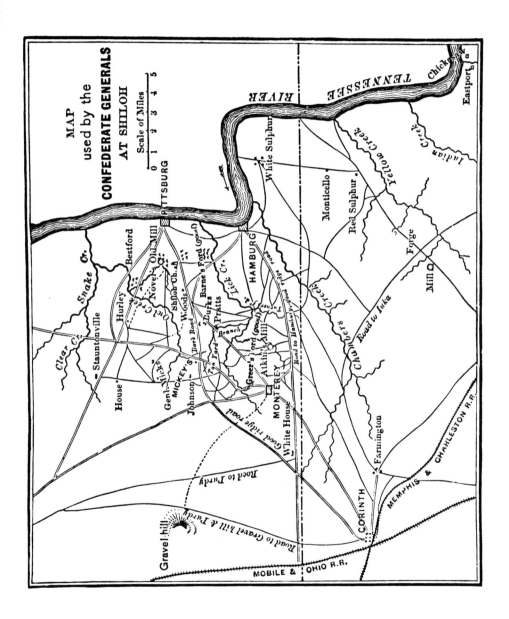

them to believe that they too would certainly experience victory while fighting under the "Sun of Austerlitz."

While the Confederates formed to advance, Johnston and Beauregard had their final brief conference. Johnston's fighting blood was up and he was eager to get to the front. At 0640 he mounted his bay horse, Fire Eater, and proclaimed, "Tonight we will water our horses in the Tennessee River." To an aide, he confided, "We must win a victory!" As prearranged, Johnston left Beauregard behind to oversee the army's rear lines and forward reinforcements and reserves to the front. Johnston showed his determination to win when he stopped to tell one of his colonels, "We must conquer this day or perish."

The noise of Powell's combat also alerted nearby Union camps. One of Sherman's soldiers, Jesse Bowman Young, described how his morning reverie was disturbed:

> The robins had been chirping in the woods since dawn, and the trees were full of music, when suddenly a sound not so melodious broke in on the ears of the soldiers, an occasional shot from the picket line a mile beyond the camp. ... [A]s the firing continued ... wild birds in great numbers, rabbits in commotion, and numerous squirrels came flocking toward the Union lines as though they were being driven from the woods.
>
> It was now almost six o'clock, and the neighboring infantry regiments showed tokens of alarm, and some of them began to form line of battle. By the time that hour actually came the firing had become quite heavy, a cannon shot now and then being heard in the midst of the musketry.
>
> An officer said, "... The rebels must be attacking our outposts."
>
> The words were scarcely spoken when a straggling squad of men came running by in great excitement, their officers in vain trying to keep them in order. They shouted the news that the Confederates were making an attack on the picket line with a heavy force.
>
> By this time the bugles had sounded, "Fall in—mount!" and the cavalry was soon in line. The long roll was beaten among the infantry regiments in every direction. The men were just at breakfast, and many of them had to spring into the ranks in a hurry, without waiting to drink their coffee or eat their hardtack.

As the sun rose higher, Powell took one look at the massing Confederate lines arrayed against him, and ordered a hasty retreat towards his camp. About half way there he ran into five companies of the *21st Missouri*, which had been sent to his support at 0615. Boldly, the combined force turned to face the

Shiloh: 6 April

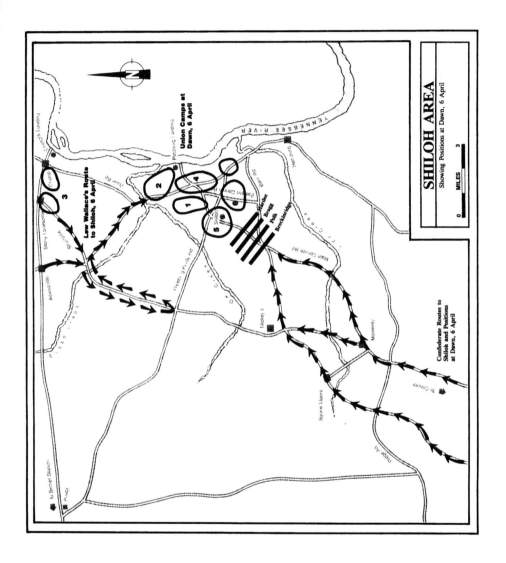

oncoming Confederate attack. By 0700 the remainder of the *21st Missouri* had come up to form alongside the survivors of Powell's command, on the eastern edge of Seay Field. Here the Yankees unexpectedly ran into the skirmishers of Shaver's fresh Confederate brigade as it was working its way across Seay Field. Shaver's first volley felled the commander of the *21st Missouri*, and this so rattled the regiment that it began to withdraw on its own. Powell saw the movement and decided it was time to pull out and return to camp for a long overdue breakfast; he would be mortally wounded only a few hours later.

The new commander of the *21st Missouri*, Lt. Col. H.M. Woodyard, withdrew slightly to the northeast corner of Seay Field. Here he was joined by three companies of the *16th Wisconsin*, which had been on picket duty. The Badgers were green troops who had been issued their first live ammunition only the night before. Woodyard's reinforced command, perhaps 400 men, was no match for Shaver's brigade of well over 2000. The Confederates outflanked Woodyard on both flanks, and began sweeping the Yankees back towards Prentiss' camps.

Meanwhile, Peabody had formed the *12th Michigan* and a few other companies to face the sound of the firing. He was just preparing to advance when Prentiss came barreling into camp. Prentiss rightly accused Peabody of bringing on a fight without orders and told him, "I will hold you personally responsible for bringing on this engagement." Peabody replied that he would take full responsibility for what he was doing.

Peabody advanced at about 0730, picking up on his way the remains of the *21st* and *25th Missouri Regiments*. His line, which was about 400 yards long, then ran right into Col. R.G. Shaver's brigade. As the two forces exchanged withering volleys, a portion of Brig. Gen. S.A.M. Wood's brigade advanced against Prentiss' right. These Confederates were caught totally unawares by Peabody's first volley. Two startled Rebel regiments broke to the rear, taking with them 800 men of the 7th Arkansas, Shaver's left regiment.

All the noise, bullets, and blood convinced the green Confederate troops that this battle was the real thing. Private Sam Watkins of the 1st Tennessee later wrote: "I had heard and read of battlefields, seen pictures of battlefields, of horses and men,

Major General Benjamin M. Prentiss' green division was overwhelmed in the first Confederate attack on 6 April. He was the highest ranking Union officer captured in the "Hornets' Nest."

of cannon and wagons, all jumbled together, while the ground was strewn with dead and dying and wounded, but I must confess that I never realized the 'pomp and circumstance' of the thing called glorious war until this. Men were lying in every conceivable position; the dead lying with their eyes wide open, the wounded begging piteously for help, and some waving their hats and shouting to us to go forward. It all seemed to me a dream; I seemed to be in a sort of haze, when siz, siz, siz, the minnie balls from the Yankee line began to whistle around our ears, and I thought of the Irishman when he said, 'Sure enough, those fellows are shooting bullets!'"

By 0815 Wood and Shaver had rallied and reformed their regiments with the aid of Brig. Gen. Thomas C. Hindman, who commanded the two brigades. The two Confederate brigades then advanced in one of the war's first great bayonet charges. Peabody's line held only about fifteen minutes against this irresistible attack. As his troops streamed rearward, Peabody, already wounded in several places, hurried to his camp to find Prentiss or reinforcements. When he could locate neither, he began rallying his men as best he could. His bravery brought him instant death when he was struck in the head by a musket ball, fulfilling his own prediction that this would be his first and last battle.

While Peabody was trying in vain to stop the surging Confederate advance, Prentiss was rushing the rest of his division into battle line. One by one he alerted his regiments, *18th Missouri, 61st Illinois, 18th Wisconsin, 16th Wisconsin,* and then sent them 300 yards south to form on the southern edge of Spain Field. By 0830 he had 3000 men in position there, supported by twelve guns in Capt. A. Hickenlooper's *5th Ohio Battery* and Capt. Emil Munch's *1st Minnesota Battery.*

The Collapse of Prentiss' Division

Prentiss' men were scarcely formed when they were struck by Confederate Brig. Gen. A.H. Gladden's brigade. Gladden was supposed to have advanced on Shaver's right, but he had lost contact with Shaver because of the woods and heavy brush that hindered his advance. Gladden's regiments were so eager to attack that they pushed forward impetuously as soon as they saw the Yankee line. Prentiss' men were no more disciplined than their foe. The *61st Illinois* began a ragged fire as soon as the Confederates came into view, without regard for the range. Wanton firing like this would prematurely exhaust the ammunition supplies of many units on both sides.

Prentiss' men had fired only a few rounds when they were ordered to withdraw to the north side of Spain Field. Prentiss had heard Peabody's brigade being driven back on his right, and was fearful of being cut off from the rest of the Union army. A withdrawal of this sort under fire would have tested veteran troops; its effect on Prentiss' raw troops was disastrous. The *18th Wisconsin* had just arrived in camp the previous day and was as green as troops could be. When it reformed on the north side of Spain Field, it had only about 150 of its 900 men still in line. Incredibly, the *15th Michigan,* another green outfit that had just arrived the previous day, had never been issued ammunition! Its men stood with fixed bayonets as long as they could before being ordered to fall back. The *15th* eagerly left the field and did not rejoin the fighting until late in the day.

Gladden's Confederates were thrilled to see Prentiss' line

Confederate troops assaulted Prentiss' camp after the division's first line was overwhelmed. None of the Union troops were surprised in their tents, as some early accounts of the battle claimed.

retreat, and they pushed on in a mad charge. As they ran forward they no longer had protection from woods and brush, but passed instead through the center of Spain Field. Prentiss' men, who were sheltered by the woods and stumps on the north side of the field, were disorganized but managed to deliver enough fire to stop Gladden's attack cold. The key to the Union line was the fire provided by Hickenlooper's and Munch's batteries. Their twelve guns swept Spain Field with canister. At about 0815 a shot from one of these batteries knocked Gladden from his horse, nearly tearing his left arm off, a catastrophic wound that would bring his death six days later. Gladden's stunned and bloodied brigade, now commanded by Col. Daniel Adams, withdrew to the southern side of Spain Field in the first Confederate setback of the day.

Prentiss' line had held temporarily, but was doomed by the collapse of Peabody's brigade on its right. Following Peabody's death, his shaken regiments held their camps only a few moments before they were driven back in confusion. Prentiss' weakened line was soon struck on its right by part of Shaver's brigade, on its front by Gladden's brigade, and on its left by that of Brig. Gen. James R. Chalmers, which was then belatedly entering the fight. Faced with these odds, the Union line simply melted away in confusion. Hickenlooper's valiant battery lost 59 of its 80 horses and was lucky to escape with four of its six guns; Munch's battery lost a gun that became wedged between two trees.

The scene in Prentiss' camp was now one of total disorder. Many Yankees who had been wounded earlier in the fighting had crawled back to their tents, only to be captured as the Confederates advanced. Other Federals who had been awakened by the fighting wandered about, dazed, in their underwear. Still other bluecoats risked death or capture in order to dash back to retrieve prized possessions from their knapsacks. By 0900 Prentiss' entire camp was in Confederate hands, along with seven Union battle flags. Many of Prentiss' men were now in pell-mell retreat towards Pittsburg Landing, and only a few isolated bands remained to offer any organized resistance along the Confederate line of advance. Altogether about two-thirds of Prentiss' original command were casualties or out of action for the day.

Sherman's Front Breaks

While the battle raged on Prentiss' front, the left wing of the Confederate army was advancing on Sherman's position. That morning most of Sherman's men had been up at 0530 hours and were preparing for their usual Sunday morning inspection. Col. Jesse J. Appler and his *53rd Ohio* were preparing for a quite different activity. Appler was posted near Rhea Field, several hundred yards in advance of the far left of Sherman's line. The noise of the Confederate attack on Peabody's position drove Appler to send a warning to Sherman in spite of the chiding he had received the day before. Sherman's response was a remark that Appler was having a bad case of the frights.

Unable to obtain specific orders as to what to do, Appler formed his regiment in battle line at 0600 and waited. About an hour later, observing that he was in danger of being surrounded

Waterhouse's Battery E, 1st Illinois Artillery, virtually destroyed Cleburne's 6th Mississippi Infantry in vicious fighting at this location early in the battle.

and swept away by several Confederate brigades, Appler wisely ordered an inglorious retreat. To his good fortune, the unit camped closest to him was Capt. A.C. Waterhouse's *Battery E, 1st Illinois Artillery*. Waterhouse's men were green, but they had six good rifled cannon and their leader was eager to fight. Waterhouse formed on a knoll dominating Rhea Field, supported by those of Appler's men who could be rallied.

Sherman was attracted by the noise of the firing to his left, and arrived at Rhea Field just after Appler's retreat. Upon seeing the field of battle, Sherman instantly exclaimed, "By God, we are attacked!" As he and an orderly, Pvt. Thomas D. Holliday, were surveying the field, a line of skirmishers from the 15th Arkansas approached, unseen, from the general's right. A volley erupted from barely fifty yards away. Holliday fell dead, and Sherman was wounded by a single buckshot that went through the palm of his right hand. The lucky general wrapped his injured hand in a handkerchief and headed to the rear to form up his regiments.

The troops facing Appler were led by Brig. Gen. Pat Cleburne, an aggressive commander who would shortly be nicknamed the "Stonewall Jackson of the West." Though Cleburne had only two of his regiments immediately on hand, he decided to press forward at 0745.

Cleburne's premature attack was quickly shattered by Waterhouse's cannon, which were belching forth smoke and canister. In only a few minutes the 6th Mississippi lost 300 of its 425 men. This loss, 71%, was a dreadful toll, exceeded by only three other Confederate regiments during the entire war.

Cleburne's attack, however, was not a total loss. At its height, Appler panicked and ordered the retreat of most of his regiment. Cleburne was unable to take advantage of Appler's retreat because he had to wait for the rest of his brigade to come up and form. In the meanwhile, Appler's former position was filled by Col. Ralph Buckland's brigade of Ohioans. Cleburne was unaware of Buckland's arrival, and ordered his 1500 men to attack as soon as all his regiments were up. Unknowingly, his brigade was attacking a force 50% stronger than itself. Nevertheless, Cleburne stubbornly persisted in his hotly contested attack for over half an hour.

At 0830 Cleburne's tiring men finally received support from the second Confederate battle line. This line, commanded by Maj. Gen. Braxton Bragg, had over 10,000 men in five brigades. Bragg had followed Beauregard's battle plan and had formed his men 1000 yards behind Hardee's front line. As ordered, he had begun his advance one-half hour after the first line moved out. But because of the rough terrain and irregular advance of the front line, Bragg's brigades had difficulty maintaining a solid line. Col. Preston Pond's brigade, on the far left, had lagged behind, and Col. Randall Gibson's was delayed by two changes in position ordered by Bragg. Because of these difficulties, only one brigade, Brig. Gen. Patton Anderson's, was ready to support Cleburne's attack at 0800.

Bragg was furious that he did not have his corps in hand when he needed it. Beauregard's battle plan had called for him to make a dashing charge with his whole corps in one magnificent line. Instead, Bragg was standing within sight of the fighting with only one brigade.

Bragg decided to wait for more of his men to come up before committing any of them to battle. About 0830 he spotted a brigade coming up the main Corinth Road. It turned out not to be one of his own units, but Col. R.M. Russell's brigade of Polk's corps. Russell was supposed to be part of Beauregard's third battle line, but in his advance along the Corinth Road he had outstripped the rest of Polk's line and even passed by several of Bragg's brigades. Bragg did not ask any questions as to how Russell had arrived so early, but simply ordered him to join Anderson in an attack on Buckland.

The attack by Anderson and Russell had difficulty passing through a swampy ravine and the heavy underbrush on Buckland's front. This terrain so disorganized the attack that only one regiment, Russell's 11th Louisiana, approached Buckland's line. In a flash, a Union volley stopped the Louisianians in their tracks. A moment later, the survivors of the 11th Louisiana were streaming to the rear. Their hasty flight broke the ranks of the regiments to their rear, and the whole Confederate line retreated in confusion. During all this mayhem Bragg himself was almost killed. A bullet perhaps intended for him struck his horse squarely in the forehead and killed the poor animal instantly. When the horse fell, Bragg injured his leg badly, but he soon mounted a fresh horse and rejoined the fight.

As Russell's main attack was being repulsed, the Confederates were having more luck against the left end of Buckland's line. Here the 13th Tennessee, which had become separated from the rest of Russell's brigade, was ordered by Bragg to assault the 57th Ohio of Hildebrand's brigade. The 13th took advantage of a ravine to get near to the Ohioans, and then began to drive them back. Meanwhile, Bushrod Johnson's brigade of Polk's corps had arrived "marching to the sound of the guns" and was committed to the attack. Johnson forced the 57th Ohio to give way, so exposing Waterhouse's battery. At about 0900 the battery had to retreat, too. By then it was so hard pressed that it had to leave three of its guns behind. As the three guns it had left were so damaged that they could not be used, the battery was knocked out of the battle. When the Confederate infantry took possession of Waterhouse's three guns, they found the body of a dead Union officer guarded by his hunting dog. Apparently,

The Confederates overran Sherman's camps near Shiloh Church late in the morning of the first day of the battle.

the officer had brought his dog with him to war. The faithful pet refused to leave his master's side and allowed no one to approach the body.

Waterhouse's retreat left only one of Hildebrand's units, the *77th Ohio*, east of the main Corinth Road. Hildebrand's left was supposed to be supported by the Illini of Col. Julius Raith's *3rd Brigade* of McClernand's *1st Division*, but Raith had deployed too far east of Buckland's line when he had advanced from his camps at about 0800 hours. When Raith saw Wood's brigade of Hardee's corps advancing from Peabody's camp, he had halted his four regiments and begun a brisk fire fight. Soon Gen. Alexander Stewart's brigade of Polk's corps arrived to support Wood, and Raith had his hands full.

Beauregard's first, second, and third lines were becoming confused and intermingled, but the combined weight of the arriving Confederate brigades succeeded in overwhelming Raith's and Sherman's lines. About 0915 half of Anderson's brigade and half of Johnson's brigade charged at what had been the center of Buckland's line in front of Shiloh Church. Their sudden attack scared away the *77th Ohio*, which was supposed

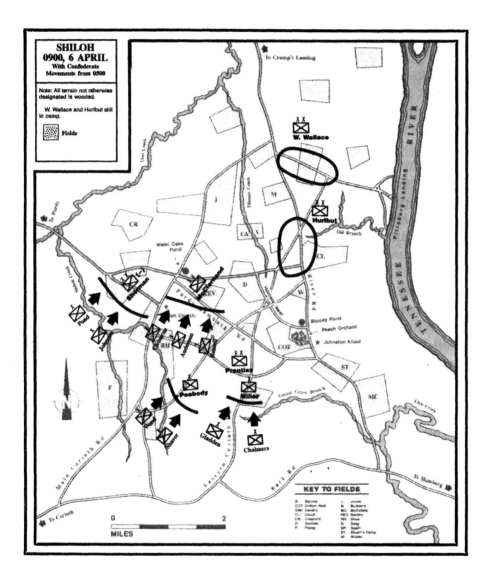

to be supporting Capt. Samuel E. Barrett's *Battery B, 1st Illinois Artillery.* Though they were deprived of their last infantry support, Barrett's artillerymen boldly continued to work their pieces. The cannon became red hot as they blasted one Confederate regiment after another with double canister. Nor did the inexperienced Confederate officers learn any lesson from their disjointed attacks. They continued sending regiment after regiment directly against Barrett's guns in unsupported attacks. Line after line of gray and butternut clad troops was smashed to pieces in vain. At about 1000, Sherman became aware of Barrett's exposed position and ordered the battery to fall back to a new line he was forming on the Purdy Road. The heroic Barrett managed to pull back all his guns just as the Confederates were moving in to outflank him.

Barrett's withdrawal signaled the collapse of Sherman's whole line. His troops had been fighting for several hours, and were running out of ammunition as well as cohesion. The deterioration of what had been Hildebrand's sector of the line exposed Raith's right and Buckland's line. Raith's troops became unnerved when they saw that they were outflanked on both the right and the left. At least one regiment, the *43rd Illinois,* fell back without orders. Other troops were running out of ammunition. One officer in the *53rd Ohio* noted, "There was a good deal of disorder here. Everybody wanted cartridges. There were three kinds of firearms in our brigade and six different types in the division, all requiring ammunition of different caliber. ... Our line was soon broken; bullets came from too many points of the compass." Finally, at about 1000 hours McClernand ordered Raith's wavering regiments to fall back to a new line being set up 600 yards to the rear. Their withdrawal quickly turned to confusion as Raith's weary men were rushed on their way by eager Confederate pursuers.

Sherman ordered Buckland to withdraw at the same time that Raith retreated; Buckland's goal was to be a new position on Raith's right. Buckland managed to withdraw in relatively good order, only to see his brigade scattered by the rout of Capt. Frederick Behr's *6th Indiana Battery.* About 0930 Sherman sent Behr from Col. John A. McDowell's *1st Brigade* to Shiloh Church to replace Barrett's battery. Sherman described what happened next: "I rode across the angle and met Behr's battery at the crossroads, and ordered it immediately to come into battery, action right. Captain Behr gave the order, but he was almost immediately shot from his horse, then drivers and gunners fled in disorder, carrying off the caissons, and abandoning five out of six guns, without firing a shot. The enemy pressed on, and we were again forced to choose a new line of defense."

The fugitives from Behr's routed battery rushed through Buckland's newly formed second line. Buckland later wrote, "We formed line again on the Purdy Road, but the fleeing mass from the left broke through our lines, and many of our men caught the infection and fled with the ... crowd. ... Colonel Sullivan and myself kept together and made every effort to rally our men, but with very poor success. They had become scattered in all directions. We were borne considerably to the left, but finally succeeded in forming a line and had a short engagement with the enemy, who made his appearance soon after our lines was formed."

Fortunately for the Union cause, McDowell's brigade had a much easier retreat than Buckland's. Throughout the morning, McDowell's three regiments had been only slightly engaged. This was because Pond's brigade, which formed the left end of the Confederate second line, never pressed its attack as it should have. For much of the morning, half of Pond's men were ordered to guard a bridge on Owl Creek out of fear that Sherman might counterattack and outflank the Confederate position. It was not until 1000 hours that Pond finally reunited his command and moved to the attack. Pond's progress was hindered when his men, many of whom were wearing blue uniforms, were fired on by supporting units.

Col. Alfred Mouton of the 18th Louisiana merely complained about this fire; Maj. Leon Querouze of the Orleans Guard Battalion went so far as to order his men to turn about and fire on the Southerners who were shooting at them! When a staff officer rushed up to tell Querouze he was firing at friendly troops, the Creole angrily replied, "I know it! But dammit, sir, we fire on anybody who fires on us!" All this confusion during Pond's advance gave McDowell time to withdraw in good order, the only Union brigade to do so of the four that had originally held this portion of Grant's front line.

Throughout the morning Sherman had been everywhere along his lines trying to stave off disaster. However improvident he had been in failing to anticipate Johnston's attack, there is no question that he was a first class fighter once the battle was joined. He knew he was abandoning his camps when he ordered McDowell and Buckland to withdraw to the Purdy Road, yet he made the order without hesitation.

Attack on the Union Left

The initial Confederate attack had met overwhelming success, despite the failure of Beauregard's tactical arrangement. The Confederates failed to achieve a decisive victory largely because of their inability to carry out Johnston's original tactical plan of pressing the Union left and driving Grant's army away from the Tennessee River. Because of the way the fighting developed in the Union center, the thrust of the Confederate attack was drawn to their left as the Rebel brigades marched to the sound of the heaviest fighting; Johnston would have much preferred a stronger push with the Confederate right.

As the battle developed, little pressure was actually put on the far Union left. Col. David Stuart's small *2nd Brigade* of Sherman's division had been put on detached duty to guard the approaches to Lick Creek. Stuart's base camp was just east of the junction of the River Road and the Hamburg-Purdy Road. When Stuart heard the early morning fighting on Prentiss' front, he formed his men and prepared to move up to guard the bridge over Lick Creek as he had been ordered to do.

Stuart's activities were being watched closely by Capt. S.H. Lockett of Bragg's staff. Bragg had sent Lockett out before dawn to scout the Federal left thoroughly. When Lockett saw Stuart form up, he was convinced that an entire Federal division was going to assault the Confederate right flank. Lockett immediately rushed to report this alarming news to his superiors. He reached Johnston about 0930. Johnston was well aware of how important it was to drive back the Federal left if his battle plan were to succeed. For this reason he directed Breckinridge to advance his Reserve Corps towards Stuart's position. Since it would take Breckinridge awhile to move up, Johnston boldly directed the two right-hand brigades of Bragg's corps, those of Brig. Gen. James R. Chalmers and Brig. Gen. John K. Jackson, to withdraw and redeploy further to the right, facing Stuart.

Chalmers and Jackson were occupying Prentiss' camps, and were preparing to move up to attack the Union line that was beginning to crystalize along the Hornets' Nest line. They received Johnston's order to move to the right at 0930 hours, but had to wait for a guide who knew the way. It was actually only 1½ miles from Prentiss' camp to Stuart's position. The most direct route, however, was blocked by a battery and part of Brig. Gen. John McArthur's *2nd Brigade* of Brig. Gen. W.H.L. Wallace's *2nd Division*. Since the intervening ground was cut up by the several ravines that fed Locust Creek, Chalmers and Jackson had to march to the south on a two-mile detour in order to reach their assigned position.

Chalmers had to wait a full half hour for a guide. An hour's march then brought him to Locust Creek, where another half hour wait was ordered while cavalry scouted the Union position. About 1100 Chalmers finally began advancing in battle line towards Stuart's position on the north side of McCuller's Field. The Yankees were ready for him. Their first volley caught the 52nd Tennessee by surprise, and the skittish regiment broke for the rear. But Stuart's men were also skittish. The *55th Illinois* was in its first battle and had difficulty forming its companies into battle line. When the firing started, most of the soldiers of the *55th* panicked and headed for the rear. Stuart managed to rally them 200 yards behind their original position, but the troops were still so panicky that they formed a hollow square to face the Confederate cavalry. An old Napoleonic formation in which the infantry formed facing outwards along each side of a square, the hollow square was relatively useless against infantry and had a distinct disadvantage against artillery.

Stuart also had trouble with another of his green regiments, the *71st Ohio*. As soon as the Confederate artillery opened fire, the *71st* melted away and was not seen again for the rest of the battle. Thus Stuart almost immediately lost the use of two of his three regiments. Only the *54th Ohio* remained to guard the whole Union left flank.

Fortunately for the Union cause, the Confederates did not press the attack against Stuart. Chalmers' men supposedly ran out of ammunition, and had to wait half an hour for more to be brought up. Jackson's brigade, which was supposed to be supporting Chalmers, was late arriving and then got held up by stiff resistance offered by the *71st Ohio* near the junction of the Hamburg-Purdy Road and the Hamburg-Savannah Road. When Jackson resumed his advance to cut off Stuart's brigade, he found his way blocked by the three regiments and a battery of Brig. Gen. John McArthur's *2nd Brigade* of W.H.L. Wallace's division, which had been sent to reinforce Stuart and arrived just in time to save the Federal left.

Meanwhile, Chalmers was desperately trying to take Stuart's position by frontal assault. His troops outnumbered Stuart's by two-to-one, but the Yankees had the distinct advantage of a strong position atop a steep ravine. Stuart held on as his men grew weary and began to run out of ammunition. Nevertheless, Chalmers was unable to dislodge him, even when reinforced by two of Jackson's regiments.

Stuart's brigade was now holding the extreme Union left by a thin thread. About 1500 Stuart correctly surmised from the sounds of battle that the Union center was being driven back. He felt he had no choice but to order his small force, the *54th Ohio* and part of the *55th Illinois*, to retreat. Immediately to his rear was a 100-foot gorge that had to be crossed. To the victorious Confederates, the scene was a veritable shooting gallery as Stuart's men dashed down one side of the ravine and up the other. Stuart then tried to rally his men, but his units were too broken to fight any more. Himself wounded, Stuart led his valiant men back to Pittsburg Landing and out of the battle.

At this point, the road lay open for Chalmers and Jackson, supported by Breckinridge, to march on Pittsburg Landing and the Union rear. However, a lack of decisive leadership brought a change of direction on the Confederate right. Instead of following Stuart's retreat to the north, the victorious Confederates shifted their attack to the northwest, following Beauregard's instructions to march to the sounds of the heaviest fighting. Here the Confederates ran directly into Brig. Gen. Jacob G. Lauman's brigade of Brig. Gen. Stephen A. Hurlbut's *4th Division*. The men of Breckinridge's Reserve Corps and Brig. Gen. James M. Withers' 2nd Division of Bragg's II Corps did succeed in driving Lauman back, thereby contributing to the subsequent Union surrender in the Hornets' Nest. Their victory, however, would have been much greater had they followed Johnston's orders to strike for the Tennessee River rather than Beauregard's unfortunate directive to march to where the fighting was heaviest.

The rout of Sherman's command severely endangered McClernand's line farther to the east. Raith's brigade of McClernand's division had already been engaged on Sherman's left from 0800 to 1000 hours. About 0900 McClernand started moving his other two brigades, those of Col. C. Carroll and Col. A.M. Hare, to Sherman's support, but he changed his mind and instead formed on a ridge slightly south of his headquarters and the Corinth Road, east of Water Oaks Pond and a half mile northeast of Shiloh Church. Though McClernand's decision deprived Sherman of badly needed reinforcements, it turned out to be advantageous. Had McClernand reinforced Sherman with his entire division, he could have helped Sherman hold his line longer, but he still would have been overwhelmed by the superior Confederate numbers that poured past both of Sherman's flanks. As it was, McClernand's presence gave an anchor for Sherman's defeated line to rally on. When McClernand ordered Raith to withdraw from Sherman's left at about 1000 hours, Raith formed on Marsh's right; Sherman's retreating forces then fell in on Raith's right.

The Confederate attack that routed Sherman's command at about 1030 also shattered Raith's unsteady troops. By now the Confederate lines were becoming dreadfully intermingled, and units from five different brigades (Russell, Johnson, Anderson, Wood and Stewart) struck Raith's regiments. Raith's line gave way first on the left, where Water Oaks Pond prevented him from linking up with the rest of McClernand's division to the east. Raith tried desperately to rally his men but was unable to do so. Soon he fell wounded by a bullet in the right thigh. Some of his men tried to carry him to the rear, but they had to leave him behind because of close enemy pursuit. Raith lay on the field for 24 hours until the victorious Union forces found him the next day. He was sent to a hospital ship where his leg was belatedly amputated. The shock and loss of blood proved to be too much, and he died on 11 April.

The Union Right Crumbles

McClernand's main position was a relatively strong one. He had two fresh brigades atop a ridge, with his right guarded by Water Oaks Pond and his center overlooking a large field known as Review Field, which had been used as a parade ground during McClernand's two weeks in camp nearby. The first Confederate attack on this line was made on the right by S.A.M. Wood's brigade. Wood's men had played a key role in defeating Prentiss earlier in the morning, but they were now becoming weary and disorganized. They were particularly disheartened by the loss of their commander during an attack on Raith's brigade at about 0930. Wood had ridden toward some Confederate regiments whose fire was striking his brigade by mistake. As he approached the 5th Tennessee, another volley rang out. Wood's horse was wounded and Wood himself was knocked down. He remained senseless for the rest of the day. As a result of his condition, Wood's men were tentative about their advance against McClernand, and they were understandably nervous about errant friendly fire from the rear. As a result, their attack lacked determination and was readily repulsed.

Soon after the repulse of Wood's brigade, Brig. Gen. A.P. Stewart ordered the 4th Tennessee to attack Capt. Edward McAllister's *Battery D, 1st Illinois Artillery*, which was the key to the center of McClernand's line. The attack of the 4th Tennessee was to be one of the most remarkable feats in this bloody battle. As Col. O.F. Strahl, the regiment's commander, put it: "General Stewart rode up and told me that General Bragg said that the battery must be taken, and asked me if I would do it. I told him we would try, and immediately ordered the men forward, bearing to the left, in order to avoid the open field in front, and marched through a thicket of small timber at double-quick. We continued to march at double-quick until we were within 30

Captain James Timony's **Battery D, 2nd Illinois Artillery,** *lost 30 men and 48 horses in just 15 minutes of fighting, and had to abandon four of its guns when it was overwhelmed late in the morning of the first day's fight.*

paces of the enemy's guns, when we halted, fired one round, rushed forward with a yell, and the battery was ours. We took two prisoners at the battery, who did not have time to escape nor courage to fight. During the whole time of this charge the battery played upon us with grape and canister, making sad havoc in our ranks, killing 31 men and wounding about 160."

Strahl's regiment was aided by more than raw courage during its charge into the mouths of McAllister's cannon. The men of McAllister's supporting infantry regiments had seen Strahl coming, but they held their fire because they thought Strahl's red, white, and blue Tennessee flag was a Federal banner. The 4th Tennessee was thus permitted to march right up to the Union front, where it let loose a devastating volley. This fire felled the colonel and lieutenant colonel of the *48th Illinois,* and soon the whole regiment scattered in confusion.

The rout of the *48th Illinois* spread down Marsh's line. As the Union infantry melted away, Capt. J.B. Burrows' *14th Ohio Battery* of six guns was engulfed and captured in its entirety. Farther to the right, four of the six guns of Capt. James P.

Timony's *Battery D, 2nd Illinois Artillery* were captured. Marsh's entire line was now shattered.

Meanwhile, Col. R.G. Shaver's *1st Brigade* of Hardee's III Corps was charging directly across Review Field towards Col. A.M. Hare's *1st Brigade*, which formed the left of McClernand's line. Shaver described what happened: "Between my command and the enemy was a large field some 200 yards wide. In making this charge my command was subjected to a heavy and destructive fire and the field was strewn with my dead and wounded. Before the woods could be reached, the enemy fled."

There was really no reason for Hare's men to have given up their position so readily. Various sources relate that one of Hare's regiments retreated after firing only one volley while another regiment ran off without firing a shot. Hare himself said only that his men "broke and retired in confusion" because they saw the troops on their right give way and the enemy was approaching in great numbers on their front.

In their hasty retreat, McClernand's routed troops literally ran through Col. James C. Veatch's brigade, which had come up from Hurlbut's division to support their line. Veatch's *14th Illinois* was thrown into disorder by stampeding horses from a battery. The *15th Illinois* broke when it lost ten of its thirteen highest ranking field officers. This left Veatch only two usable regiments, the *46th Illinois* and *25th Indiana*. These fought on, as did a few other scattered units up and down the line.

Veatch slowly withdrew his now mixed command down the Corinth Road towards Pittsburg Landing. He was pursued by parts of Shaver's and Stewart's brigades. Elsewhere on this flank there was complete mayhem. Sherman's troops and the rest of McClernand's men streamed north until they were rallied near Jones' Field. On their part, the victorious Confederates were almost as disorganized as their defeated foes. The Confederate left had. been fighting since dawn and had crushed three separate Union positions: Peabody's, Sherman's first line, and then the McClernand-Sherman line. Many regiments were intermingled or separated from their brigades, and almost all the Confederate units were low on ammunition. Numerous valuable officers of all ranks had been lost, and many regiments had lost over half of their men in action, not counting stragglers or those who stayed behind to loot the captured Union camps. In addition, there was no overall commander on this flank at the moment. Hardee and Bragg had gone to the right, and the senior general present, Brig. Gen. Thomas C. Hindman, had been put temporarily out of action by a shell that disemboweled his horse.

For all these reasons, the Confederates were unable to mount any sort of pursuit of the routed Union forces in their front. About all they could do was try to catch their breath, find some fresh ammunition, and await reinforcements.

The Lines Stabilize

From 1100 to noon, Sherman rallied all the forces he could about one-half mile north of his previous line. These troops consisted primarily of McDowell's relatively fresh brigade, a portion of Marsh's brigade, and fragments from Buckland's, Raith's, and Veatch's brigades. Sherman had certainly had a rough morning. Besides being surprised and driven from two separate positions, he had received two slight wounds and had three of his horses killed. Much to Sherman's surprise, Grant rode up about noon for a quick conference. Sherman expected a thorough tongue-lashing for being so completely surprised and routed, but Grant simply told him that he had fought well and should continue to hold on! Lew Wallace had been ordered to his support and fresh ammunition was being sent forward.

Grant's reassuring words so emboldened Sherman that he promptly began a counterattack to recover Hare's camps. His bold move met success at first, but soon met increasing resistance from the reforming Confederate lines. For almost an hour the two sides banged away at each other in an even combat. Then the balance was tipped by the arrival of Col. Robert P. Trabue's "Orphan Brigade" of Breckinridge's Reserve Corps, and Capt. W.I. Hodgson's battery, the 5th of Louisiana's famed Washington Artillery (the "Orphan Brigade" was composed mostly of regiments from Kentucky that were unable to return home after their state fell into Union hands). Hodgson's artillerymen bravely held their ground unsupported and blunted Sherman's advance. While his comrades were stubbornly trying

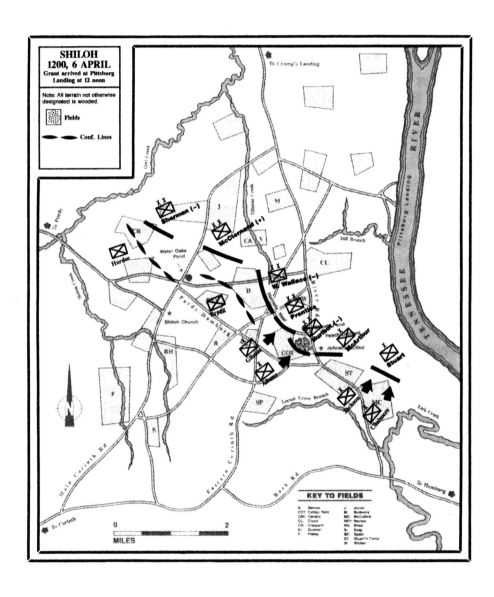

to hold their line, the commander of the *46th Illinois* took his tired and hungry men out of line because he found they were near their original camp; they simply left the battle line to go and get some lunch.

Meanwhile, Trabue was beginning to meet with success against McDowell's brigade on the left end of Sherman's makeshift line. In a short while, however, his advance was checked by a new wave of Federal attackers, the *15th* and *16th Iowa Regiments*. Both units were green and had received their first issue of ammunition only that morning; indeed the *15th Iowa* had reached Pittsburg Landing only a few hours earlier. The troops advanced reasonably well until enemy fire began taking a toll of their officers. They also used up all their limited supply of ammunition too quickly, and soon had no choice but to halt their advance.

Just at this crisis, Confederate Maj. Gen. William Hardee arrived on the scene. He noted that the Union lines were wavering and decided to take advantage of the situation. He gathered four reliable regiments and hurled them in a mad charge against the left wing of McClernand's line. This unexpected blow sent McClernand's regiments flying. Further to the left, Trabue saw what was happening and ordered a bayonet charge against McDowell's brigade. Soon the remainder of the tired Confederate line joined the attack, and the whole Union line broke for the rear.

The Confederates were not able to take advantage of Sherman's retreat because of problems of their own. Many units were out of ammunition, and others for various reasons headed east instead of north. Hardee sent Col. John A. Wharton's Texas Ranger Cavalry Regiment in pursuit of Sherman's men, but the Texans retreated when their commander was wounded. The only Confederates to really harass the Yankees were Capt. John Hunt Morgan's small squadron of Kentucky cavalry. Morgan made several successful charges before being stopped in Perry Field by canister from Hickenlooper's battery.

By 1500 hours Sherman was forming the remains of his own and McClernand's divisions facing west along the Hamburg-Savannah Road. After a day's heavy fighting, he had only skeletons of brigades; most of his men who had not fallen casualty

McClernand's division held its original line along the Purdy Road until noon, when it was forced to retreat about a mile and reformed adjacent to Jones Field.

had by now run for safety to Pittsburg Landing. Fortunately for Sherman, his line was not attacked again after the repulse of Morgan.

Veatch's command, a quarter mile to the south of Sherman, was not so fortunate. During the Union retreat, Veatch had managed to rally the *14th Illinois* and *25th Indiana Regiments* along with three of McClernand's units on the east side of Cavalry Field. About 1600 he was attacked there from two different directions, by Pond's brigade from the northwest and by Trabue's brigade from the southwest. Here, a bit of confusion on the Confederate side permitted Veatch to escape his predicament. It seems that Pond's left regiment, the 18th Louisiana, was wearing blue uniforms that day. When Trabue's men saw these Louisianians, they opened fire, thinking they were Yankees. By the time this error was corrected, Veatch was well aware of the location of the two Confederate brigades. For the moment Trabue's men were too shaken to renew their attack immediately, so Pond went in alone. By bad luck he had to cross a field squarely in front of two 24-pounder howitzers of McAllister's battery. The attack was bloodily repulsed and relative peace began to settle over this part of the battlefield.

Defense of the Hornets' Nest

While Sherman and McClernand were fighting to defend the Union right, an even more desperate drama was being played out in the Union center. Here a whole new line was formed by two fresh Union divisions and the remains of Prentiss' men, the Hornets' Nest.

When the battle began Brig. Gen. Stephen Hurlbut formed the men of his *4th Division* in their camps along the River Road, about a mile southwest of Pittsburg Landing. About 0730 he received a plea for help from Sherman, and sent Col. James G. Veatch's *2nd Brigade* to the front. Half an hour later Hurlbut received a desperate plea from Prentiss, and began marching his two remaining brigades, Col. N.G. Williams' *1st* and Brig. Gen. Jacob G. Lauman's *3rd*, to the south. By chance, Hurlbut arrived in Prentiss' rear about 0830, just when Prentiss' line was collapsing under intense Confederate pressure. Hurlbut immediately saw that there was no sense in proceeding farther, and formed his troops in a large cotton field immediately south of a blooming peach orchard. Hurlbut placed Mann's *Battery C, 1st Missouri Artillery*, under Lt. Edward Brotemann, in the center of his line, with Williams' brigade and the *2nd Michigan Battery*, under Lt. C.W. Laing, on the left, and Lauman's brigade and Capt. John B. Meyers' *13th Ohio Battery* on the right. Both wings were bent back, giving the division a convex line facing the enemy.

Hurlbut's biggest mistake was a tactical one. He permitted Capt. John B. Meyers to put the five guns of his *13th Ohio Battery* about 150 yards in front of Lauman's brigade, in a position that offered neither support nor cover. The Confederates got their artillery into position soon after Hurlbut's men came up. Amazingly, the first Rebel shots were right on target. One shell killed Williams' horse, knocking him senseless. Other shells landed right on Meyers' battery and scared away many of his horses. This unnerved Meyers' green cannoneers, who fled without firing a shot. (For this poor showing, the battery was disbanded

Hurlbut's division repulses the first Confederate attack on the Peach Orchard in the early afternoon of 6 April. This line was soon overwhelmed, exposing the Hornets' Nest line to capture.

soon after the battle and Meyers was fired from the army.) The hasty retreat of Meyers' men left the pieces in no man's land, a tempting target for the advancing Confederate infantry.

The omens did not bode well for Hurlbut's line. On the right, several of Lauman's regiments were temporarily disorganized by Meyers' stampeding horses. On the left, many of Williams' men were scattering to seek what shelter they could from the Confederate artillery barrage.

Fortunately for Hurlbut, luck turned temporarily in his favor. Of the five Confederate brigades that had routed Prentiss, only one was left to face Hurlbut. Wood's and Shaver's brigades had already drifted off to the left to aid in the attack on McClernand and Sherman. Chalmers and Jackson were preparing to assault Hurlbut when they were ordered by Johnston to withdraw and move to attack Stuart's brigade on the far Confederate right. This left Col. Daniel W. Adams (now commanding Brig. Gen. A.H. Gladden's brigade) by himself facing Hurlbut. Adams was able to send forward only a reinforced skirmish line. His men were simply too disorganized from their earlier fighting and charge through Prentiss' camps to enable them to mount a new attack immediately.

The Confederate generals ordered Breckinridge's Reserve Corps to move up to support their enter, but Breckinridge's nearest troops were more than an hour's march away. The resultant delay in assaulting Hurlbut's line perhaps cost the Confederacy the battle. The Confederates failed to follow up on the advantage they had gained by routing Prentiss, and they lost any temporary advantage they might have had against Hurlbut's unsteady line.

Hurlbut took advantage of the lack of Confederate pressure on his front to withdraw his line 300 yards to the north. This withdrawal began accidentally when Col. Isaac C. Pugh, commanding Williams' brigade, withdrew his far left regiment slightly for fear of being outflanked by Chalmers and Jackson. Hurlbut saw the move and thought it was not a bad idea. He promptly had his whole line fall back to a fence line on the north side of the cotton field he had originally held. This position had three advantages: the stabilizing influence of the protective fence line, the shelter provided by a woods on the right of the line and a peach orchard on the left of the line, and the increased distance over which the attacking Confederates would have to advance, most of it open fields.

Hurlbut's line was soon lengthened and reinforced. A few intact units of Prentiss' division formed a tentative line along an old road on Hurlbut's right. Prentiss' men were exhausted but they had been resupplied with ammunition and they were determined to do their duty. In addition, they were reinforced by a new regiment, the 23rd Missouri, fresh from Pittsburg Landing.

The heaviest reinforcement Hurlbut received was W.H.L. Wallace's 2nd Division, which doubled the strength of the new line. Wallace, who had been camped close to Pittsburg Landing, had formed up his men soon after breakfast. Shortly after 0900 he advanced all his brigades to the front. Wallace sent Brig. Gen. John McArthur's 2nd Brigade to the left, where he extended Pugh's line on the east side of the Peach Orchard. Wallace then took his two remaining brigades, Col. James M. Tuttle's 1st and

Brigadier General W.H.L. Wallace (upper left) directing the defense of the Hornets' Nest line before he received his mortal wound (from the Shiloh Cyclorama).

Col. Thomas W. Sweeney's *3rd*, to Prentiss' right. Here he formed along an old road. His position was a strong one, with woods for shelter and the large Duncan Field in front. At this point the whole Union line in the center was a rather strong one, with over 11,000 mostly fresh men and 38 cannon holding a bowed line about one-half mile long. The line's only major weaknesses were it exposed flanks, and the fact that its center was held by Prentiss' worn-out troops.

The best way for the Confederates to attack this newly formed line in the Union center would have been to outflank it, or to gather all available troops for a massive charge. At first the Confederates did neither, and they paid a bloody price for their mistake.

The first new Confederate unit to arrive opposite the Union center was Brig. Gen. B.F. Cheatham's 2nd Division of Polk's corps. After being originally posted in the third Confederate line of battle, Cheatham arrived at the front just as Prentiss was being driven back. He continued on and reached the south side of Duncan Field about 1000 hours. Cheatham then began an artillery bombardment of Wallace's line and anxiously awaited reinforcements so that he could attack. Finally about 1100 he saw Col. Randall L. Gibson's brigade of Bragg's corps coming up. This was the support Cheatham wanted, and he eagerly began his charge. The result of this attack was predictably disastrous. Cheatham described it: "I at once put the brigade in motion at double-quick time across the open field, about 300 yards in width, flanked on one side by a fence and dense thicket of forest trees and undergrowth. So soon as the brigade entered the field the enemy opened up upon us from his entire front a terrific fire of artillery and musketry, but failed altogether to check our movement until we reached the center of the field, when another part of the enemy's force, concealed and protected by the fence and thicket to our left, opened a murderous cross-fire upon our lines, which caused my command to halt and return their fire. After a short time I fell back to my original position."

As Cheatham retreated, he was pursued briefly by the *12th* and *14th Iowa Regiments* in one of the few Union counterattacks of the day. These bold Union regiments then retreated when they met elements of Gibson's brigade moving into position. Gibson then prepared to make an attack of his own. This got off to a terribly bad start when his left regiment, the 4th Louisiana, was mistakenly fired on by the 9th Tennessee of Cheatham's brigade and lost over 100 men, a blow which understandably shook Gibson's brigade, which consisted of only three regiments.

The undaunted Gibson nevertheless continued to form for an attack on the Union center. It was about noon when he began moving through the thick underbrush towards Prentiss' position. Gibson's visibility was so limited that he was upon the Union line before he really knew it. A sudden volley erupted from the Yankee position and thoroughly scattered Gibson's Louisianians. Thus the second Confederate attack on the Union center failed miserably.

Braxton Bragg personally witnessed Gibson's attack, and was greatly annoyed to see the Louisianians retreat so readily. He responded by sending Gibson an order to attack again. Without

*The **44th Indiana** of Hurlbut's division defended a portion of the Hornets' Nest line during the afternoon of 6 April. The firing was so intense that the underbrush caught fire in places.*

thinking, Gibson formed his men up and charged right up to the mouth of Hickenlooper's tired but game *5th Ohio Battery*. When the smoke cleared, the Confederates were again in retreat. Piles of ghastly mangled bodies marked the line and limit of their advance. The canister and bullets had flown so thickly that the attackers likened them to hornets. Thus the Union line received the now famous nickname Hornets' Nest.

Amazingly, Bragg ordered Gibson to attack yet again! Once more the valiant little brigade charged up to Prentiss' line in an attempt to maintain its honor. This time the attack did slightly better, if only because the Union defenders on this part of the line were getting tired and were running out of ammunition. Yet, courage and flesh could only avail so much against lead and iron. Back streamed Gibson's men a third time. Still, the indomitable Bragg was convinced that Gibson had been repulsed only through lack of effort. Fortunately for Gibson, Bragg then left to

Prentiss' troops and Hickenlooper's battery repulse one of Hardee's attacks during the height of the fighting at the Hornets' Nest (from the Shiloh Cyclorama).

supervise the Confederate right. If he had stayed, he might have ordered Gibson to make a fourth attack!

While Gibson was hurtling his men against the Union center, Breckinridge's troops were coming up from the Confederate rear. Breckinridge originally had formed at 0730 hours, near the intersection of the Corinth Road and the Bark Road. He was not ordered forward until 0830, when Beauregard ordered him to send one brigade to the left and two to the right. Accordingly, Breckinidge sent Col. Robert P Trabue's brigade to the left and Col. W.S. Statham's and Col. John S. Bowen's to the right. Two hours later Johnston sent for Breckinridge to come to the right, and was surprised to find most of his force already there.

Bowen and Jackson began arriving at the front shortly after 1100 hours. They were drawn up facing McArthur's brigade, which formed the far left of the Hornets' Nest line. Jackson's brigade had previously made little progress attacking here, largely because he had loaned two of his regiments to support

One of Gibson's three attacks on Hurlbut's portion of the Hornets'
Nest line (from the Shiloh Cyclorama).

Chalmers' attack on Stuart. Though they outnumbered McArthur's thin line, Statham and Bowen were slow to develop their attack. Their main problem was the many ravines they had to cross in order to reach the Union line. They also had some difficulty with their raw troops. For example, in one regiment a lieutenant accidentally wounded himself with his own weapon. Next the 45th Tennessee mistakenly let loose a volley into the 20th Tennessee. It then took Breckinridge, Johnston, and Tennessee Governor Isham G. Harris quite awhile to restore Bowen's and Statham's lines to order.

Shortly before 1400, Bowen, Statham, and Jackson were finally in position for the first massed attack against the Union center. In one of his last orders, Johnston ordered the attack to be made with the bayonet against the left end of the Union center. The weight of Confederate numbers overwhelmed McArthur's defenders, who had been engaged here for about three hours. One by one, McArthur's regiments withdrew with heavy casualties. Sometime during this attack, Johnston was struck by a stray bullet and bled to death before help could be secured. His death at the height of the battle deprived the Confederate army of his strong leadership just when it was needed most.

Farther to the left, Stephens' brigade of Maj. Gen. B.F. Cheatham's division (Polk's I Corps) enjoyed less success in its attack on Lauman's brigade. Stephens' regiments charged right up to the guns of Ross' *2nd Michigan Battery*, but were driven back bloodily. As Hurlbut surveyed the situation, he knew he had to do something to bolster his left at the Peach Orchard. At 1430 he boldly pulled Lauman's brigade out of line and formed it in a field north of the pond behind the Peach Orchard. Here Lauman, joined by the *32nd Illinois* of Pugh's brigade, was struck immediately by three Confederate brigades, those of Col. W.S. Statham, Brig. Gen. John S. Bowen, and Brig. Gen. John K. Jackson. These were soon joined by a fourth brigade, Brig. Gen. James R. Chalmers', which turned westward after chasing Stuart's brigade away from the Union right. The *32nd Illinois* was the first Federal unit to be overwhelmed. The Confederates then struck Lauman's brigade in Wicker Field. Lauman fought tooth and nail, supported by Willard's *Battery A, 1st Illinois Artillery*. Lauman then managed to stall the onrushing Confederates temporarily by ordering the *57th Illinois* and *31st Illinois* to make a bold counterattack. However, renewed Confederate pressure forced him to order a general retreat at about 1530.

The Confederates had now broken the back of the Union center, but they did not realize it. The ground was too rough to see what needed to be done, and the temporary vacuum in high command created by Johnston's death at 1430 left no one to give the needed orders. In addition, many of the attacking Confederate regiments were disorganized and low on ammunition and line officers.

Regiments were peeled back from the left. Here one of McArthur's regiments, the *9th Illinois*, lost 365 of its 617 men, the highest percentage battle loss of all Union units in the battle. McArthur himself was wounded in the foot. By 1400 his whole brigade was in retreat.

The Confederate forces now pivoted the direction of their attack and headed across the Hamburg-Savannah Road for the Peach Orchard, which was held by Col. Isaac C. Hurlbut's *1st*

Brigade, now under Pugh. When the men of the *41st Illinois*, Pugh's own regiment, saw what was coming, they promptly withdrew to the rear, claiming they were out of ammunition. Soon Pugh's whole line was in retreat. A few of his regiments managed to form between the Peach Orchard and a pond. There they halted the now disorganized Confederate attack for a moment.

Collapse of the Hornets' Nest Line

About 1600 Bragg tried to give the Confederate attack the push it needed to overwhelm the Union position. Bragg found Gladden's battered brigade, under Col. Zach Deas now that Gladden was dead and Col. Daniel W. Adams wounded, resting to catch its breath. Reluctantly, Deas formed up his men and headed for the Union line to the left of the Peach Orchard. This position had been abandoned by Lauman's brigade an hour and a half earlier, but was now held by the *3rd Iowa*, the only regiment of Pugh's brigade still on the field. Seeing that they were outnumbered, the Iowans withdrew a few hundred feet and then put up a heavy resistance to Deas' worn-out troops before falling back once more.

During its next withdrawal, the *3rd Iowa* fell in on the left end of a new line that had just been formed by Prentiss. Prentiss had seen the rout of the troops on his left, and was determined to hold his position at all costs, as he had been ordered by Grant. He understood that the troops to his right were still in good shape, and he had been told by Grant that Lew Wallace's division would be up at any time. For these reasons he had his men turn about and form at a hairpin angle to their former line, facing east-northeast only 150 yards or so northeast of W.H.L. Wallace's line, which was facing southwest along the northeast side of Duncan Field.

Unknowingly, Prentiss and Wallace were in for a lot more trouble than they expected. Their hairpin line was outflanked by over half a mile on the left, where Chalmers' brigade was advancing northwest after routing Lauman, and on the right, where Russell and Trabue were advancing southeast after routing Sherman. Less than one-quarter mile separated the two

Confederate wings, which were now closing in on the main Corinth Road, the only remaining Union line of retreat. Nor did Wallace and Prentiss have much to work with in forming their last line. Prentiss had less than 1000 men left from several exhausted regiments of various brigades, and Wallace had only five full regiments (the *7th* and *58th Illinois* of Col. Thomas W. Sweeny's brigade and the *2nd*, *7th*, and *12th Iowa* of Col. James M. Tuttle's brigade). The rest of his regiments had been sent to the left to meet one temporary crisis or another.

Facing Wallace's line was one of the few really effective moves that the Confederates made in the entire battle. During the early afternoon, Brig. Gen. Daniel Ruggles, of Bragg's corps, had formed a few cannon on the southwest side of Duncan Field. He then began peppering the Union lines with good effect. At midafternoon, he witnessed two more fruitless assaults on the center of the Hornets' Nest line. About 1500 Shaver's brigade was brought in obedience to Bragg's order to march to the sounds of the heaviest fighting. Shaver charged up the eastern Corinth Road, only to be blasted away by Union guns at close range. The Confederates were not any more sure of the Union position than they had been two hours before, and their formations were severely hindered by the thick scrub and brush they had to pass through. The smoke had just cleared from Shaver's attack when Patton Anderson was ordered to assault the same sector at 1600 hours. This was the sixth unsupported Confederate attack that day on the center of the Hornets' Nest line. Anderson met with no more success than had his predecessors. His men could not see where they were going, and they moved so slowly in the brush that they were mowed down by the Union defenders.

Finally it was clear to everyone on this front that the Confederates would need more than unsupported infantry to carry the Hornets' Nest line. Around 1600 Ruggles began gathering all the batteries he could to form one massed battery along the southwestern edge of Duncan Field. Many batteries were available for use; indeed several had been left behind during the Confederate advance, and others had not been deployed because of the ravines and rough, woody terrain. By 1700 Ruggles had 62 cannon from eleven and one-half batteries pounding the Union

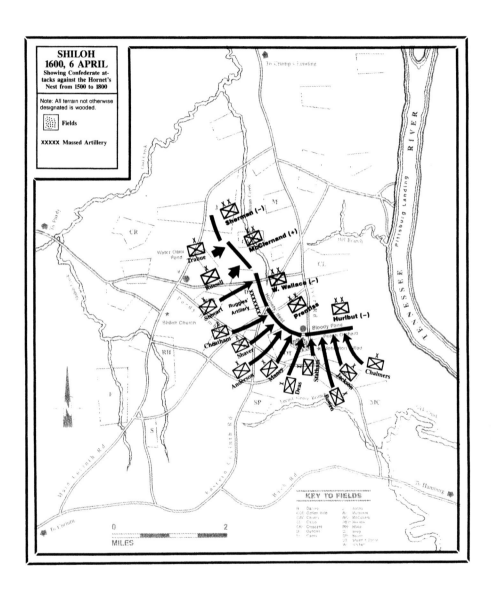

The western end of the Hornet's Nest line was defended by W.H.L.
Wallace's division (from the Shiloh Cyclorama).

center. Facing the thicket at the center of the Hornets' Nest line
were 26 guns, and an additional 36 were adjacent to Duncan
Field.

Even while Ruggles was positioning his cannon, the Confederates were making a seventh attack on the Hornets' Nest.
About the time that Anderson was being repulsed, Col. Marshall
J. Smith led two regiments, his own Crescent Louisiana and the
38th Tennessee, across Duncan Field towards the *7th* and *58th*
Illinois of Sweeny's brigade. Smith was sent into action by
Beauregard, who was persisting in his tactic of throwing regiment after regiment against the Union lines. This attack met
more success than its predecessors, largely because Sweeny's
two regiments were located in an unsupported and unprotected
position in the center of Duncan Field. In addition, the Union
troops were almost out of ammunition. Smith's attack at first
drove Sweeny's units back to the northeastern edge of the field,
to the line they should have been holding in the first place.

At this juncture, the Confederates finally began putting
pressure on Sweeny's vulnerable right flank. Polk came up with

several new regiments and directed them to join the Crescent Regiment's attack against Sweeny's right. The *7th Illinois* saw what was coming and withdrew to the northeast and safety; the *58th Illinois* retreated a quarter mile to the east in its quest to escape. Sweeny, who had lost his right arm in the Mexican War, went down after being wounded in his good left arm, but by then he had practically no troops left to command.

Disaster was now ready to break loose on the exhausted defenders of the Hornets' Nest line. The Yankees were outflanked on both sides, and were being pounded by Ruggles' artillery on the other side of Duncan field. W.H.L. Wallace realized the desperateness of the situation when Sweeny's command was turned and driven back. Quickly he sent the word for Col. James Tuttle to withdraw the remains of the Iowans of his *1st Brigade*. Wallace was then struck by a ghastly mortal wound through his left eye. Wallace's order must have come as a surprise to Tuttle. He had been successfully repulsing Confederate attacks all afternoon and was still holding his assigned sector of the line.

As Tuttle's regiments began to retreat, they were pressured by Anderson's brigade, which was attacking again from the south, and by Smith's command, which was coming from the west. Their only way out of this trap was by the main Corinth Road, but this avenue was soon blocked by the Crescent Regiment, the 38th Tennessee, and two newly arrived regiments of Stewart's brigade that had been hurried forward by Ruggles. Total confusion reigned. Bullets from the rear notified the Union officers that they were surrounded. Soon white flags began to appear among the scattered and trapped Union regiments. One by one their surrender was accepted: the *58th Illinois, 12th Iowa, 18th Missouri, 3rd Iowa*. Numerous other Yankees were captured individually or in groups.

The same scenario was being played out on Prentiss' portion of the line. Shortly before 1700, Prentiss' right wing was broken by a totally unexpected attack, a mounted cavalry charge by Col. Nathan Bedford Forrest's Tennessee Cavalry Regiment. Forrest routed the *23rd Missouri*, but was unable to capitalize on his success because his men could not ride through the thick brush. Gladden's brigade, now under Col. S.C. Deas, had advanced to support Forrest, but was stopped and driven back by Federal artillery fire. It fell to Col. George Maney to deliver the knockout blow. Around 1630 Maney formed up Stephens' three best remaining regiments, the 1st, 9th, and 19th Tennessee, and moved to the support of Forrest and Deas. To Maney's good fortune, all the Union defenders in this sector were otherwise occupied. Maney's men reached the Hornets' Nest in intact lines without being fired on. The Tennesseans thus were able to charge into the Hornets' Nest with a full head of steam. They easily broke the Union line and drove it back in confusion. Prentiss' units were now thoroughly disorganized, and had nowhere to retreat. Breckinridge's command, led by Chalmers' brigade, had reached the main Corinth Road and was literally shaking hands with Trabue's and Russell's brigades, advancing from the west. As soon as he realized he was surrounded, Prentiss ran up a white flag to surrender all the trapped troops; he was the ranking officer on the front after W.H.L. Wallace had been mortally wounded. One by one the Yankee units laid down their arms as they got word of the surrender. Col. Madison Miller, commander of Prentiss' *2nd Brigade,* surrendered at 1726, and the last Union troops gave up their arms by 1800 hours. Many Union soldiers smashed their guns against trees rather than surrender them. Others wept openly that their gallant defense seemed to have been in vain. A few overly jubilant Confederates further insulted their prisoners by dragging the flag of the *12th Iowa* through the mud. They also ripped to pieces the flag of the *14th Iowa.*

The Confederate success was indeed a significant one. Altogether some 2,320 Yankees were captured behind the Hornets' Nest. This number included only about 300 men of Prentiss' actual command; a few came from Hurlbut's division and most came from the *8th, 12th,* and *14th Iowa Regiments* of W.H.L. Wallace's division. Nevertheless, Prentiss' name is connected most closely with the Hornets' Nest, largely because he was the highest ranking officer captured there. Confederate captures also included more than just prisoners. Trabue's Kentucky brigade alone picked up 1,393 rifles in the area, in addition to eleven swords and four cannon. Many of the rifles were new

Enfields, which the Kentuckians eagerly traded for their own inferior weapons.

Impressive as the Confederate victory had been, it did not come cheaply. Hundreds, even thousands of unnecessary casualties had been lost in the numerous ill-conceived frontal charges that had been launched against the Hornets' Nest. Altogether some 18,000 Confederates had been arrayed against the 4,300 defenders of the Hornets' Nest, but the Confederates had never used more than 3,000 at any one time in any of their twelve attacks. In addition, the Union defense here had attracted almost all available Confederate battle forces and sidetracked them from their assigned goal, the capture of Pittsburg Landing.

Grant's Last Line

Throughout the day, there had been a steady stream of wounded and demoralized Union soldiers heading for the rear of the army and Pittsburg Landing. As the day progressed, the stream became a rivulet. When the Hornets' Nest line collapsed, it was as if a dam had burst, and a veritable flood of individuals and broken regiments swept to the rear. If Grant hoped to salvage the battle, he had to somehow form a new line before his entire army, and military career, were washed into the Tennessee River.

The so far victorious Confederates were in many ways as exhausted and disorganized as the retreating Federals. The Southern divisions and brigades had already become hopelessly intermingled earlier in the day; now regiments and companies were scattered in the confusion that followed the surrender of the Hornets' Nest. An immediate difficulty was gathering the captured Yankees for movement from the field. This task was finally given to the 18th Alabama, which needed half an hour to form up the surrendered Northerners. Numerous private soldiers thought the battle was over and began plundering the Union camps and the captured prisoners. Other Confederate units were without ammunition or had lost so many officers that they could not form up.

Amidst all this confusion, the Confederate generals realized that they had to push on to make their victory complete. A quick meeting of generals Bragg, Polk, and Breckinridge at about 1800 produced a simple and direct strategy for the remainder of the day: "Sweep everything forward and drive the enemy into the river."

As the Confederates formed up, control of the center of their renewed advance fell to Ruggles' command, which proceeded with its left on the Corinth-Pittsburg Landing Road. To Ruggles' left, across the road, was Trabue's Orphan Brigade. Many of Trabue's Kentuckians were newly rearmed with captured Enfield rifles. Jackson's brigade, on Ruggles' immediate right, was less fortunate. Most of the men in this unit were out of ammunition. Nevertheless, they were ordered to advance with bayonets fixed. On Jackson's right was Chalmers' brigade, which was also low on ammunition. To the rear of this first line was formed a second line made up of intermingled units from numerous different brigades.

Grant knew that he was in a desperate situation. All afternoon he had been waiting frantically for the arrival of Lew Wallace's division and Buell's army. When it became apparent that neither would arrive in time to help, Grant began putting together a last ditch line as best he could. Late in the afternoon he had stabilized the right flank of his final line along the Hamburg-Savannah Road. Here the remains of McDowell's, Hildebrand's, Buckland's, Marsh's, Hare's, and Veatch's brigades were lined up facing west. However, there was no great pressure from the Confederates here. The main Confederate thrust was forming to the south, between the main Corinth Road and the river. This was the front on which Grant had the fewest men. Tuttle's brigade and portions of Hurlbut's division had formed on the main road to the Landing, but big stretches of the line were not defended at all.

Grant rapidly hurried to throw every unit he could into his new line. Hare's and Veatch's brigades were pulled back from the right to fill the gap between Tuttle's front and the Hamburg-Savannah Road. Grant then boldly formed the left of his line from scattered artillery units that were gathered from all available sources. Several were the remnants of batteries which had been roughly handled earlier in the day; others were reserve

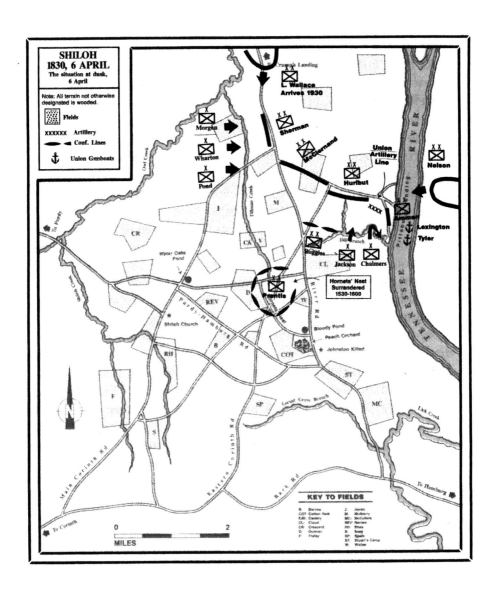

batteries that had been encamped near the Landing. Among these batteries were several huge guns. Two 20-pounder Parrott rifles of the *8th Ohio Battery* were placed on the bluff adjacent to the river to anchor the far left of the line. Near the line's center, five gigantic 24-pounder siege cannon were dragged into position. They had been brought along for use in the anticipated siege of Corinth, but would now be used for a quite different purpose. To the left of the siege guns were lined up twelve rifled guns (six 10-pounder Parrotts and six 20-pounder Parrotts) of *Batteries D, H,* and *K of the 1st Missouri Artillery.* The result was a nasty-looking line which bristled with about fifty guns, though lacking infantry support. Altogether, Grant's final line covered about a mile in length.

Grant had literally thrown his line together during the time bought for him by Prentiss' last efforts in the Hornets' Nest. Additional time had been bought by a few valiant units that sacrificed themselves to slow the Confederate advance. One of these units was Ross' *2nd Michigan Battery.* During his retreat, Ross had stopped to try to halt the advance of Col. A.J. Lindsay's 1st Mississippi Cavalry, which was having a field day gathering in prisoners. The exhausted men of the battery were not able to get into position quickly enough, however, and were overrun by the charging enemy cavalry. Ross' five guns were captured intact with their horses, harnesses, and crew. Flushed with this success, Lindsay rushed ahead with thirty or forty of his men to try to capture another battery. He had to give up this chase when his quarry reached the safety of Grant's infantry line. Lindsay ended up taking part of his regiment to the banks of the Tennessee River. Here his thirsty mounts drank deeply, fulfilling Johnston's morning wish, "Tonight we will water our horses in the Tennessee River!"

At the last minute Grant received additional much needed reinforcements from Buell's army. Buell's leading unit, Col. Jacob Ammen's *10th Brigade* of Brig. Gen. William "Bull" Nelson's *4th Division,* had reached Savannah on the evening of 5 April. Ammen's men had been hearing the sounds of battle since dawn of the 6th, and by 0700 they were preparing for action. All they lacked were orders to march. Generals Buell and Nelson were both present at Savannah, but they wanted precise instructions from Grant before moving forward. However, when Nelson went to Grant's headquarters for orders, he found that Grant had already left for the front. He had, though, left the following note for Nelson: "An attack having been made on our forces, you will move your entire command to the river opposite Pittsburg. You can obtain a guide easily in the village."

Nelson and Buell promptly ordered Ammen's men to form up, and then began looking for a guide. Much to their surprise, none was immediately to be found. Some of the locals reported that there were a few trails through the swamps south of Savannah, but most of the good roads were on the western side of the river. The only person who really knew the way was the local doctor, who had gone on a call and would not be back until noon.

While they waited for the doctor to return, the anxious Union commanders decided to send out a cavalry patrol to explore the roads south along the Tennessee's eastern bank. They also kept their eyes open for any transports that might arrive from the north or be despatched from Pittsburgh Landing to carry them across the river. As the morning wore on, the sounds of the battle grew louder. Yet there were no signs of any boats, any doctor, or any good news from the cavalry patrol. Finally, the doctor arrived. The column got under way sometime after 1300 hours. On the doctor's advice, Ammen left behind his cannon and his baggage because of the muddy condition of the roads.

Ammen's march was one of the great forced marches of history. As his men proceeded south, the sound of the battle grew louder, showing that Grant's army was being pushed back to the river. The situation was obviously urgent. To their dismay, the route being taken was far from speedy. The road recommended by the doctor had been washed out by recent rains, and Ammen ended up proceeding through what appeared to be pure swamp. Nevertheless, Ammen continued to drive his men, like Blucher leading the Prussians to Waterloo. When messengers began arriving with news of Grant's defeat, Ammen had them led aside so that his men would not be disheartened by the bad news.

Finally, after three hours of toil, Ammen's leading regiment, the *36th Indiana*, began to reach the banks of the Tennessee

The road to Pittsburg Landing was extremely congested all day as wounded and stragglers headed to the rear and ammunition wagons tried to make their way to the front.

opposite Pittsburg Landing. It was 1630 hours, and the cannon of both sides were already banging away at each other along Grant's last line. Nelson, who had marched with Ammen's vanguard, signaled a sutler's boat and commandeered it to take four companies of the *36th* across the river. The scene Nelson found on the western riverbank was one of total bedlam: "I found cowering under the riverbank when I crossed from 7,000 to 10,000 men, frantic with fright and utterly demoralized, who received my division with cries, 'We are whipped; cut to pieces.' They were insensible to shame or sarcasm—for I tried both on them—and, indignant at such poltroonery, I asked permission to open fire on the knaves." These dispirited creatures were in fact so huddled along the shore that there was no room for Nelson to land his men. Nelson was able to secure a landing area only by advancing a detachment with lowered bayonets.

The four companies of the *36th Indiana* rushed up the hill, fighting a stream of disheartened fugitives from Grant's army. When they reached the top of the hill, the Hoosiers were posted in support of Grant's thin artillery line that was on the bluffs above the river. The remainder of Ammen's brigade followed as quickly as they could be transported across the river. At 1730, as they were advancing to the front, Grant's 24-pounder siege guns began to fire, joining the chorus of shrieking shells being launched by the gunboats *Lexington* and *Tyler*.

While Grant's line was growing stronger with every moment, the Confederates were having difficulty mounting their last attack. Their problems were threefold. Firstly, they had only a few batteries up to engage Grant's long line of artillery. This meant that most of the Union artillery pieces were not suppressed, and could concentrate their fire on the advancing enemy infantry. Secondly, the Confederate troops were greatly unnerved by the thundering gunboats in the nearby Tennessee River. The gunboats' shots made more noise than harm because of their undirected fire into the deep ravines, but their presence was literally awe inspiring. Thirdly, the Confederates were approaching the Union lines from the wrong angle. Braxton Bragg, who now had command on the Confederate right, was leading most of the army's available infantry against Grant's left. Here the terrain was more unfavorable than at any other point along the whole Union front. Any Confederate advance would have to cross the deep ravines formed by Dill Branch and its tributaries; in addition, these streams had swampy bottoms that made any organized advance virtually impossible. Once these obstacles were crossed, the attackers would be charging right into the muzzles of Grant's artillery, now supported by Ammen's newly arrived fresh regiments. Prospects of success for such an attack were not high given the exhausted condition of most of the attackers. All things considered, Bragg would have been better advised to strike the center or right of Grant's line, where there might have been a chance of routing the exhausted survivors of the earlier stages of the battle.

As it was, Bragg urged his men forward for one last charge to sweep the Yankees from the field. Because of the rough terrain, he was not able to coordinate his advance. Chalmers' brigade attacked first on the right. He advanced nobly, but he had the

The last Confederate attack on the evening of 6 April did not get as far as this sketch suggests.

Field where General A.S. Johnston died at around 1430 on 6 April. Johnston was the highest ranking Confederate officer killed during the war.

misfortune of hitting the exact spot occupied by Ammen's fresh troops. The fighting grew hot as Chalmers made several charges. In the end, he suffered terribly from the flanking fire of the Union artillery and had to give up his effort as darkness fell. He later wrote: "In attempting to mount the last ridge we were met by a fire from a whole line of batteries protected by infantry and assisted by shells from the gunboats. Our men struggled vainly to ascend the hill, which was very steep, making charge after charge without success. ... This was the sixth fight in which we were engaged during the day, and my men were too much exhausted to storm the batteries on the hill."

Chalmers had made his attacks virtually unsupported. Jackson's brigade had come up on his left, but it was in no shape to pose a serious threat to the enemy. One of Jackson's regiments had been detached to guard prisoners, and the other three had little or no ammunition. Nevertheless, they were ordered to charge with fixed bayonets. Quite understandably, Jackson's men balked when they ran into heavy Union artillery fire. They then refused to advance without support. Jackson's supporting unit, Ruggles' command, had been prepared to advance, but did not do so because of new orders from Beauregard.

It seems that Beauregard was taking seriously his new role as army commander. Once he got over the immediate shock of Johnston's death, he wired the War Office in Richmond: "We this morning attacked the enemy in strong position in front of Pittsburg, and after a severe battle of ten hours, thanks be to the Almighty, gained a complete victory, driving the enemy from every position. Losses on both sides heavy including our commander-in-chief, General A.S. Johnston, who fell gallantly leading his troops into the thickest of the fight."

Beauregard then spent the rest of the late afternoon trying to rally and reorganize the troops that were milling around in the Confederate rear and in the captured Union camps. About sunset he decided there had been enough fighting for the day. He ordered his troops to stop fighting and go into camp. If Grant's line were still there in the morning, it could easily be pushed into the river then.

When Beauregard's order reached the front, it obviously undermined all that Bragg was trying to do. Bragg wanted to rush all available troops forward for one last glorious charge. Instead, he saw Ruggles' line withdraw from the field, and then Jackson's. By the time Bragg found out why this was happening, it was too late to countermand the order and return Ruggles and Jackson to the front. Thus the Confederates lost their last chance to win the battle.

Night, 6-7 April

As darkness descended upon the battlefield, most of the Confederate troops retired to spend the night in the captured Union camps. During the hours of darkness, units tried to reassemble as best they could, but all organizations from corps down to companies had been scattered and disorganized by the long day's fighting. Many of the Confederates feasted on delicacies found in the captured Union camps. Pvt. Henry Stanley, like many others, sought solace in an exhausted sleep. Their sleep was fitful at best. At 2100 the Federal gunboats *Lexington* and *Tyler*, which had earlier taken up a station at Pittsburg Landing, began firing every ten or fifteen minutes, a barrage that would continue all through the night. The firing was ordered by Nelson for the deliberate purpose of disturbing the Confederates' sleep. Evidence, however, suggests that this shelling may have harmed the Union troops as much as the Rebels. The gunboats' booming cannon kept the Yankees awake too, and many of the shells landed among wounded Union troops. One shell found its mark in a tent where some Rebels were playing cards; the bodies of the card players were found the next morning with their cards still in their hands.

More discomfort came from a steady rain that began at 2200, and lasted until 0300 on the 7th. Private Stanley was fortunate enough to be able to crawl into a captured tent to escape the wetness. Many of his comrades, and most of the thousands of wounded on the field, were not so lucky and had to endure the night as best they could. North of the Peach Orchard some of the wounded crawled to a small pond in order to quench their overwhelming thirsts. Several of them bled to death there, staining the waters of the pond. In this way the pond earned the dreadful nickname "Bloody Pond," still used to this day.

This sketch accurately reflects the confusion as Grant struggled to form his last line of defense at the end of the first day's fight.

*The Union gunboats **Lexington** and **Tyler** used their big cannons to help Grant hold his last line on the night of 6-7 April.*

Grant was severely criticized for not being with his army when it was first attacked. He had been spending the nights at Savannah, 9 miles away, and reached the field at 0900 aboard his headquarters boat, Tigress *(shown here, second from left, at Pittsburg Landing after the battle).*

Bragg and Beauregard spent the night, ironically, in Sherman's former headquarters tent. When reports came in that there was much enemy activity at Pittsburg Landing, the generals assumed that Grant was retreating. One Confederate leader did not believe these reports. Col. Nathan Bedford Forrest decided to send scouts dressed in captured Union overcoats to see exactly what was happening in the Union rear. These scouts carried out their mission successfully, and returned with the disturbing news that the enemy was being heavily reinforced. Forrest reported this to Hardee and Breckinridge, and was told to give the facts to Beauregard. Unfortunately for the Confederate cause, Forrest was unable to locate his army commander. Thus Beauregard was completely unaware of what he would face in the morning. He went to sleep believing that Grant might

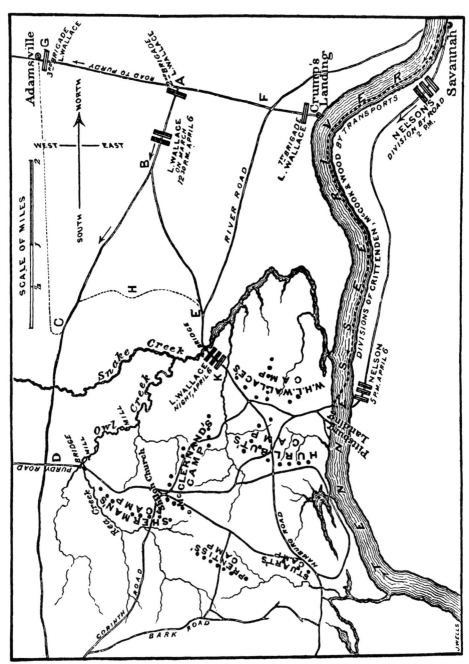

Grant's Reinforcements

The heavy guns of Grant's siege battery, which formed an important part of his "east line."

have left the field, and had made no dispositions to meet a greatly reinforced foe.

Grant had a much less restful night than his Confederate counterparts. He knew how close he had come to utter destruction that day, and he tried to deal with the strain of defeat. In addition, his foot still hurt from a fall from his horse on 4 April. To make matters worse, the noise of a field hospital near his headquarters kept him awake. He ended up spending the night curled up under a tree.

Meanwhile, the men of Buell's *Army of the Ohio* were arriving all night and needed posting. The remainder of Nelson's *4th Division* arrived by 2100 and was posted on Ammen's left, supporting the artillery line north of Dill Branch. Soon after, Brig. Gen. Thomas L. Crittenden's *5th Division* began arriving aboard steamers from Savannah. When the boats had finished ferrying Crittenden's men, they began bringing Brig. Gen. Alexander McCook's *2nd Division.*

Before this, at about 1930, the head of Lew Wallace's long lost *3rd Division* of Grant's own *Army of the Tennessee* finally began to cross Snake Creek on the far Union right. By 0100 on 7 April Wallace had his men formed along the Hamburg-Savannah Road north of Sherman.

The arrival of these 22,000 reinforcements buoyed Grant's spirits, and he determined to make a massive counterattack the next day. When Lt. Col. J.B. McPherson asked him if the army were going to retreat that night, Grant seemed annoyed and responded, "No, I propose to attack at daylight and whip them."

Johnston's Last Hours

Gen. Albert Sidney Johnston, overall commander of the Confederate army at Shiloh, was determined to face death in his desperate effort to defeat Grant and save his reputation after his loss of Kentucky and most of Tennessee in February of 1862. Once the army marched north from Corinth, he was ready to trust the "iron dice of battle" and fight the enemy "if they were a million."

Johnston was up before dawn on 6 April and heard the opening shots of the battle of Shiloh while he was eating breakfast. At 0514 he mounted Fire Eater, his horse, and proceeded towards the front. He stopped to set up a headquarters at the junction of the main Corinth Road and the Bark Road. First Beauregard and then some other generals came up for some last minute instructions. At 0640 Johnston again mounted up, and proclaimed "Tonight we will water our horses in the Tennessee River."

Johnston rode up to Hardee's front lines and encouraged the troops to remember their heritage and use the bayonet. Throughout the early stages of the fighting he took direct command of one brigade after another as he led them into advantageous positions and launched their attacks. About 0930 he received Capt. S.H. Lockett's report of a possible threat posed by the Federal left. He then made the snap decision to send Chalmers' and Jackson's brigades, plus Breckenridge's Reserve Corps, to bolster the Confederate right and ensure success there. Johnston then spent most of the rest of the morning waiting for Breckenridge to come up.

When Breckenridge's brigades finally began to arrive, at about noon, Johnston helped post them in line, and then helped rally them as they wavered under their first fire. Shortly before 1400 he ordered Jackson, Statham and Bowen to make a grand bayonet charge. Johnston was elated as the charge swept the Yankees from the field. He had been under heavy fire himself, but miraculously had not been felled. Or so it seemed.

During this attack, Johnston was struck four times, and his horse twice. The only bullet that Johnston was aware had hit him tore the sole of his left boot. He joked about it with Governor Isham Harris of Tennessee, who was a volunteer aide on his staff, and continued to direct the battle.

A few minutes later Harris noticed Johnston grow pale and slouch in his saddle. He rushed up and supported the general and asked him if he were hurt. Johnston replied that he thought so, badly. Harris and another officer led Johnston to a nearby ravine and took him off his horse. Unluckily, Johnston's personal staff surgeon, Dr. D.W. Yandell, was not at hand. Johnston had left him in some captured Union camps earlier in the day to care for captured Union wounded.

Governor Harris sent for a doctor and attempted to locate the general's wound. Johnston did not know where he had been hit, nor could Harris find the wound. The general breathed his last at about 1430 hours.

Harris and some other officers sent the sad news to Beauregard so that he could take command at the front. They then wrapped the general's body in a blanket so that the troops would not find out and panic. His body was placed on Fire Eater, though the poor animal was so badly wounded that he could hardly walk. The gloomy entourage then returned to Johnston's morning headquarters, which the general had so optimistically left only eight hours earlier.

About 2100 or 2200 that night Beauregard ordered Johnston's body taken to Corinth. It was accompanied by several important staff officers, all of whom would consequently be absent from the second day's battle. From Corinth, Johnston's body was taken to New Orleans for burial in St. Louis Cemetery. After the war it was removed from there to Austin, Texas, where it rests today.

When the battle ended the next day, the Yankees found what they thought was Johnston's body near McClernand's headquarters. The body showed no signs of rank, since it had been stripped of its clothing. Nevertheless, several captured Confederate officers and some former friends of Johnston identified it as the Confederate commander. Brig. Gen. William "Bull" Nelson ordered the body to be cleaned and then buried it in one of his own shirts. Later it was learned that the body was not Johnston's, but that of Capt. Thomas W. Preston, a member of Confederate Brig. Gen. A.P. Stewart's staff.

Controversary still rages over how and why Johnston died. Post-battle examination of his body showed that he had been slightly wounded by a Minié ball in his right calf directly behind the knee. The wound itself was not major, and Johnston proably never knew that he had been hit; he had nerve damage in his leg as a result of a wound received in a duel in 1837. The only damage the bullet made was significant—it tore open the major popliteal artery. Johnston then slowly bled to death without knowing it. Indeed, no one quite understood why he died until his right boot was later removed from his body. It was filled with blood, and the death-dealing bullet was found still in his leg, near the shin bone.

Shiloh historian Wiley Sword proposed the theory that Johnston was felled by his own troops. Sword cites as evidence the fact that Johnston was struck by a bullet from an Enfield rifle, a weapon that many of the Confederate troops were carrying. In addition, Johnston was wounded in the back of his leg while leading a charge. These points, however, cannot be proved. The fateful shot could just as well have been fired from a Yankee Enfield while Johnston never knew that he had been hit. Modern medical interpretation suggests that, from this type of wound, Johnston would have remained conscious for about thirty minutes; he could have survived only about an hour. The only way that his life could have been saved would have been by putting a tourniquet on the injured leg. This was not done because the wound was not suspected—let alone located—in time.

A final controversy concerning Johnston's death concerns the exact location where he died. In April of 1896, Governor Harris visited the battlefield and located the death site under an oak tree near the intersection of the Hamburg-Savannah Road and the Hamburg-Purdy Road. It seems from other evidence that Harris, who was 78 years old in 1896, was mistaken. More contemporary evidence suggests that Johnston fell on ground covered by the right of Statham's brigade in its final attack on the Union left center. The exact location seems to have been slightly east of the Hamburg-Savannah Road, about 200 yards north of Sarah Bell's cabin.

The Hornets' Nest

The sunken road in Shiloh's famous Hornets' Nest was not as deep a natural trench as some veterans have claimed. It was actually no more than a depressed cart path through the edge of a woods. As such, it offered no great defensive advantage as did the Bloody Lane at Antietam. Instead, it furnished a reference point for forming the Union line and a handy route for lateral movement. The strength of the position came from the fact that it offered wooded shelter to its defenders, while its attackers had to advance through the open ground of the cotton field or Duncan field, or through the stubble and heavy undergrowth that was south of the center of the Hornets' Nest line.

Because of th intensity and length of the fighting in the Hornets' Nest, there are more anecdotes and strange battle incidents associated with this sector than with any other part of the battle.

During the fighting in the Hornets' Nest, one green Union soldier forgot to remove the ramrod from his gun after he loaded it. He did not notice his mistake until he fired and the ramrod speared a Rebel advancing against him.

At one point a Union soldier in the Hornets' Nest became unnerved and ran to hide behind a big tree in the rear of the line. Soon other soldiers followed and hid behind the same tree. In not too much time there was a long line of soldiers, snakelike, stretching behind the tree like the tail of a kite being flown in the wind. Later a crazed officer withdrew to this tree also, and paced back and forth along the length of the line of cowering men.

One Iowa soldier saw his brother killed in the battle line. He calmly walked over to the body, kneeled, and began firing at the enemy. He remained in this position until his regiment was forced to retreat.

Another soldier was astonished to see a rabbit bolt out of the woods from dread fear of the noise of the battle. The rabbit darted right up to the soldier and snuggled up to him for protection.

As the Confederate 4th Louisiana of Gibson's brigade was moving forward in preparation for its first assault on the Hornets' Nest, some of its men saw an officer carrying a Union flag right towards their line. A quick volley felled both the officer and his horse. Later the Louisianians discovered that the officer was not a Yankee as they had thought, but a Confederate officer who was riding back to his own lines with a captured Union flag. Thus he was killed in his moment of triumph.

During the fighting one sixty-year-old private from the Union *9th Illinois* of McArthur's brigade became separated from his regiment and refused to retreat. He then fought alongside several other units, and rejoined his regiment that night. He carried with him notes signed by several officers showing that he had been fighting all day and not skulking.

When Prentiss surrendered the remains of the Union line at the Hornets' Nest, a mounted Union officer rode up to a line of infantry to order them to stop firing at their own men. The line turned out to be Confederates, and the officer and his horse were shot dead.

The Twelve Attacks on the "Hornet's Nest"

TIME	CONFEDERATE BRIGADES	SECTOR ATTACKED
1100	Cheatham	west
1200	Gibson I	center
1300	Gibson II	center
1400	Bowen, Statham, Jackson	east
1430	Stephens	east
1500	Shaver	center
1600	Anderson	center
1600	Deas	east
1630	Forrest	east
1630	Smith	west
1645	Maney	east

Note: The Hornets' Nest line was surrendered between 1730 and 1800, after it was outflanked on both the left and the right. It was not captured by direct assault.

West Sector: north of the cotton field, near the Peach Orchard
East Sector: north of Duncan Field
Center Sector: north of the wooded area between Duncan Field and the cotton field

Of Green Troops and Stragglers

In order to understand the battle of Shiloh fully, we must remember how green and untrained most of the troops engaged there were. Of the 110,000 men in the battle, only about one-fifth—mostly in four of Grant's six divisions that had been engaged at Fort Donelson—had previously seen serious combat. This means that most of the troops and generals on both sides had not been under fire in a large scale battle. Some units in both armies had been organized for less than a month, and a few regiments had been armed for less than a week. As a result, numerous units had difficulty going through the simplest maneuvers even on the parade ground. Trying to keep order and move in the noise and confusion of battle was next to impossible for many units. For this reason, there are numerous accounts of regiments melting away before hardly firing a shot. Other units broke for the rear under even light enemy pressure and could not be reformed. The difficulty in moving and holding lines was deepened by the wooded and rough nature of the battlefield. All too often companies and individuals who became separated from their units honestly could not locate their parent commands. This was particularly so in the Union army, where many units were caught by the Confederate surprise attack and so never did form up properly. Then too many weakhearted individuals simply got scared and bolted for the rear, or all too readily offerred to escort wounded comrades away from the fighting.

As the battle developed on Sunday morning, 6 April 1862, a steady stream of wounded, demoralized, and cowardly Yankees began to flow from the front lines to Pittsburg Landing and safety. By mid-morning this stream had grown to a river as various Union regiments were shattered and driven from their camps. At noon Grant observed thousands of stragglers huddling near the riverbank. The sight so angered him that he ordered a picket line to be set up to keep additional stragglers from reaching the rear. This line, though, was not very effective against the hordes that pressed against it. Almost all the stragglers and slightly wounded who reached the riverbank were out of action for the day. No amount of threats or curses could bring them back to action.

This huge number of stragglers caused such confusion at Pittsburgh Landing that Grant had difficulty moving his forces around, especially his artillery, in the preparation of his last line. They also crowded the riverbank so much that Buell had difficulty in landing his troops and advancing to the front. Nelson, who was with the first of Buell's troops to land, had to clear a landing spot by sending his men into the straggler mob with lowered bayonets. Buell said of the situation, "On the shore I encountered a scene which has often been described. The face of the bluff was crowded with stragglers from the battle. The number there at different hours has been estimated at from five thousand in the morning to fifteen thousand in the evening. The number at nightfall would not have fallen short of fifteen thousand, including those who had passed down the river, and the less callous but still broken and demoralized fragments about the camps on the plateau near the landing. At the top of the bluff all was confusion. Men mounted and on foot, and wagons with their teams and excited drivers, all struggling to force their way closer to the river, were mixed up in apparently inextricable confusion with a battery of artillery which was standing in park without men or horses to man or move it. The increasing throng already presented a barrier which it was evidently necessary to remove, in order to make way for the passage of my troops."

The Confederates also had straggler problems, but of a different nature. Because their attacks were initially successful, they lost fewer demoralized men heading for the rear than the Union army did. Still, they too lost numerous wounded and slightly wounded soldiers who headed to the rear with eager helpers. In addition, many of the South's green soldiers were soon sickened by the blood and gore and simply fell out of line. Others unintentionally became separated from their commands and milled aimlessly around the battlefield. The most serious Confederate straggling, though, came when the hungry troops stopped to pillage the Union camps that were captured early in the fighting. Many of these camps had breakfast still cooking on the fires, an all too alluring temptation for those Rebels who had run out of food the day before; having left Corinth with three days' rations early on 3 April, they had run out because the attack was postponed for two days. Other Confederates simply wandered about gathering souvenirs. One historian has estimated that at least one-third of the Confederate soldiers were engaged in some form of pillaging on the first day. Pvt. Sam Watkins of the 1st Tennessee later heard tales of Confederate soldiers finding lost Yankee money on the battlefield on 6 April, especially in the captured camps, "But they thought it valueless and did not trouble themselves with bringing it in."

"Bull" Nelson

William "Bull" Nelson (1824-1862), commander of Buell's 4th Division at Shiloh, received his colorful nickname from the fact that he was 6'4" tall and weighed 300 pounds. He had little pre-war military experience other than a stint as an ordinary sailor during the Mexican War.

At the start of the Civil War, Nelson received a commission as a brigadier general largely because his brother was a good friend of President Lincoln. His first real action was at Shiloh. In the vanguard of Buell's army, Nelson had to push his men in order to reach Grant in time to "save the day" on the evening of the 6th. He then did a reasonably good job leading his men in action on the 7th. After being promoted to major general in July, he was wounded at the battle of Richmond (Kentucky) in August. He was then sent to Louisville to recuperate, and in September took command of the so-called *Army of Kentucky*.

While at Louisville, Nelson had an altercation with a subordinate that led to his eartly demise. It seems that Buell did not get along at all well with Brig. Gen. Jefferson C. Davis (no relation to the Confederate president). On 20 September 1862 the two generals happened to meet in the lobby of a Louisville hotel. Davis had harsh words with Nelson over some matter, and Nelson responded in kind. When Davis threw a crumpled card in Nelson's face, Nelson slapped him. Davis then went to fetch a pistol, and dealt Nelson a mortal wound. Curiously, Davis was never punished for his crime. His friend Governor Oliver P. Morton of Indiana had witnessed the entire episode, and Morton used his political influence to shield Davis. In addition, Davis was respected for his military abilities, while Nelson's temper was well known. The case remains a strange one to this day.

Don Carlos Buell

Shiloh was the high point of the career of Maj. Gen. Don Carlos Buell (1818-1898). Buell was a West Point graduate (1841) who had been wounded and decorated in the Mexican War. At the beginning of the Civil War, he received command of the *Army of the Ohio*. While Grant was besieging Forts Henry and Donelson, Buell was busy capturing Bowling Green. He then advanced on Nashville, which was defenseless after Fort Donelson fell. Without doubt Buell's timely arrival at Shiloh saved the battle for the Union cause. On the second day of the battle, Buell's three divisions carried the weight of the fighting and Buell himself did a good job directing them.

After Shiloh Buell's career went downhill. His campaign in Tennessee was sidetracked by Bragg's invasion of Kentucky. He failed to commit all his troops at Perryville on 8 October 1862, even though he greatly outnumbered the Confederate army there. Popular outcry over his failure to destroy Bragg's army was so great that he was replaced by W.S. Rosecrans. Buell never again held command. He spent six months defending his campaigns before a board of inquiry and then was sent to Indianapolis to await orders. After a year of waiting, he resigned from the army in June of 1864.

Generally regarded as a very competent commander, Buell's personality was not dynamic enough to inspire his men or his subordinates. He was also a bit too cautious to ever risk decisive action. In post-war years, Buell remained critical of the performance of Grant and Sherman at Shiloh, so gaining more unpopularity. His name now stands in relative obscurity, one of the war's many disappointments.

Lexington and *Tyler*

The gunboats *Lexington* and *Tyler* were stalwart members of the Union western flotilla and played key roles in the campaign and battle of Shiloh. The *Tyler*, which was built in Cincinnati in 1857, was a side wheel steamer of 575 tons. She was one of the original boats bought to form the Mississippi River flotilla in 1861. When the ship was converted to military use, there was an unsuccessful effort to change her name from *Tyler*, the former U.S. president who had cast his lot with the Confederacy, to *Taylor*, the successful Mexican War general and U.S. president. *Lexington* was a sidewheel steamboat built in Pittsburgh in 1860. She was made of wood and was 177 feet long. Despite her 448 tons, she had a draft of only seven feet and so was well suited for the river war in the West.

Both vessels were active in almost every riverine engagement in the West. *Lexington* was present at Grant's occupation of Paducah, Kentucky, in September of 1861. Here they helped hold off the advancing Confederate army while Grant's routed command escaped across the Mississippi on transports. The next spring, the two warships helped capture Fort Henry and assisted in the capture of Fort Donelson on 16 February. They took part in the campaign against Island No. 10 and in

several reconnaissances on the Tennessee River that preceded the battle of Shiloh. The most significant of these was their shelling of the Confederate fortifications at Eastport, Mississippi, on 12 March.

They rendered excellent service at Shiloh. When the Confederates attacked early on the morning of 6 April, *Tyler* was anchored near Pittsburg Landing and *Lexington* was four miles downstream at Crump's Landing. Since Grant was not then on the field and there was no one to give the gunboats any orders, naval Lt. James Shirk of *Lexington* and naval Lt. William Gwin of *Tyler* were left to act largely on their own. About 0945 Gwin moved *Tyler* to a position one mile upstream from Pittsburg Landing, where he could support the infantry lines. He was joined there about 1045 by *Lexington*, which Shirk had brought down to see how the battle was going. Shirk then steamed back to Crump's Landing to support Lew Wallace's division.

Gwin waited impatiently as the battle drew closer to the river. Finally at 1325 he sent an officer ashore to get permission to bombard some Confederate troops he saw near the river. Union General Stephen Hurlbut, commander of Grant's *4th Division*, applauded the idea. At 1450 Gwin opened fire with his huge eight-inch naval guns that fired 53-pound shells. He fired at the Confederates for an hour but probably did not cause many casualties because he could not locate the enemy positions precisely in all the smoke of battle. But the noise of his firing certainly unnerved the Confederates and gave confidence to Grant's hard-pressed men.

At 1550 *Tyler* withdrew to Pittsburg Landing, where Gwin sought orders from Grant. Being no naval man, Grant simply directed Gwin to do whatever he thought best. Gwin took a position in the river near the left flank of Grant's infantry line. Here he was joined at 1600 by *Lexington*, which had left Crump's Landing after Lew Wallace departed for the battle front. Within a few minutes the two gunboats were blasting away in support of Grant's final line. Their first barrage, from 1610 to 1640, silenced several enemy batteries. Their most significant contribution to the battle came at 1735, when the two gunboats helped turn back the last Confederate attack of the day. Shirk described this action in his battle report: "We again, with the *Tyler*, opened fire upon them, silencing the enemy, and, as I hear from many officers on the field, totally demoralizing his forces and driving them from their position in a perfect rout, in the space of ten minutes."

Tyler shelled the Confederate right again from 1800 to 1825, and then paused to rest for awhile as the noise of the land battle subsided. Shirk took advantage of the lull to return to Crump's Landing and check things out there. About 2100 Nelson suggested to Gwin that he

fire a shell into the Confederate lines every ten minutes to keep the enemy from sleeping. Gwin began firing at 2100 and continued until 0100, when *Tyler* was relieved by Shirk's *Lexington*. *Lexington* then kept up the fire at fifteen-minute intervals until dawn, when the battle resumed and there was too much danger of hitting friendly troops. There can be no question that the gunboats' fire gave the Confederates an uncomfortable night, yet their firing also kept the Northern troops awake. Those Yankees who were camped closest to the river were almost knocked over by the naval gun blasts, which caused many of the infantrymen to have a ringing in their ears for several weeks after the battle. One scholar has pointed out that the undirected fire from the gunboats probably killed as many wounded Yankees lying on the battlefield behind the Confederate lines as it did Rebels.

The two gunboats continued to be active after Shiloh. *Tyler* was the mainstay of the Union defense of Helena, Arkansas, in July of 1862, where she fired 413 rounds in eight hours to help drive off a Confederate attack. Her gallantry earned the gunboat the respect of her enemies, who called the *Tyler* "the most formidable gunboat in the Union river fleet." Both vessels took part in the early stages of the Vicksburg campaign. *Lexington* also fought at Arkansas Post in early 1863 and in the Red River campaign in the spring of 1864. She was sold by the government in August of 1865 when her warlike qualities were no longer needed. The *Tyler* was also sold after the war.

Artillery Losses

During the battle, Grant's army lost 34 guns on the first day, while the Confederaets lost 17 guns on the second day—a net gain of 17 for the Confederates—quite a substantial haul, but nowhere near the number lost at Fort Donelson and Island No. 10.

Union Batteries	Total Pieces	Pieces Lost
Army of the Tennessee	119	34
Army of the Ohio	131	0
Confederate Batteries		
Army of the Mississippi	108	17

Guns Lost or Abandoned in the Battle

UNION

Bat. D., 1st Ill. (McAllister)	1 24 pd. howitzer
Bat. E., 1st Ill. (Waterhouse	2 4½ in. James Rifles
	1 3.67 in. James Rifle
Bat. D., 2nd Ill. (Dresser)	4 3.67 in. James Rifles
Bat. E., 2nd. Ill. (Schwartz)	2 12-pd. smoothbores
6th Ind. Bat. (Behr)	2 12-pd. howitzers
	3 6-pd. smoothbores
2nd Mich. Bat. (Ross)	2 10-pd. Parrots
	2 20-pd. Parrots
	1 6-pd. smoothbore
5th Ohio Bat. (Hickenlooper)	2 guns
13rh Ohio Bat. (Myers)	2 6-pd. Wiard Rifles
	2 12-pd. Wiard Rifles
TOTAL	34 guns (21 rifles)

CONFEDERATE

Gage's Ala. Bat.	1
Ketchum's Ala. Bat	2
Girardey's Ala. Bat	1
Cobb's Ky. Bat.	2
Smith's Miss. Bat	3
Stanford's Miss. Bat	4
Bankhead's Tenn. Bat	2
Polk's Tenn. Bat.	2
TOTAL	17

CHAPTER VI

The Second Day, 7 April

Both sides had the same plans for battle on Monday 7 April 1862. Beauregard apparently planned to bring his troops out of their camps and attack Grant's last line, if indeed Grant still remained on the battlefield. Because he was unaware that Grant had been reinforced, Beauregard anticipated a quick completion to the battle and had made no special plans for the new day. About the only serious military work Beauregard did on the night of 6-7 April was to rearrange his command structure. Since the Confederate brigades, divisions, and corps were too intermingled to be separated, he just assigned different sections of the line to his top generals. Bragg got command of the left, and Hardee was switched from the left to the right. Polk was to hold the center, aided by Breckinridge. These assignments were quite different from those with which they had started or ended the battle on the previous day. Few of the generals knew where their troops were; unknown to any of them, Maj. Gen. B.F. Cheatham had withdrawn his division to march back to his campsite of 5-6 April, some three miles from the front.

Beauregard might have learned more of Grant's situation had he carefully interrogated his highest ranking prisoner, Brig. Gen. Benjamin Prentiss. Prentiss spent all night bragging to anyone who would listen that Buell would join Grant that night and thump the Rebels soundly the next day. His listeners, however, refused to believe him. They had fresh but erroneous evidence from scouts that Buell was headed for Decatur, Alabama, and not Shiloh.

Grant also had no precise plans for the morning of the 7th. His

Major General Don Carlos Buell's Army of the Ohio arrived late on 6 April just in time to save Grant's army from total defeat. Buell was so disgusted with Grant's performance that he refused to communicate with him during the fighting on 7 April.

intention was simply to form up his men alongside Buell's and attack vigorously to regain his old camps and the honor he had lost the previous day. During the night he made no arrangements for battle, and he issued no battle orders until near to dawn.

Of the three principal generals on the field, only Buell appears to have had definite plans for the 7th. Because of the disorganized state of Grant's troops, Buell had his men form up 300 yards in front of the center of Grant's "Last Line." He then issued orders for a dawn attack. At no point, though, did he meet with Grant. By all accounts, Buell was quite disgusted with the performance of Grant's command on the 6th. He considered himself the commander of a separate army, answerable to Halleck but not to Grant. He would cooperate with Grant on the 7th, but he would not go to him for orders.

Attack and Counter Attack

Buell's attack began before dawn on the 7th. Leading the way was Nelson's *4th Division* of three brigades. Nelson's men stumbled forward in the darkness for over half an hour, expect-

The causes of Major General Lew Wallace's late arrival at the battlefield on 6 April are still heartily debated today.

ing to meet the Rebels at every step. Finally, about 0520, they ran into skirmishers from Forrest's cavalry on the northern edge of Cloud Field. The Confederates readily gave way, and Nelson pushed on another one-half mile to the southwest, where he reached the rear of the previous day's Hornets' Nest line. About 0600 Col. William B. Hazen's brigade was fired on by Chalmers' Confederate brigade, which had encamped between Wicker Field and Bloody Pond. Chalmers had the initial advantage over Hazen, but he was unwilling to advance without support from Jackson's brigade, which was expected momentarily. Nelson also was unwilling to force more combat against an enemy of undetermined strength. He decided to wait for Crittenden's *5th Division*, which was coming up on his right. As a result of this impasse, the two sides sat still and rested for over an hour and a half (0630 to 0800) while their skirmishers peppered each other across Wicker Field.

Meanwhile, fighting had developed on its own farther to the west. Here, Lew Wallace had formed his three brigade division by 0100 on the far right of Grant's line. Wallace's men had not yet been engaged in the fighting, though they were worn out from a full day of marching on the previous day and the excitement of the moment. Facing Wallace's line was Col. Preston Pond's 3rd Brigade of Ruggles' 1st Division, from Hardee's III Corps. It seems that Pond was the only commander in the Confederate army not to have received Beauregard's withdrawal order of the previous evening. Consequently, he prepared his men to renew the battle at dawn on the 7th, not knowing that he was about a mile north of his nearest supports.

When the sun rose on 7 April, Wallace's Unionists and Pond's Confederates were surprised to find themselves so close together—only about 400 yards separated their lines. As soon as it was light enough to see, Capt. Noah Thompson's *9th Indiana Battery* opened fire on Capt. William Ketcham's Alabama Battery, which was still in its night camp. The Confederates quickly recovered from their rude awakening and held off until more Union guns joined the fray. Ketcham then retired his guns, leaving the way open for Wallace to advance. Pond was then ordered to withdraw and go to the support of the troops opposing Buell's advance.

Pond's withdrawal left the defense of the Confederate left to Wharton's cavalry command, which was posted in Sowell Field, and Wood's and Gibson's brigades, which were formed on the southern edge of Jones Field. Here another impasse developed. Wallace was unwilling to advance farther until he received support. Hurlbut, who was supposed to be supplying this, was delaying sending in his division until he could find provisions for his men, and Sherman was unwilling to advance until Buell made more progress on his left. Consequently, both sides halted. They skirmished with each other for about an hour. Then the Confederates briefly took the initiative. About 0900 Ruggles directed Gibson and Wood to charge across Jones Field to seize Thompson's battery, which was posted without apparent supports a quarter mile north of the Confederate line.

The Confederate attack did not go well. Wood's men were hit by flanking fire from Sherman's line, and soon gave way. Gibson's brigade continued its charge towards the battery, not knowing that Wallace had replaced Thompson's battery with Lt. Charles H. Thurber's fresh *Battery I, 1st Missouri Artillery*. Gibson's 1st Arkansas Regiment rushed the battery and man-

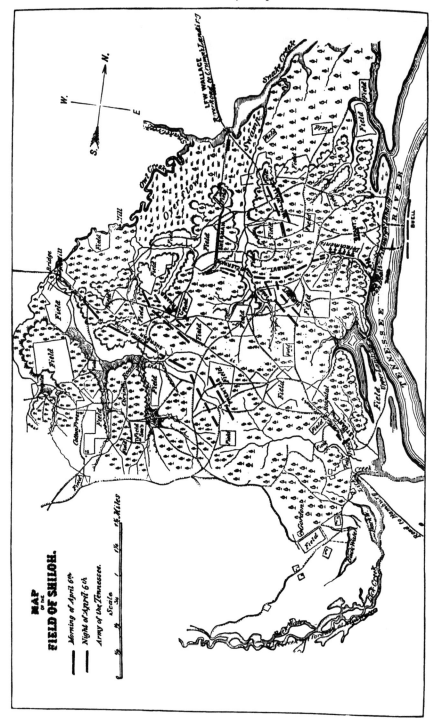

aged to capture one cannon, but before the Razorbacks could drag off their prize they were driven back by heavy fire from Col. Morgan Smith's *1st Brigade*. Meanwhile, Wharton's Texas Rangers, who had joined the attack on Gibson's left, were repulsed by Col. John M. Thayer's *2nd Brigade*. The failure of these attacks, and the knowledge of increased Union pressure all along the line, then persuaded Beauregard to order Ruggles to withdraw a half mile to the Corinth Road.

Meanwhile, action had resumed on Buell's front. By 0800 Crittenden's *5th Division* and Brig. Gen. Lovell Rousseau's *14th Brigade* of McCook's *2nd Division* had come up to extend Nelson's line west from Wicker Field to the northwest corner of Duncan Field. When Buell finally began his advance about 0800, he at first met no opposition. It seems that Chalmers' men had run out of ammunition, and Chalmers had withdrawn them to seek a fresh supply. Their withdrawal permitted Nelson to reach the Peach Orchard in good order. Here he formed on the line held by Hurlbut's division just 24 hours earlier.

At 0900 Buell attempted to advance beyond the Peach Orchard. He met unexpectedly stiff opposition. During the previous lull in the morning's fighting, the Confederates had organized a new line along the Hamburg-Purdy Road, facing the Peach Orchard. Brig. Gen. John S. Martin's brigade (formerly Bowen's) held the left end of this line, and a makeshift brigade under division commander Brig. Gen. J.M. Withers was on the right. Buell's main effort was made by Col. Sanders Bruce's *22nd Brigade* in the center. As Bruce advanced, he ran into increasingly heavy fire from the Confederate infantry. Then Hodgson's battery of the Washington (Louisiana) Artillery opened up on Bruce's left flank. Hodgson was posted with Martin's brigade, and could not have been in a better position to enfilade the Union attack. Several well placed shots routed Bruce's *1st* and *2nd Kentucky Regiments*, and Bruce had no choice but to retreat.

Hardee, who was personally overseeing the Confederate defense in this sector, decided to take advantage of Bruce's retreat and ordered a counterattack. Martin's brigade rushed forward, led by the 2nd Confederate Regiment. Buell saw them coming, and ordered Hazen's brigade to attack their left flank. It was a masterful move. His counterattack jolted Martin's regiments and sent them streaming to the rear. In a short time the victorious Yankees even managed to capture three of Hodgson's cannons.

By now the battle was becoming wild. Just as Hazen's attack was spending its force, the Crescent (Louisiana) Regiment led yet another Confederate counterattack. Hazen's men at the time were disorganized from their mad charge, and they were suddenly demoralized by fire coming into their rear by some of their own troops. When Hazen's men saw the Crescent Regiment charging at them, they abandoned their newly captured cannons and scattered to the rear. Hardee then brought forward another new unit, a makeshift brigade led by Col. John Moore of the 2nd Texas. Moore was cautioned as he advanced not to fire on the Crescent Regiment in his front; the Louisianans were wearing blue uniforms and could easily be mistaken for Yankees. For this reason he did not challenge a large force he met in the woods. This proved to be a fatal mistake. The force turned out to be a part of Nelson's command. A sudden Union volley shattered Moore's entire line, which melted away to the rear.

Meanwhile, Chalmers' brigade reentered the fight on the Confederate right. About 1100 Bragg ordered Chalmers to attack Ammen's brigade on the left flank of Buell's line. Chalmers' men made some progress, but were unable to sustain a fire fight with the Federals. It seems that the night's rain had wet their cartridges, and no one had thought to obtain any dry ammunition. Soon Chalmers was forced to retreat under heavy enemy pressure.

The confused fighting on Buell's front reached a new crescendo about noon, when Bragg threw into the fray Col. George Maney's brigade (formerly Stephensen's) of Cheatham's division. Maney entered the attack with only half of his command. Most of the 9th Tennessee had been separated from the brigade the previous day and still had not been located. In addition, the 7th Kentucky had been mistakenly left behind the previous night, when Cheatham returned to his pre-battle camps. Since the 7th's colonel had accompanied Cheatham, the regiment was fighting on a different front under the command of a captain. Aided by the 154th Tennessee of Col. Reston Smith's brigade (formerly Bushrod Johnson's), Maney pitched into Ammen's right flank. He probably would have routed Ammen's line, if he had not suffered badly from the fire of Capt. William Terrill's *Battery H, 5th U.S. Artillery.* Terrill's two 10-pounder Parrott rifles and four Napoleons were posted just south of the Peach Orchard, and poured a destructive fire into Maney's attacking line. After some desperate fighting, Maney finally had to give way about 1230.

During all this intense fighting, Bragg managed to bring Nelson's division to a standstill. The heavy commitment of troops to their right, however, left few Confederates to hold the center of their line. For this reason, Crittenden's and McCook's fresh Union divisions had a relatively easy time when they finally began their attack across Review Field about 1100.

The only Confederate opposition to Crittenden and McCook was three separated brigades. The best organized of these was Trabue's Orphan Brigade, which was posted east of Duncan Field with Byrne's Kentucky battery. Russell's brigade was loosely stationed south of Duncan Field, and Patton Anderson's brigade was lined up west of Duncan Field.

Curiously, the first attack in the central portion of the battlefield had been made by the Confederates, not the Yankees. Around 1000 hours Bragg ordered Trabue to support Hardee's attacks by assaulting Crittenden's Union division. Trabue promptly advanced over the same rough ground that had broken up so many attacks on the Hornets' Nest the previous day. This day the results were the same. Trabue was easily repulsed, and Smith's Union brigade began a counterattack. Fortunately for the Confederates, the same rough terrain that had hindered their attack also delayed the Federal advance. This gave Trabue time to withdraw and reform.

The most decisive Union advance of the day occurred on McCook's front. Here again, it was the Confederates who made the first move. About 1030 Bragg sent Russell's brigade to support Trabue's attack. Russell's men, however, had no brush to cover their advance. In about fifteen minutes their attack was checked and driven back. McCook promptly ordered a counterattack by Rousseau's *4th Brigade.* Russell's men retreated so quickly that Bragg had no choice but to withdraw Anderson to a new line being thrown together a half mile to the rear.

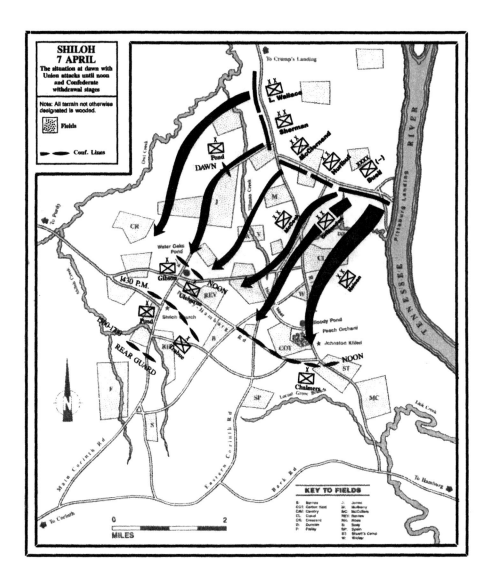

The **8th** *and* **18th Illinois** *regiments of McClernand's division captured a Confederate battery near the Purdy Road on 7 April.*

At this point, a unified advance by all of McCook's and Crittenden's men could have broken the Confederate center to pieces. However, the Union commanders remained cautious because of the heavy battle raging on Nelson's front. Nevertheless, their advance met steady success. About 1300 Brig. Gen. Jeremiah Boyle's *11th* and Col. William S. Smith's *14th Brigade* rushed Russell's brigade and captured two guns of Cobb's Kentucky battery. Bragg managed to stall the advancing Yankees with a brief counterattack. The situation appeared to be so critical to McClernand that he ordered Col. August Willich to lead his *14th Wisconsin* in a sacrificial bayonet attack. Willich's attack achieved its purpose, but at a bloody cost; his regiment was driven back after a sharp fifteen minute struggle. When Willich's attack was followed up by a charge of the *Louisville Legion (5th Kentucky)*, the Confederate line began to give way. Bragg had used up his reserves and had no more troops to throw into the fray. Soon Rousseau's entire brigade was advancing up the road that led from Duncan Field to the main Corinth Road. Supported by very accurate fire from Capt. John Mendenhall's combined *Battery H/M* of the *4th U.S. Artillery*, Rousseau's advance bent back the entire Confederate center. The stiffest resistance to Rousseau's advance was offered by Stanford's Mississippi Battery. Stanford felled hundreds of Rousseau's men and held on even after his infantry supports were driven back. Finally, Stanford had no choice but to withdraw what he could of his command. He had only enough horses left to pull away two of his six guns. At the same time the Yankees managed to capture all six guns of Cobb's Kentucky Battery.

Well after 1400, in the woods northwest of Shiloh Church, Bragg gathered all the troops he could as a last resistance to the advance of McCook's and Crittenden's divisions. For a time his front stalled the Yankees, and a brief counterattack met limited success. By now many of the blue clad regiments were disorganized or out of ammunition. The Confederates simply lacked the strength to take advantage of the situation. When Morgan's Kentucky cavalry attempted to charge Mendenhall's battery, many of the Confederate saddles were emptied in vain. By now the Confederates, too, were running out of ammunition, and their men were exhausted from two days of constant fighting.

Meanwhile, the Confederate left had been driven steadily rearward towards Shiloh Church. After Ruggles had withdrawn from Jones Field, Lew Wallace and Sherman made a concerted advance with the whole Union right flank about 1000. Bragg was desperate to stop the Union juggernaut. About 1100 he ordered Cleburne to make an assault on Sherman's left. Cleburne did not think much of the order; at the time he had with him only 800 of the 2,700 men with whom he had started the battle. Despite this small number, Cleburne met temporary success because his opposition, assorted Union companies that had survived the previous day's fight, was more disorganized than his own command.

General Beauregard, at his headquarters at Shiloh Church, issues orders at 1400 on 7 April for his army to begin retreating from the field.

Soon the Confederates received their last reinforcements from the rear, a portion of Cheatham's division. Cheatham fell in with Cleburne's command, and was then joined by Patton Anderson's brigade. This Confederate line formed just north of Water Oaks Pond, and was one of the strongest the Confederates formed that day. It fought Sherman and Wallace to a standstill for an hour beginning at noon. The Confederates then began to give way from exhaustion and the weight of superior Union numbers. They especially felt pressure from Rousseau's brigade advancing against their right flank. By 1400 Rousseau was driving back the entire Confederate left and center, which by then had been compressed into one line.

Beauregard now had all he could do to rally his worn-out

During the second day of the battle, Buell's men recovered about 20 cannons lost by Grant's batteries on 6 April. Here the 1st Ohio Infantry *is shown after it recaptured several guns of Behr's 6th Indiana Battery.*

troops. To his good fortune, the pressure from Wallace's front slackened when Wallace stopped his advance and sent Col. Charles Whittlesey's *3rd Brigade* on a broad flanking movement to the west. Beauregard took advantage of this brief respite to bring up Pond's brigade from Shiloh Church. Pond had received five different sets of orders during the day and had been marching and counter-marching ever since his early morning clash with Wallace. Beauregard also gathered up several other stray regiments from Trabue's brigade and other commands. Finally, he had six regiments in line for a counterattack. The men were grim and unenthusiastic, but still followed orders to fix their bayonets.

At 1430 hours Beauregard ordered Pond and his supports forward in the last Confederate counterattack of the battle. Their charge caught Col. Edward N. Kirk's *5th* and Col. William S. Gibson's *6th Brigade* of McCook's division completely unaware. Kirk was wounded, and the whole Union line wavered. But the Confederates suffered heavy casualties, too, especially from Union artillery fire. Soon the charge spent its force and began to give ground under pressure from Union counterattacks. Led by the *32nd Indiana*, Buell's regiments put so much pressure on Beauregard's line that many Confederate units simply broke up and headed for the rear.

Beauregard was aware that the battle was now over. When his aide, Col. Thomas Jordan, asked, "General, do you not think our troops are very much in the condition of a lump of sugar, thoroughly soaked with water, but yet preserving its original shape, though ready to dissolve? Would it not be judicious to get away with what we have?", Beauregard responded, "I intend to withdraw in a few moments." Soon Beauregard organized a holding force of a couple batteries and 2000 men from stray regiments, and posted this conglomerate command on a ridge south of Shiloh Church. He then ordered a general retreat for the whole army.

Beauregard's order to retreat came as a surprise to Hardee's command on the army's right wing. After the intense attacks and counterattacks of the late morning, both sides on this end of the battlefield were exhausted and had settled down to long range fire fights. It was not long then until many of the Confederates began running out of ammunition. Nobody knew where the army's reserve ammunition wagons were, so entire brigades had to be pulled out of line to search for cartridges in the captured Union camps.

Around 1300 Withers had found his line so reduced that he decided it was best to withdraw to the southwest. His move to a new position near Prentiss' old camps was part of the tendency of the entire Confederate army to collapse on its center that day. Buell saw Withers' retreat and quickly ordered his men to advance in pursuit. Nelson was slow in mounting his attack; the only successful charge during his pursuit was made on his far right by the *2nd Kentucky* of Bruce's brigade. This regiment charged right up to Harper's Mississippi Battery, which was posted just east of Barnes Field. Harper lost so many men and horses that he had to leave two guns behind when he was forced to retreat in haste.

The most glorious moment in a battle is for a regiment to capture an enemy flag or cannon. The hard earned glory of the *2nd Kentucky* was all too short lived when the unit was struck by a counterattack led by Martin's brigade. Martin's men had been in the rear scrounging for ammunition when Buell's afternoon advance began. Bragg hurried them to the front, and they quickly overwhelmed the *2nd Kentucky*, which had no supports. This attack broadened when Breckinridge advanced a reinforced brigade across Barnes Field in support of Martin's attack. At the north end of the field, Breckinridge ran into Col. George Wagner's *21st Brigade* of Brig. Gen. Thomas J. Wood's *6th Division* posted along the Purdy Road, 2000 strong and fresh from Pittsburg Landing. Breckinridge was momentarily repulsed, but reformed his men for yet another charge.

The End

It was at this moment—around 1515—that Bragg received orders from Beauregard to retreat. Bragg was reportedly surprised at the order, but he must have been aware of the odds against him. In addition, the sounds of battle must have told him how poorly things were going on Beauregard's front. Bragg posted a small rear guard and began withdrawing toward Mickey's. At the same time, Beauregard's troops were sullenly marching south along the main Corinth Road, thoroughly dejected after their high hopes of the previous day. In their despair, they set fire to all the captured enemy camps they passed. The resulting fire and smoke added to the day's plentitude of gunpowder smoke and gave a totally hellish appearance to the battlefield.

As the Confederates disengaged and withdrew, a few Union troops conducted a limited pursuit. On the Union right, Lew Wallace advanced cautiously and then called off his men. In the center, Grant sent only a few reserve regiments forward. They advanced until they ran into Breckinridge's rear guard, and then pulled back. Buell mistakenly thought that the Confederates had withdrawn along the Hamburg-Savannah Road, so he sent Nelson's division off in that direction. When he found no Confederates there, Buell formed near Stuart's old camp for an expected third day of fighting. The only determined pursuit was by Brig. Gen. James A. Garfield's *20th Brigade* of Wood's *6th Division*. Garfield's command had been the last of Buell's army to reach the field, and so it was the only totally fresh unit on the battlefield. Yet, there was not much Garfield could do with a late start and only three regiments. He was soon recalled, to his disappointment, before his men could fire a shot.

Grant later claimed that his men were too exhausted and disorganized for a determined pursuit of the enemy, saying, "I wanted to pursue, but had not the heart to order the men who had fought desperately for two days, lying in the mud and rain whenever not fighting, and I did not feel disposed to positively order Buell, or any part of his command to pursue." Besides, he had only a few cavalry units available, and many of his men were out of ammunition. Yet, had it been later in the war, an effective pursuit would have been pushed forward without question. Hundreds of prisoners could have been snatched up, though it is likely that no heavy damage could have been done to the Confederate army because of its head start and the lateness of the day. Then, on top of everything else, it began to rain again. Grant gave up all hope of pursuing the Confederates, and formed up his men for a possible renewal of fighting on 8 April.

Where Was Grant?

Maj. Gen. U.S. Grant, commander of the Union forces at Shiloh, was not present on the battlefield during the opening stages of the battle on the early morning of 6 April 1862. He spent the night before the battle at his headquarters in Savannah, some nine miles downstream from Pittsburg Landing. In fact, he spent almost every night at Savannah after he arrived in the area on 17 March. Almost daily he went to Pittsburg Landing to inspect his troops, but he preferred to spend his nights at Savannah in order to keep in better touch with Buell's army, which was approaching from Nashville. In retrospect, Grant's decision to return every night to Savannah was one of the several major mistakes he made before the battle.

Grant spent the night of April 5-6 at his headquarters in the Cherry House in Savannah. He got up around 0630 and began reading his morning mail before breakfast. About an hour later an orderly interrupted his breakfast to report the sound of firing from the direction of Pittsburg Landing.

Grant immediately boarded the steamboat *Tigress* to go to Pittsburg Landing. It took *Tigress* a while to raise steam, and then she had to make her way against the Tennessee's current. About 0815 *Tigress* pulled in near Crump's Landing, four miles north of Pittsburg Landing, so that Grant could have a short conference with Maj. Gen. Lew Wallace, commanding the *3rd Division*, which was stationed there. Grant ordered Wallace to be ready to march on a moment's notice and then resumed his trip to Pittsburg Landing.

Grant reached the Landing about 0900, a little more than four hours after the battle started. He immediately mounted his horse and headed inland. There he ran into W.H.L. Wallace, who briefed him on the progress of the battle. Grant continued on to the battlefront to confer with Sherman and his other division commanders. Upon seeing the desperateness of the situation, he sent orders for Lew Wallace and Buell to hurry to join him. He then waited frantically all afternoon for these reinforcements to arrive. When Lew Wallace failed to show up, Prentiss' line at the Hornets' Next was captured, and Grant barely managed to hold on to his last line on the bluffs above the Tennessee River.

Grant's absence during the morning's surprise attack dogged him for the rest of his life. His superior, Halleck, took command of Grant's and Buell's combined armies soon after the battle, effectively relieving Grant of command. At one point the offended Grant was ready to resign. His friend Sherman persuaded him to stick around, and Halleck finally left for Washington in July. In this way Grant was returned to command. He went on to take Vicksburg, relieve Chattanooga, capture Richmond and Lee's whole army, and ultimately become president. All this might have turned out quite differently had things gone a bit better for the Confederates on the first day of Shiloh.

Where Was Lew Wallace?

For most of the aftenoon of 6 April, Grant and his weary troops waited desperately for Lew Wallace and his *3rd Division* to come up from Crump's Landing and reinforce their hard-pressed lines. Grant himself kept looking to the north, and sent messenger after messenger to hurry Wallace onward. Yet Wallace did not appear until near nightfall, when the day's contest had ended. Where had he been all day?

Wallace had been at Crump's Landing, some four miles north of Pittsburg Landing, for about three weeks before the battle. His purpose was twofold: to guard the river landing and nearby Savannah as important communication centers, and to keep an eye on the Confederate troops at Bethel Station, 118 miles west of Crump's Landing on the Mobile and Ohio Railroad. As Grant's army began to concentrate at Pittsburg Landing, Wallace was kept at Crump's in order to guard the army's northern flank. His continued presence there also helped alleviate the crowded conditions that began to develop at Pittsburg Landing.

About 0600 hours on 6 April Wallace was awakened by one of his men, who told him of the sounds of combat coming from the army's main camp near Pittsburg Landing. Wallace promptly mobilized his division at Stoney Lonesome, two miles west of Crump's Landing. Here he would be able to defend against any attack coming from the direction of Purdy, or he could march more quickly to Pittsburg Landing if so ordered. Wallace himself remained at Crump's so as to receive any orders from Grant more quickly.

About 0830 hours Grant arrived at Crump's aboard the steamer *Tigress*. Grant was on his way from Savannah to Pittsburg Landing, but wanted to stop to give Wallace personal instructions. In a brief conference in midstream near the landing (Wallace had boarded a transport in order to meet Grant aboard the *Tigress*), Grant directed Wallace to hold his troops ready to march when the order came. For the moment Grant hesitated to order Wallace forward for fear of a Confederate attack from Purdy. In addition, he did not know precisely where the battle was being fought at the main camp, or where Wallace's help would be needed.

After Grant sailed for Pittsburg Landing, Wallace joined his 4,000 troops at Stoney Lonesome. There the men waited anxiously as the noise of battle increased to the south and drew closer to the river. No messengers came from Grant. As he waited, Wallace sent out scouts to the west and found that he was in no danger of an attack from the direction of Purdy. Yet, without precise orders from Grant, he was hesitant to advance to the south on his own authority.

Wallace's long awaited orders were indeed on their way. Upon reaching Pittsburg Landing about 0900 hours, Grant had immediately realized the severity of the situation. He at once sent a staff officer to order Wallace to proceed to join him and form his division on the right of the army in a line at right angles to the river. Grant's messenger took *Tigress* down to Crump's, and then reached Stoney Lonesome by horseback. Wallace received the order about 1130, but did not proceed immediately. Amazingly, he decided that the troops needed lunch first! When a second courier arrived from Grant with orders to hurry up, Wallace told him not to worry, he was on his way.

Needless to say, Grant was greatly annoyed when his courier returned to report that Wallace's men had not set out before noon. He then sent yet another aide to get Wallace moving immediately. Ths aide, Capt. W.R. Rowley, took the river road all the way to Crump's Landing and was amazed to find no trace of Wallace's "lost" division. Rowley finally found out that Wallace had taken the Shunpike. After a frantic ride, he located Wallace at about 1400 hours. Seeing Wallace's men taking a rest and being no closer to Pittsburg Landing than when they had started out, Rowley asked Wallace what was going on. When Wallace replied that he was marching to Sherman's camp as he had been ordered, Rowley exclaimed "Great God! Don't you know Sherman has been driven back? Why, the whole army is within half a mile of the river, and it's a question if we are not all going to be driven into it."

Wallace was dumbfounded and did not think clearly. He knew that the route he was on would lead straight to the Confederate rear and probably disaster, so he would have to reverse his direction to go by another route. But instead of ordering his men to turn around and have the rear troops lead the way, he decided to have the whole line wait while his lead brigade doubled back to continue at the head of the column. This decision forced most of Wallace's men to sit still for an hour while the lead troops countermarched past the three-mile-long column. Even then, Wallace's march was slow because he had to keep pace with his batteries and wagons.

By then Grant was growing panicky. Wallace was desperately needed to shore up the Hornets' Nest line, but nobody seemed to know where he was. At 1430 Grant sent yet more staff officers to find Wallace. They also took the River Road, and found no trace of him. Retracing their steps, they sent down the Purdy Road and found Wallace at 1530 at Overshot Hill. Wallace had spent three and one-half hours marching up and down the Shunpike, and was still about five miles from Grant's army.

Even now, Wallace did not march as if the outcome of the battle depended on his presence. Though he had heard the sound of Grant's guns booming, Wallace nevertheless made several stops to scout the road ahead or to allow his rear troops to catch up. Finally about 1915 hours his troops began crossing Snake Creek on the northern edge of the battle area. His men had marched 14 miles in seven hours and had taken three times as long to reach the battlefield as they should have.

Wallace's tardiness in reaching the battlefield put a blotch on his record that would haunt him for the rest of his life. For a time Grant blamed Wallace's absence for the army's defeat on 6 April. Wallace's late arrival certainly did affect the way the battle was fought. Yet, it probably did not materially affect the course of the battle. Had he arrived earlier, Wallace may just have been swept away with the rest of Grant's divisions by the onrushing Confederate tide.

Afterwards Wallace at one point darkened his reputation by taking the stand that he deliberately marched towards the Confederate rear in order to take them by surprise, but was recalled from this daring mission by Grant. This interpretation should be viewed as a total fabrication by Wallace in a desperate attempt to account for his actions.

There can be no question that Wallace was guilty of not reaching the battlefield quickly enough. His frequent halts, order of march, and error in reversing his line of march all contributed to his tardiness. However, he was not late on purpose, nor did he show negligence enough to be disciplined after the battle.

The person primarily responsible for Wallace's lateness in reaching the battlefield was not Wallace, but Grant. The main reason Wallace got off to a late start was that he did not receive marching orders from Grant until nearly noon. Grant had had the opportunity to order Wallace forward at 0830 hours, but he delayed in sending for him until after he reached the battlefield. Most significantly, Grant erred by not writing out Wallace's orders himself, and by not specifically directing him to take the River Road. When Grant sent for Wallace he naturally assumed that

Wallace would come via the River Road, a route that was three miles shorter than the one Wallace took using the Shunpike. Grant even admitted his error in his memoirs, where he wrote, "I never could see and do not see now why any order was necessary further than to direct him to come to Pittsburg Landing, without specifying by what route." Nevertheless, Wallace took the Shunpike route because he honestly felt that it was the most direct route to Sherman's camp.

We have no way now to tell exactly how Grant's order to Wallace was worded. Grant kept no copy of it, and he later could not remember its wording precisely. The paper on which it was written was lost during the battle. Grant's aide who wrote out the order later said that it directed Wallace to take the River Road, but Wallace insisted to his dying day that he was told to form on Sherman's right. The weight of the evidence seems to favor Wallace's assertion that he was told where to go, but not how to get there.

After Shiloh Lew Wallace's military career took a definite downturn. He spent two years on various military boards and did not take the field again until the spring of 1864, when he was assigned to command the *VIII Corps* in Maryland. There he lost the battle of Monocacy on 9 July 1864, during Jubal Early's raid on Washington.

Wallace's life after the war was definitely more productive. In 1865 he served on the court that tried Lincoln's assassins, and he was president of the court that tried Henry Wirz, the former commander at Andersonville prison. Later in that same year, he tried to help the Emperor Maximilian in his successful attempt to seize control of Mexico.

Wallace won his greatest claim to fame in 1880 while he was serving as governor of New Mexico Territory. It was then that he wrote the lengthy novel *Ben Hur, A Tale of the Christ*, a story later made into excellent movies starring Ramon Navarro and, several generations later, Charlton Heston.

How the Newspapers Saw the Battle

The first detailed news of the battle of Shiloh was carried on 9 April 1862 by the *New York Herald*. It seems that an enterprising reporter named W.C. Carroll scooped his rivals by taking a steamboat to Fort Henry, which was the closest telegraph station to the battlefield. Carroll's account boasted of a great victory, but was inaccurate in many of its details. He overestimated the losses on both sides (18,000-20,000 US and 35,000-40,000 CS), and falsely claimed that Grant himself had turned the tide of battle by personally leading a charge on the second day. Carroll's article was not overly long, so the *Herald* padded it with long biographies of the principal generals involved. Following the practice of the times, numerous other Northern papers quickly reprinted the *Herald's* article.

A quite different account of the battle surfaced a couple days later in the *Cincinnati Gazette*. It was written by Whitelaw Reid under the pen name "Agate." Reid by chance had been at Crump's Landing with Lew Wallace when the battle began. When Grant stopped to see Wallace while on his way from Savannah to the battlefield, Reid sneaked aboard *Tigress* and arrived at the battlefield at the same time as Grant. Here he was astonished at all the confusion, and became convinced that the army was poorly led and had inexcusably been taken by surprise on 6 April. After the battle he hurried all the way back to Cincinnati before writing out his version of the battle. Because of its detail and shocking accusations, Reid's account of the battle is the one that most caught the country's attention. Reid's primary charge was that the army had been surprised so badly that men were bayonetted in their tents or forced to fight in their underwear. He charged that Grant did not arrive on the battlefield until after several divisions had been routed, and that Grant was late in ordering up Lew Wallace. In Reid's opinion, the real hero of the battle was Buell, who saved Grant's army on the second day.

Reid's charges were supported by many soldiers who had been in the battle; it was clear to them that the rout of Grant's army had been due to poor generalship and not to any fault of their own. The lieutenant governor of Ohio even went so far as to scream that "Grant and Prentiss ought to be court-martialed or shot." Several influential newspapers, including the *Chicago Times* and the *Cincinnati Commercial*, repeated the charges of incompetency against Grant and his subordinates.

The furor caused by Reid's article took a long time to die down. In retrospect, we know today that several of his principal arguments were incorrect. Reid claimed that the Union troops were surprised in their camps, when they all actually had plenty of time to form up and deploy for battle. He also stated that Prentiss' division was captured at 1000, whereas Prentiss did not actually surrender until 1730.

Grant tried to defend himself against these charges by writing a confused letter to the *Cincinnati Commercial*. Sherman took the accusations more personally, since he was responsible for the deployment of the Union troops into the positions that the Confederates surprised, resulting in the rout. He charged that the exaggerated stories of the Union "disaster" had been fabricated by stragglers and cowards "who ran away and had to excuse their cowardice by charging bad management on the part of the leaders."

The bad feelings against Grant and Sherman did not begin to settle down until Henry Halleck, commanding head general in the West, reported to the War Department that he did not consider Grant or Sherman guilty of any of the charges leveled against them by Reid. As the war continued, the fervor over Shiloh subsided and the newspapers took up fresher controversies. Nevertheless Reid's accusations colored the nation's view of Shiloh, and in some ways still do.

Civil War Medicine

Over 16,000 men were wounded at Shiloh. Many of those who died in the days and weeks after the battle could now have been saved. As with everything else in the Civil War, medical care for the troops had to be improvised. And as with everything else, the process of developing an efficient system for caring for the sick and wounded was slow, difficult, and literally painful. To begin with, the practice of medicine in the United States then was primitive even by the standards of the times. The intellectual and humanitarian currents that had already begun to establish medicine on a scienfitic basis in Europe had barely affected the United States. Medical education was poor; most physicians and surgeons were trained largely through service as apprentices. The few formal medical schools were not much better; Harvard, which may have been the best in the country, is said to have owned neither a microscope nor a stethoscope until after the war. There was little supervision over the profession and little organization within it. Fads and fashions and frauds were common. Nevertheless, most medical personnel, all but a handful male, were honest, dedicated, and hardworking.

The physicians of the age did their best and were actually fairly good at treating some problems. But, with the existence of bacteria barely known in Europe and not even rumored in America, there was no scientific understanding of the nature of the various conditions, and no systematic basis for treatment. Thus, many fevers were thought to be caused by "various atmospheric influences, such as products of vegetable or animal decomposition." Surgery was the most advanced branch of medicine at the time. This was fortunate, for the usual method of dealing with wounds required cutting, and amputation was frequent. Knowledge of anatomy was adequate and the surgeon's tools were well developed. Chloroform and ether were known and used, often excessively, but antisepsis was unheard of. As a result, a patient's chances of survival hinged not on the skill of the surgeon as much as on whether or not he could avoid serious infection. Drugs were drawn largely from those of folk medicine. Some of these (calomel, arrowroot, acacia, camphor, belladonna, mustard, assafoetida) had limited applications, while others (mercury, strychnine, ammonia, potassium arsenate, lead acetate, turpentine) were downright dangerous. Nevertheless, some progress had been made. It was understood that an adequate and balanced diet had something to do with health; a notion had arisen of the relationship between cleanliness and health; and many genuine medicines had been discovered, including quinine, iodine, and opium.

Disease was the biggest killer of the war, not enemy gunfire. Union records show that of 359,528 deaths recorded among the troops, only 67,058 were killed in action (18.65%). There were also 43,012 officers and men who died of wounds, making a grand total of 110,070 battle-related deaths (30.6%). Disease accounted for 224,586 officers and men (62.57%). The balance, 24,972 (6.9%) was due to all other causes, including homicides (520), execution (267), drownings (4944), accidents (4114), and so forth, including a large category of unknowns (12,121). Thus, disease caused nearly 50% more deaths than did battle.

The greatest losses from disease, however, came in the earlier part of the war, particulartly in the first two years, when everyone was learning to be a soldier. Camp sanitation was terrible; food was usually of poor quality; clothing and tentage were often shoddy and insufficient. The armies learned in time, though only the North had the resources to cope adequately with the problem of disease. In the Mexican War the average annual death rate from disease had been 10.2% of strength. In the Civil War, this figure declined to 6.2%, at least for the Union forces. The Medical Department of the Confederacy tried its best, but despite great efforts, it could not really cope with a persistent shortage of resources, including surgeons, medicines, and supplies. Although records are inadequate, it appears the Confederate deaths from disease and wounds were relatively higher than were Union ones. However, even at the end of the war a Union soldier was still more likely to succumb to disease than to bullets.

At the beginning of the war, many physicians volunteered to fight, just as everyone else did. Soon, however most took on the status of volunteer surgeons, either as commissioned officers or under contract. Surgeons usually served as majors or captains, while contract surgeons held the temporary rank of lieutenant. Some were inept and some were unsuited to the military, but most did their jobs as best they could. At many battles they worked under appalling conditions. Many of the wounded at Shiloh did not receive adequate treatment until they had been transferred to Savannah or Corinth. One significant advance in the treatment of the wounded occurred on the second day of Shiloh (7 April), when Union surgeons established a tent field hospital for treatment of the wounded as close to the fighting as possible. This was the first such field hospital in the war.

Initially medical services were organized on a regimental basis. Each Union regiment had a surgeon, two assistant surgeons, and a hospital steward, while Confederate regiments had ony one surgeon and one assistant surgeon. These doctors would set up regimental hospitals as needed to deal with the sick and wounded. The system proved inadequate because quite often regiments had more casualties than their doctors could care for. This situation was improved in the East by Dr. Jonathan Letterman, who became medical director of the *Army of the Potomac* in mid-1862. Dr. Letterman established field hospitals at the bri-gade level, pooling the personnel of the regiments in each brigade. Still later he based medical service in divisional hospitals, equipping each division with field ambulances, storage wagons, and cooking facilities. These arrangements worked very well by making sure that all personnel were fully employed, and by facilitating the complex supply arrangements needed by medical units. Initially there were no arrangements for the collection of wounded men. If they could not get themselves to a field hospital, they remained on the field until someone took pity on them. One result of this was that men would often leave the firing line to carry a wounded comrade to the hospital. This practice was not conducive to military efficiency since the faint hearted could and did use it as a ready excuse to get away from the firing line. Dr. Letterman later organized an ambulance corps for the *Army of the Potomac*. This was a disciplined body of men whose sole task was to recover the wounded and bring them back to the field hospitals. Each regiment, brigade and division had its ambulance corps detachment, all under the control of the medical director of the corps. In an infantry regiment, the ambulance detachment consisted of a sergeant, nine privates, and three ambulance wagons with drivers; they were assisted by band members in those regiments that had a band. Letterman also decided that it was better to avoid moving the wounded as much as possible. For this reason he established regular hospitals to treat the worst of the wounded in place rather than evacuate them great distances, as was done so harmfully at Shiloh. Letterman's arrangements worked so well, that a wounded man who received treatment actually had a fair chance of survival—of the wounded who received medical assistance only 13.3% died, despite the inadequacies of the medical science of the day. Letterman's system worked so well that it was later extended to all Union armies.

The scandalous medical situation that prevailed at the start of the war sparked considerable public interest in the problem. Women joined various nursing organizations, and some (such as Clara Barton, Anna M. Holstein, and Anna Etheridge) even went into the field to aid the troops. Several volunteer organiza-

tions were set up to render aid to the soldiers when the government failed them. These groups, such as the United States Sanitary Commission and the Christian Sanitary Commission, soon began to wield considerable political clout. These organizations did not hesitate to use their power, and with the whole-hearted support of the men in the field, they virtually took over the direction of medical affairs from the Medical Department. The War Department began to implement changes, the most notable of which was the appointment of Dr. Joseph K. Barnes as Acting Surgeon General in early 1863. Barnes began a thorough reform of the Medical Department, greatly improving services to the sick and the wounded.

The Gallant Mrs. Wallace

One of the most heart-rending stories of Shiloh concerns Ann Wallace's surprise visit to her husband Brig. Gen. William H.L. Wallace, commander of Grant's *2nd Division* (not to be confused with Lew Wallace, commander of Grant's *3rd Division*). "Will" had recently been sick, and Ann decided to make an unannounced visit to cheer him up. She arrived at Pittsburg Landing aboard the steamer *Minehaha* just before daylight on 6 April. No sooner had she landed than she heard the sounds of fighting. The battle was under way. Mrs. Wallace realized that she would be unable to go to the front until the fighting ceased, so she waited anxiously all day as

wounded streamed to the landing and the din of battle crept nearer.

Late in the day, Mrs. Wallace finally received news of her husband. This news came from none other than her brother, Lt. Cyrus Dickey, who was a member of Will's staff. Dickey had the sad task of telling his sister that her husband had received a mortal wound in the head during the fighting at the Hornets' Nest. Dickey had tried to bring him off the field, but had been unable to do so because the Union line soon collapsed completely. Mrs. Wallace was left alone with her grief, then selflessly spent the night nursing the wounded.

She was rewarded the next day.

191

During the morning's fighting, the Union forces rolled back Beauregard's army and recovered much of the ground they had held the previous day. During a lull in the fighting, Mrs. Wallace's brother went back to look for Wallace's body. He found the general about 1100. Much to his amazement, Wallace was still breathing. Some Confederate troops had put a blanket around him, but the general was suffering terribly from his wound.

Dickey had Wallace carried back to the landing carefully and quickly.

He then found his sister, who rushed to the side of her stricken husband. Will was conscious, and Ann hoped things might turn out well after all.

The general was taken to Grant's former headquarters in Savannah, the Cherry mansion. Ann nursed him with all her devotion. His pulse was strong, but he began to develop a fever on the 10th, four days after being wounded. He faded quickly, and passed away the same day. His poor wife had recovered him only to lose him again.

CHAPTER VII

Afterwards

On the morning of 8 April, all the Union troops were exhausted and wet. Most of Grant's men had been fighting for two straight days, and Buell's men had left their packs behind during their forced march to the battlefield. Many of the Yankees were fearful of yet another enemy surprise attack. Indeed, this seemed to be happening soon after daylight when firing broke out all along the Union lines. Actually, no Confederate fighting troops were then anywhere near Grant's lines. What had happened now appears rather silly. It seems that some of Garfield's men had fired their weapons to clear them of moisture after the night's rain. The noise of this firing alarmed adjacent units, which interpreted the shots to be coming from a Confederate attack. Soon nervous troops up and down the Union line were firing wildly at imagined Confederates in their front. It took the Union officers a great deal of time to halt this "battle." Some units had fired as many as ten rounds before they were informed of their mistake!

When the firing finally died down, Grant sent out a reconnaissance force consisting of the *4th Illinois Cavalry*, Wood's division, and two brigades of Sherman's division. This force left about 1000 and advanced steadily until it reached a small Confederate cavalry force about noon. This Confederate command was small, perhaps 350 men, but it was led by one of the war's best cavalry leaders, Nathan Bedford Forrest. Forrest saw signs of indecision in the Union troops that faced him, and boldly ordered his men to charge. The Confederate troopers overwhelmed several companies of the *77th Ohio*, and then routed the supporting Union cavalry. Sherman, who was caught up in all the confusion, was almost killed or captured; he and his staff hastened ingloriously to the rear. It was then Forrest's turn to be surprised. As his cavalrymen pressed on, they ran right into Col. Jesse Hildebrand's brigade of Sherman's division. Many of the cavalrymen fell casualty, and Forrest suddenly found himself alone within fifty yards of the enemy. He tried to ride off and was wounded in the side. Nevertheless, though his horse was also badly wounded, Forrest managed to ride to safety. He would be the battle's last official casualty.

Sherman stopped his pursuit after this encounter with Forrest, and returned to his camp at nightfall. Meanwhile, the Confederate army limped into Corinth. A more dispirited lot could hardly be seen. The roads were incredibly muddy, and the exhausted troops had almost no organization and few supplies. Things were little better at Corinth. Wounded were everywhere, and little food or drinking water was to be found. Beauregard strove mightily to reorganize his army, now numbering about 30,000, in anticipation of a renewed advance by Grant and Buell.

The two armies now paused to tally their losses. Altogether some 23,746 men had been casualties, over 20% of the 111,511 men engaged on both sides. The Yankees had lost the most men, 13,047 to 10,699 in the Confederate army; all but 2103 of the Union losses were in Grant's command. Over 16,000 men on both sides had been wounded, and many of them still lay on the field, suffering in the rain from exposure. Others were crowded in crude field hospitals. The usual procedure for dealing with wounds in the extremities was amputation. Piles of severed arms and legs lay near the field hospitals as the exhausted surgeons labored over their work. Statistics show that perhaps three of every four amputees died from their wounds or the stress of the amputation. Many of the wounded who could be moved, both Union and Confederate, were transferred from the battlefield to Union hospitals in Savannah. The Confederate wounded who were evacuated by their own forces on the 6th or 7th had to endure a jolting wagon ride back to Corinth, where they filled all available buildings. One of the wounded Confederates taken to Corinth was a Tennessee captain named Benjamin Vickers. When his fiancee, Sallie Houston, heard of his

Burning dead horses near the Peach Orchard after the battle.

plight, she insisted on visiting him in the hospital and exchanging their marriage vows. So the couple were wed ten days after the battle. Vickers died a few days later.

There also remained the problem of dealing with the dead bodies that covered the field. The warm spring weather hastened their decay, and the smell on the battlefield was soon almost unbearable. Over 3400 dead (1654 Union and 1728 Confederate) lay on the field. All were buried by the Union forces on the 8th and 9th. When Beauregard asked for a truce on the afternoon of the 9th in order to retrieve or bury his dead, Grant replied that the unpleasant job had already been completed. Confederate dead were buried in long trenches, six feet wide, four feet deep, and up to fifty or more feet long. One trench near McClernand's camp held 571 dead in seven layers. Union dead were buried with more care. Individual graves were provided for those soldiers who could be identified. Others were buried by regiment or brigade. After the battle some of the identified bodies were retrieved and taken home by grieving families. Today 3695 Union dead from Shiloh and other battles rest in the Shiloh National Cemetery. The Confederate dead still rest on the battlefield in their mass graves.

Besides the human dead and wounded, there were over 500 dead horses on the battlefield to be dealt with. These were too big for the exhausted soldiers to bury, so they were covered with brush where they fell and were burned.

Leadership losses at all levels were particularly high at

Shiloh. Unlike later wars, leaders in this battle felt that their duty was to lead their troops in person. All too many actually led charges and paid for their boldness with their lives.

The highest ranking officer killed was, of course, Gen. Albert Sidney Johnston of the Confederate army; he was, in fact, the highest ranking Confederate officer killed during the war. The Confederates also lost Brig. Gen. A.N. Gladden, who led a brigade in Bragg's corps. Maj. Gen. William Hardee, leader of the III Corps, was wounded, as were two division commanders in the I Corps, Brig. Gen. Charles Clark and Maj. Gen. Benjamin Cheatham. Altogether nine Confederate brigade commanders were wounded: Brigadier Generals Bushrod Johnson, A.M. Wood, and John S. Bowen; Colonels Preston Smith, William Stephens, Daniel Adams, Zach Deas, and R.G. Shaver. Among the mortally wounded was Kentucky's Confederate Governor-in-Exile George W. Johnson. Johnson was serving as a volunteer officer in Trabue's Kentucky Orphan Brigade on 7 April when he received two serious wounds. He lay on the battlefield until the next day, when a Yankee recognized a Masonic sign he was giving. Johnson died on 9 April aboard a Union hospital ship. His captors had thought he was former U.S. Vice-President Brig. Gen. John C. Breckinridge and were disappointed to find out that he was only a governor.

In Grant's army, three of the six division commanders were casualties: Brig. Gen. W.H.L. Wallace was killed, Brig. Gen. Benjamin M. Prentiss was captured, and Brig. Gen. William T. Sherman was wounded. Grant's army also lost two brigade commanders killed, Colonels Julius Raith and Everett Peabody; and five brigade commanders wounded, Brig. Gen. John MacArthur and Colonels Abraham Hare, Thomas Sweeney, Nelson Williams, and David Stuart. In addition, one brigade commander, Col. Madison Miller, was captured. Buell's army lost one brigade commander wounded, Col. Edward Kirk. Maj. Gen. U.S. Grant himself had come close to being killed twice, once when a nearby aide was decapitated by a cannon ball, and a second time when his scabbard was broken just below the hilt by a bullet.

Shiloh was by far the bloodiest battle of the war up to that time, and continued to rank as one of the war's costliest battles.

The battlefield during and after the conflict offered enough strange and gory sights to sicken even the strongest men. In several places, including the camp of the *14th Michigan*, fires had started that consumed the wounded and partially or totally burned their bodies. In one ravine, a dead Union bugler was found leaning against a tree. Someone had stolen his bugle; in his hand he held a letter from his wife that he must have been reading when he died.

Brig. Gen. James A. Garfield of Buell's army, who would later become a martyred president, wrote after the battle, "The horrible sights that I witnessed on this field I can never describe." Even Grant was overwhelmed by the intensity of the fighting: "Shiloh was the severest battle fought in the West during the war, and but few in the East equalled it for hard, determined fighting. I saw an open field, in our possession on the second day, over which the Confederates had made repeated charges the day before, so covered with dead that it would have been possible to walk across the clearing, in any direction, stepping on dead bodies, without a foot touching the ground."

The sight of all these dead and wounded particularly shocked the green troops, many of whom would become accustomed to similar sights before the war's end. One soldier in the *6th Ohio* later gave his impression of one section of the field, "A considerable number of wounded had crawled or been carried to one of the ravines, out of range of the fire which swept the slopes above. Many had died there, and others were in the last agonies as we passed. Their groans and cries were heart rending. One poor fellow begged most piteously to be put out of his misery and another kept repeating, 'O God, have mercy! O God, O God!' until we passed out of hearing. The gory corpses lying all about us, in every imaginable attitude, and slain by an inconceivable variety of wounds, were shocking to behold."

Culmination of the Campaign

After burying the dead, Grant's and Buell's battered armies licked their wounds for several days as they awaited the arrival of Halleck. When Halleck reached Shiloh on 11 April, he took command of all the forces there and made Grant his second-in-

Major General Henry W. Halleck took command of Grant's, Buell's and Pope's combined armies after Shiloh and led a labored but successful advance against Corinth, Mississippi, which fell on 30 May 1862.

command. This situation in no way pleased Grant, for he now had no troops to command. In a short while he was so upset about having nothing to do and not being told what was going on, that he was ready to resign. He would have done so if his friend Sherman had not talked him out of it.

Altogether Halleck spent some three weeks preparing his army for the final drive on Corinth, Mississippi. During this period he was joined by Pope's *Army of the Mississippi*, plus several newly raised units. These reinforcements raised his total strength to over 100,000 men and 200 cannon. Halleck organized his army into four wings. The right wing, commanded by Maj. Gen. George H. Thomas, consisted of four of Grant's former divisions (Sherman's, Hurlbut's, W.H.L. Wallace's, and Prentiss') plus Thomas' from Buell's army. The bulk of Buell's army, still under Buell, formed Halleck's center division. Pope's army comprised the left wing. A small reserve, consisting of McClernand's and Lew Wallace's division of Grant's old army, was commanded by McClernand. Neither Sherman nor Grant was given any special responsibility because of the cloud surround-

When Halleck finally began his long delayed advance against the Confederate forces at Corinth, his men were slowed by heavy rain and deep mud.

ing them over their responsibility for being surprised on the first day of Shiloh.

Beauregard was also being reinforced at this same time. Van Dorn's veteran army of 17,000 finally arrived from Arkansas, and new troops were called in from assorted garrisons and recruiting depots. Nevertheless, Beauregard still had only about half the strength available to Halleck. His base at Corinth was a strong one, but it was only twenty miles from Halleck's army at Shiloh. The best that Beauregard could hope for was to capitalize on some major mistake by Halleck or his subordinates.

Halleck was by nature too cautious to make any such mistakes. He finally began moving at the end of April. He kept the wings of his army close together, and dug entrenchments every night in order to avoid a surprise attack. The lessons taught by Shiloh had been well learned. By such cautious advances, it took him almost a month to reach Corinth.

Beauregard was prepared for the inevitable. When Halleck's troops began moving into a position to attack his Corinth defenses on 27 May, he drew up orders for an evacuation. For three days the Confederates frantically removed all the supplies they could. Then on 29 May Beauregard devised a clever ruse to extricate his infantry. He ordered that "whenever the railroad engine whistles during the night near the entrenchments, the troops in the vicinity will cheer repeatedly, as though reinforcements had been received." Pope fell for it.

When he heard the cheers, he deduced that Corinth was being reinforced. In reality, Beauregard was using these very same trains to remove his troops from Corinth. At dawn on 30 May, Pope sent skirmishers to test the enemy's strength. They were surprised to find the Confederate works unoccupied. A series of explosions at 0600 revealed that the Confederates were destroying what supplies they could not take with them. Halleck immediately occupied Corinth, while Beauregard moved on to Baldwin, some fifty miles to the south.

Thus the Shiloh campaign ended with Union triumphs on every front. Halleck's campaign had secured all of Kentucky and most of Tennessee for the Union, and he had reached his primary objective at the key transportation center of Corinth, Mississippi. Nashville, Tennessee, had been captured, along with Lexington and Bowling Green, Kentucky, and other important financial and industrial towns. And there was an important bonus, for New Orleans had been so stripped of defenders to reinforce Johnston's army before Shiloh, that it was easily captured by the Union navy on 25 April. New Orleans was by far the largest and most economically important city in the Confederacy, and its loss would be felt deeply.

Halleck's penetration to Corinth cut off much of the Confederate defenses along the Mississippi River. Fort Pillow, the last obstacle north of Memphis, was evacuated on 1 June, and the Union forces occupied Memphis on 6 June. The road to Vicksburg lay open, as did the route to Chattanooga and

Atlanta. Yet, it would take the Northern armies a year to reap the advantages of the position they gained by the victory at Shiloh. In July, Halleck was called east to become the commander of all the Union armies, and his large command in Tennessee and Mississippi was broken up into two smaller armies and numerous garrisons. In Tennessee, the *Army of the Cumberland* would be ineffectively led by Maj. Gen. William S. Rosecrans for over a year. In Mississippi, Maj. Gen. U.S. Grant's *Army of the Mississippi* would after numerous attempts finally break the back of the Confederacy at Vicksburg on 4 July 1863.

Given the strategic situation Johnston faced in March of 1862, it now appears that he made the right decision in attacking Grant's army at Shiloh. His bold gamble, aided by Grant's and Sherman's errors, came within a whisker of victory. Had the battle been better managed, with more men sent to break Grant's left and less attention paid to assaulting the Hornets' Nest, Johnston might well have won the battle before Buell arrived to turn the tide. Such a victory would have forced Buell to withdraw to Nashville, so relieving the pressure on Memphis. It would also have permanently ruined the careers of both Grant and Sherman, who would have been held responsible for the success of the Confederate surprise attack on 6 April. But such was not to be. Instead, Johnston paid for his gamble with his life, and Grant and Sherman pieced together their shattered reputations to become the North's two greatest commanders at the end of the war. As one contemporary Southern writer put it, the South "was never really glad again after that awful day of Shiloh."

Sharing the Blame for Shiloh

The noted historian Otto Eisenschiml once wrote of Shiloh that it was a "Battle of Big Blunders... of the four commanding generals, one died; the other three, Grant included, should have been court-martialed either for disobedience of orders, almost criminal negligence, downright stupidity, or for all of them." Eisenschiml's accusations run true, and the cases against the principal generals at Shiloh can easily be stated.

Maj. Gen. U.S. Grant, commander of the Union *Army of the*

Tennessee, was probably the most negligent of the principal leaders at Shiloh. Grant's greatest error was permitting his army to encamp at Pittsburg Landing, a position in enemy territory with its back to the river. Grant's orders from Halleck were to await the arrival of Buell's *Army of the Ohio* before advancing against Corinth. It would have been much wiser for him to have made his base at Savannah, which was much more accessible to Buell because it was on the eastern bank of the Tennessee River. If Grant had encamped at Savannah, there is practically no way he could have suffered a surprise attack from the enemy. Instead, he accepted Sherman's recommendation to use Pittsburg Landing as a base. Pittsburg Landing did indeed offer a clear approach to Corinth, some 20 miles to the south, but it also gave the Confederates easy access to the Union camp.

Once he allowed his army to concentrate at Pittsburg Landing, Grant made no special effort to form a defensive position. Instead, he let Sherman locate the camps, which were situated more with an eye to hygiene and water supply than to defensive needs. There were two especially improvident mistakes in the posting of Grant's army at Pittsburg Landing. One was the stationing of Lew Wallace's division at Crump's Landing, some four miles from the rest of the army. Supposedly Wallace was guarding the army's right flank and keeping an eye on the Mobile and Ohio Railroad, but his exposed position posed a constant concern to Grant, who feared that Wallace might be set upon by the Confederates. The second gross error in the posting of Grant's army was the fact that his veteran divisions were posted nearest to Pittsburg Landing simply because they got there first. His two greenest divisions, Sherman's and Prentiss', were then posted farthest from the landing—and closest to the Confederates. The green troops should have been kept near the landing, and the more veteran divisions shifted to the outer campsites.

The most serious charge against Grant was the fact that he did not order his army to entrench. In his *Memoirs*, Grant took pains to explain how he had directed his engineers to prepare a line of entrenchments. However the line they recommended did not include all the camps and was too far from good water sources, so it was not constructed. In addition, Grant claimed that his men needed more practice with drill than with digging. Nevertheless, the simple truth is that Halleck had ordered Grant to entrench, and Grant did not do so. Grant recognized this error afterwards, and wrote, "The fact is, I regarded the campaign we were engaged in as an offensive one and had no idea that the enemy would leave strong entrenchments to take the initiative when he knew he would be attacked where he remained."

Grant was also guilty of not paying close enough attention to the strategic situation of his army at Pittsburg Landing. He did not spend enough time with his troops, and slept each night at Savannah, some seven miles upstream on the opposite bank of the Tennessee River. Savannah was a convenient place to meet Buell's troops as they arrived from Nashville, but it was not suitable for a command post for an army encamped at Pittsburg Landing. This was made especially clear on the morning of 6 April, when Grant did not reach the battlefield until about four hours after the fighting had started. His absence meant that the Union forces fought most of the morning with no real overall supervision. Grant himself admitted in his *Memoirs* that he should have been paying more attention to his troops, and that in the early days of April he was more concerned with Buell's pending arrival than he was with his army's condition or possible enemy movements.

Grant also failed to keep an accurate picture of the enemy's strength and intentions. It is all the more amazing that Grant allowed his army to be in an exposed position at Pittsburg Landing when he thought that Johnston's strength was 100,000 (Civil War commanders had a bad habit of seriously overestimating the size of the enemy's forces). Grant failed to send out adequate scouting parties to determine Confederate positions and movements, and relied too much on Sherman's inaccurate evaluation of conditions between Shiloh and Corinth. Grant had enough cavalry available for daily or extended patrols, but he did not order many simply because he could not imagine the Confederates making any moves against him. Only Lew Wallace, who was posted in an isolated camp at Crump's Landing, was enterprising enough to send spies to Corinth to try to find out what Johnston was doing.

The final charge against Grant was not provable at the time

and has been hotly debated ever since—the charge that he failed to give clear orders to Lew Wallace when he was at Crump's Landing, and so was responsible for Wallace's delayed arrival that prevented him from participating in the first day's battle at Shiloh. From today's vantage point, the collected evidence seems to find Grant in error in his orders to Wallace on 6 April.

One thing is clear, that Grant was not drunk at the time of the battle, as several newspapers later charged. He certainly had a reputation for drinking, dating from some unhappy days on the West Coast in 1854, when he was depressed about being absent from his family. Supposedly, charges of drunkenness were connected to his resignation from the army in 1854. Nobody had ever really seen him drunk, and we do not even know his favorite brand of whisky. Nevertheless this stigma followed him all his life.

Rumors of Grant's drinking surfaced in the winter of 1861-62 and kept plaguing him throughout the war. Early on, Col. John A. Rawlins, Grant's assistant adjutant general, took it on himself to be a watchdog over Grant's drinking habits. His letters to officials in Washington made it clear that Grant was only drinking socially or for medicinal reasons. Rawlins was certain that any rumors of the general's overindulging had been started by Grant's rivals or by rejected army contractors.

Soon after Fort Donelson fell, the drinking rumors started flying again. These and other reasons led Halleck to suspend Grant from command for two weeks in March 1862. When the rumors proved false and the crisis passed, Grant was returned to command.

When rumors began to circulate after Shiloh that Grant had been drunk there, his supporters immediately came to his defense. Capt. William Rowley of his staff wrote, "As to the story that he was intoxicated at the battle of Pittsburg, I have only to say that the man who fabricated that story is an infamous liar." Col. J.E. Smith of the *45th Illinois* agreed, "I see also that Grant is severely censured by the public for drunkenness, got up no doubt by those who are jealous of him. There is not foundation for his report." This opinion was also supported by Col. Jacob Ammen, a brigade commander in Buell's army, I am satisfied Grant was not under the influence of liquor, either of the times I saw him."

Grant's most important supporter was Illinois Representative Elihu B. Washburne. Soon after the battle of Shiloh, Washburne praised Grant's achievements in an address to the Congress. Washburne did not hesitate to address the drunkenness issue head on: "There is no more temperate man in the army than General Grant. He never indulges in the use of intoxicating liquors at all. He is an example of courage, honor, fortitude, activity, temperance and modesty, for he is as modest as he is brave and incorruptible."

Washburne's words helped Grant weather this storm, but drinking rumors continued to follow the general. The most notable case occurred in early June of 1863 during the Vicksburg campaign. a reporter named Sylvanus Cadwallader claimed that Grant had gone on a 48-hour drunken spree, but no other direct evidence can be found to substantiate the charge. (See a modern debate on the issue in the August 1956 *American Heritage*.) Rawlins at the time expressed concern that Grant was drinking too much wine, but no one actually saw him drunk. Grant's habits improved when Vicksburg fell. Apparently he liked an occasional slug when times were tough; it is certainly clear that he drank no more than other generals of those hard-drinking days.

The accumulated charges against Grant—particularly his failure to entrench—were enough to put him under a cloud of suspicion after the battle, even though the battle was victorious. Halleck effectively shelved him in late April by making him his second-in-command, so giving Grant little authority and no troops to command. If Grant had not done so well at Forts Henry and Donelson, he no doubt would have been replaced permanently after Shiloh. And he surely would have been court-martialed if he had lost at Shiloh.

The charges against Maj. Gen. W.T. Sherman for incompetence at Shiloh are much more succinct. Sherman, as Grant's alter ego, was the actual Union camp commander at Pittsburg Landing. It was Sherman who laid out the camps as they were, and Sherman who set up the pickets and cavalry patrols; Grant simply approved Sherman's arrangements. It seems today almost unbelievable that Sherman misread or ignored so many evidences of the pending Confederate attack. He was clearly led to a false sense of security by the constant Confederate probings of his position, and he had no patience for the skittishness of his volunteer army brigade and regiment commanders. At one point he even told one regimental commander to take his "damn regiment back to Ohio;" several of his subordinates were so gun shy of him that they did not dare to go near him with any news of enemy activity. Sherman's failure to scout the enemy positions adequately and his inattention to what was actually going on in his front show that he was clearly guilty of negligence. He should indeed have been court-martialed, and certainly would have been if the North had lost the battle. That he was not court-martialed was due to three reasons—the skill he showed while under fire in the battle, his close friendship with Grant, and the fact that the North won the battle.

As it was, Sherman had to write a raft of letters to show that he was not as guilty of negligence as he was charged. He was especially angered at Whitelaw Reid's account of the battle. For a time the whole affair threatened to get out of control. Sherman had no liking for reporters because he had a "fatal flaw" that played right into their hands. In late 1861 he had buckled in to the pressures of command in Kentucky. He had felt he was assigned an impossible position against superior enemy forces. He claimed that every time he tried to move, the newspapers informed the enemy. When he began denouncing reporters right and left, a correspondent sent him a story that Sherman had the manners of a Pawnee. After Sherman objected to the comparison, the reporter apologized in print to the Indians. Affairs came to a head when Sherman had the equivalent of a nervous breakdown and was temporarily relieved of command. On 11 December 1861, the *Cincinnati Daily Commercial* ran the headline, "General Sherman Insane!" Sherman then threatened to shoot one of Horace Greeley's reporters, but calmer heads eventually prevailed. Sherman's brother John, a member of Congress, and his powerful relatives, the Ewing family, used their influence to defuse the situation, and Sherman was reassigned to Illinois.

When Sherman's old quarrel with the newspapers erupted again after Shiloh, his family and friends again came to his support. Finally his brother John urged him to calm down, "I see newsmen are fighting with you again. Why can't you keep on good terms with them? They are very useful if you allow them to be, but if not they have a power for evil that no one can stand against. I see no reason for you to quarrel."

The charges of incompetency raised against Gen. P.G.T. Beauregard, Johnston's second-in-command, concern the way Beauregard organized and directed the battle.

The awkward way that Beauregard arranged the Confederate attack did not materially aid the Southern forces in the battle. Instead of assigning each Confederate corps a sector of the line, Beauregard, as Johnston's chief of staff, arrayed the army in three long lines, each a mile in length. The first line comprised Hardee's corps, the second Bragg's, and the third Polk's, with Breckinridge's in reserve. This whole arrangement was inspired by Napoleonic tactics and looked very good on paper. However, it did not take into account the roughness of the terrain or the difficulty each corps commander would have trying to control so broad a front. As brigades became engaged, some lost their direction in the woods or even lost contact with their division and corps commanders, especially on the flanks. In other areas, units from the second and third lines that advanced along roads reached the front much more quickly than the other units of their lines. As a result of the intermingling of commands and attack waves, by afternoon of the first day the Confederate leaders agreed on an *ad hoc* command structure—Hardee and Polk took charge of the army's left, and Bragg and Breckinridge directed the right. This restructuring led to confusion when some brigade leaders did not know what superior to report to. The restructuring also caused confusion on the night of 6 April, when nobody notified Pond to withdraw his brigade from its advanced position on the army's far left flank, and Cheatham withdrew his division several miles without anyone in the army's high command knowing it.

The second charge against Beauregard is much more serious. By his early morning statements, Johnston made it known to his subordinates that his battle plan was to lead with his right and drive Grant's army into Owl Creek, away from its base at Pittsburg Landing. Throughout the morning and early afternoon Johnston directed reinforcements to his right, and it was on this front that he received his mortal wound. Beauregard, however, was working at cross purposes to his commander all day. Beauregard's initial plan appears to have been to push with equal weight all along the line and simply overwhelm Grant's army. When this failed to happen, partly because of the depth of the Union position and partly because of the obstinacy of Prentiss' line, Beauregard began shifting units to the west in an effort to push Grant's line into the Tennessee River. This was contrary to what Johnston wanted, and served only to help Grant's situation. As Grant's army withdrew, its line became shorter and stronger as it formed nearer to Pittsburg Landing. This position was also the most convenient spot to meet Buell's reinforcing army.

Beauregard was not later specifically censured for these shortcomings at Shiloh. He was, however, removed from command of the Army of the Mississippi later that summer because of the loss at Shiloh and his subsequent loss of Corinth.

Confederate commander Gen. A.S. Johnston himself made several tactical errors in running the battle. The most significant of these were two. The first was approving Beauregard's grandiose Napoleonic order of battle, already discussed. The second was insisting on driving Grant's army away from the Tennessee River and into Owl Creek. About 1415 on 6 April Johnson lost the Confederates what was perhaps their best chance to win the battle. Jackson's and Chalmers' brigades had defeated Stuart's brigade, which had been tenuously holding the Union far left all day. As Stuart retreated, the road lay open for Jackson and Chalmers to grab Grant's supply and transportation base at Pittsburg Landing, about two and one-half miles to the north of their position. Johnston, however, chose not to send Jackson and Chalmers north. Instead, he ordered them to wheel and attack the flank of the Hornets' Nest position. This movement followed his plan to drive the Yankees into Owl Creek, but did not take advantage of the momentary golden opportunity that had been offered. Johnston apparently never realized the chance he missed; in about an hour he lay dead. His death and the stubborn resistance of the Hornets' Nest line gave Grant a chance to form and protect Pittsburg Landing, so snatching victory from the jaws of defeat.

The Battle Sites Today

Shiloh National Military Park, which now contains 3,908 acres, was established in 1894. It was the second western battlefield park created (the first was Chickamauga-Chattanooga). The park museum and library are located near Pittsburg Landing. Shiloh is one of the most pristine Civil War battlefield parks, with much of the battlefield preserved in natural wartime condition. It has few modern intrusions like Gettysburg, and no major highways bisecting it, like Bull Run and Chickamauga. Numerous tablets and markers erected by the states and the U.S. government tell the history of the battle.

After the battle of Shiloh, the Union and Confederate dead were interred in mass burials in separate trenches. Four years later the Union dead were transferred to the newly created Shiloh National Cemetery, which embraces ten acres on a bluff overlooking the Tennessee River. The cemetery now contains some 3,856 bodies, two-thirds of which are unidentified. (This number also includes Union casualties from other nearby battles and hospitals, as well as soldiers from the Spanish-American War and later.) Curiously, the cemetery contains only two Confederate burials. Most of the Confederate battle casualties at Shiloh still lie in the five large burial trenches where they were buried by Union troops right after the battle. The largest, located about a mile west of the Hornets' Nest, contains 721 bodies stacked seven deep.

Cherry Mansion, Grant's headquarters in Savannah before the battle, still stands intact. Two Union generals, C.F. Smith and W.H.L. Wallace, died here while the mansion was being used as a hospital after the battle.

Fort Donelson National Military Park, which was established in 1928, contains about 550 acres, which constitute about one-third of the battle area. Several impressive sections of the fort's ramparts still remain, and several batteries have been reconstructed, as has the historic Dover Hotel. Little remains of nearby Fort Henry, most of which was inundated fifty some years ago by the waters of Kentucky Lake, which was created by a Tennessee Valley Authority dam on the Tennessee River downstream from the fort. Some 655 Union soldiers (504 unknown) are interred in the Fort Donelson National Cemetery, which dates to 1867; total burials there now number 1761.

The site of the Confederate fortress at Columbus, Kentucky, is now nicely preserved as a state park. Its high bluffs offer a panoramic view of the Mississippi. The park contains trenches, samples of early artillery pieces, and a huge six-ton anchor that was used to secure an iron chain that was stretched across the river to stop Union shipping.

Belmont battle field is almost as poorly preserved as Fort Henry. Part of it lies under water because the Mississippi River has changed its course somewhat. Most of the rest of the battlefield is covered by swamps and fields that are highly unlike the heavily wooded terrain Grant fought on in 1861.

The final major site associated with the Shiloh Campaign, Corinth, Mississippi, preserves several houses that were used as headquarters and hospitals in 1862. Among these is Rose Cottage, the house to which A.S. Johnston's body was brought after he was killed at Shiloh on 6 April. Many of the fortifications built here by the Confederates in early 1862 are also preserved; they ironically were defended by Union troops when the Confederates attacked Corinth on 3-4 October 1862.

The Shiloh Cyclorama

In the late 1800s, huge circular paintings called "cycloramas" were popular, especially when they contained Civil War subjects. These large paintings were usually 50 feet high and 400 feet in circumference, and offered a 360 degree view of their subjects when viewed from the inside. Of the several cycloramas created after the war, two still survive in excellent form and popularity; one is at Gettysburg and the other at Atlanta. All the rest have been lost, though photographs still survive of some of their scenes. Among the lost cycloramas was one on the battle of Shiloh. It did not depict the entire battle, but focused on the combat at the "Hornets' Nest." This cyclorama was painted by a Parisian artist named Theophile Poilpot, who was aided by a crew of twelve assistants. It was first displayed in Chicago on 3 July 1885, and remained there for two years. At one time Maj. Gen. Benjamin Prentiss, who had commanded a division at the Hornets' Nest and was captured there, was on hand to give lectures on the painting. The whole work later disappeared and its exact fate is unknown. There is a partial reconstruction of the cyclorama in *Military Images*, Vol. 4, No. 4, pages 112-19. In addition, some scenes are shown in *Battles and Leaders of the Civil War*, Vol. I, pages 504-505 and 510-511.

Johnny Shiloh

One of the youngest soldiers on the battlefield was little John Lincoln Clem (1851-1937), an eleven-year-old dummer boy serving with the *24th Ohio Infantry* of Ammen's Brigade in Buell's *4th Division*. During the battle, his drum was smashed by an artillery shell, and he gained fame in the newspapers as "Johnny Shiloh." Later he served as a drummer boy for the *22nd Michigan* in several battles, including

Chickamauga and Chattanooga. At Chickamauga he is reported to have picked up a musket and served with the infantry. At one point he was isolated and approached by a mounted Confederate colonel, who shouted, "Surrender, you damned little Yankee!" Clem responded by shooting the colonel dead. Later in the battle he was captured, but escaped by falling down and pretending to be wounded. This bravery earned him the nickname "Drummer Boy of Chickamauga."

After the war, Clem tried to enter West Point but could not win an appointment because of his lack of formal education. Support from George ("Rock of Chickamauga") Thomas and President Grant then won him an appointment as a lieutenant in the Regular Army in 1871. He rose to the rank of colonel, and was retired in 1916 as major general, the last man on active duty to wear the blue and gray Civil War campaign ribbon. He died in 1937 and was buried in Arlington Cemetery.

The Drummer Boy of Shiloh

"Look down upon the battlefield,
O Thou, Our Heavenly Friend,
Have mercy on our sinful souls."
The soldiers cried, "Amen."
There gathered 'round a little group,
Each brave man knelt and cried.
They listened to the drummer boy,
Who prayed before he died.

"Oh, Mother," said the dying boy,
"Look down from heaven on me.
Receive me to thy fond embrace,
Oh, take me home to thee.
I've loved my country as my God.
To serve them both I've tried!"
He smiled, shook hands—
  death seized the boy,
Who prayed before he died.

Each soldier wept then like a child.
Stout hearts were they and brave.
They wrapped him in his country's flag
And laid him in the grave.
They placed by him the Bible,
A rededicated guide
To those that mourn the drummer boy
Who prayed before he died.

Ye angels 'round the throne of grace,
Look down upon the braves,
Who fought and died on Shiloh's plain,
Now slumbering in their graves.
How many homes made desolate,
How many hearts have sighed.
How many like that dummer boy,
Who prayed before he died.
  —Will S. Hays

Guide for the Interested Reader

The battle of Shiloh has been written about extensively, but not nearly as much as Gettysburg. By far the most detailed recent study of the battle is Wiley Sword's *Shiloh: Bloody April* (New York: 1974). This account presents the battle blow by blow at regimental level, but is at times confusing because of its mass of detail. A more focused and readable, but less detailed, history can be found in *Shiloh: In Hell before Night* by James Lee McDonough (Knoxville: 1977). The best of the older histories of the battle is M.F. Force's *From Fort Henry to Corinth*, which is Volume II of Scribner's *Campaigns of the Civil War Series*, first published in the 1880s, with several recent reprints. David W. Reed's *The Battle of Shiloh and the Oganizations Engaged* (Washington: 1903) gives a dry but accurate account of the battle. A most interesting approach to the study of the battle is provided by *"Seeing the Elelphant": Raw Recruits at the Battle of Shiloh* by Joseph A. Frank and George A. Reaves (New York: 1989).

Those who wish to find out how the generals involved fought the battle (or claimed to have fought the battle) are encouraged to read the official battle reports of both sides published in Series I, Volume 10 of *War of the Rebellion: A Compilation of the Official Records of the Union and Confederate Armies* (129 volumes, Washington: 1880-1901). Other valuable accounts were written later by key participants for the *Century Magazine* and were republished in *Battles and Leaders of the Civil War* (New York: 1887-1888, with several more recent reprints). Volume I deals with the Shiloh campaign. Additional contemporary accounts can be found in Volume IV of Frank Moore's *Rebellion Record* (New York: 1862, reprinted 1977).

It is interesting to note how the interpretations of the battle have changed through the years. The nation's first view of the battle was colored largely by reporter Whitelaw Reid of the *Cincinnati Gazette*, who emphasized the losses suffered by Grant's army from the initial Confederate surprise attack. Grant's alleged incompetence was emphasized by his rival Don Carlos Buell, who exaggerated the role of his own *Army of the Ohio* in saving Grant's men on the evening of the first day. Grant responded in his *Personal Memoirs of U.S. Grant* (New York: 1885) that "The presence of two or three regiments of Buell's army on the west bank before firing ceased had not the slightest effect in preventing the capture of Pittsburg Landing." Grant also tried to blame the loss of the first day's battle on Lew Wallace's tardy arrival on the evening of 6 April. Lew Wallace defended his actions in *An Autobiography* (New York: 1906). Another important Union autobiography is Sherman's *Memoirs of General W.T. Sherman* (New York: 1875).

On the Confederate side, after the war Bragg blamed Beauregard for calling off the last Confederate attack that might have won the battle at dusk of the first day. Bragg's claim, however, seems to have originated in a long standing feud between him and Beauregard. At the time of the battle, Bragg complained only of the exhausted condition of his troops, and he did not really begin to complain about Beauregard's withdrawal order until ten years after the war. Beauregard himself claimed for some time after the battle that, despite his retreat on the second day, the battle had actually been a victory because he smashed up Grant's army and disrupted Halleck's plans. This illogical position caused Beauregard's star to fade even more in Southern eyes. A.S. Johnston's view of the battle, of course, was lost when he was killed on the first day.

More recently, the battle has been studied in much greater detail from the Southern viewpoint than the Northern. An overview of the battle's relationship to the progress of the war in the western theater can be read in Thomas L. Connelly's *Army of the Heartland* (Baton Rouge: 1967) and Stanley Horn's *The Army of Tennessee* (New York: 1941). The role of the artillery in the battle can be studied in George F. Witham's *Shiloh, Shells and Artillery Units* (Memphis: 1980), and Larry J. Daniel's *Cannoneers in Gray: The Field Artillery of the Army of Tennessee, 1861-1865* (University of Alabama: 1984). The only similar surveys of Union troops at the battle are the study of the Federal artillery in George Witham's book cited above and a brief discussion of the Federal cavalry in Volume III of *The Union Cavalry in the Civil War* by Stephen Z. Starr (Baton Rouge: 1985). The best survey of the campaign from the Union viewpoint is still probably Bruce Catton's *Grant Moves South* (Boston: 1960). By far the most thorough study of the early stages of the Shiloh campaign is *Forts Henry and Donelson: The Key to the Confederate Heartland*, by Benjamin F. Cooling (Knoxville: 1987). Also recommended is *The Battle of Fort Donelson* by James Hamilton (New York: 1968).

Additional information on Shiloh can be found in biographies of various individuals who fought at the battle, notably:

Grant: A Biography by William S. McFeely (New York: 1981).

William Tecumseh Sherman by James M. Merrill (New York, 1971).

Sherman: A Soldier's Passion for Order by John Marszalek (New York: 1993).

Beauregard: Napoleon in Gray by T. Harry Williams (Baton Rouge: 1955).

Breckinridge: Statesman, Soldier, Symbol by William C. Davis (Baton Rouge: 1974).

Braxton Bragg and Confederate Defeat by Grady McWhiney (New York: 1969)

Braxton Bragg: General of the Confederacy, by Don C. Seitz (Columbia, SC: 1924).

A Battle from the Start: The Life of Nathan Bedford Forrest, by Brian Wills (New York: 1992).

Morgan and His Raids, by Cecil F. Holland (New York: 1942).

The Man who Presumed: A Biography of Henry M. Stanley, by Byron Farwell (New York: 1957).

The Autobiography of Sir Henry Morton Stanley (New York: 1909).

From the viewpoint of the fighting man, the best battle

accounts can be found in the numerous regimental histories published after the war. Representative of these are:

The Story of the 55th Regiment Illinois Volunteer Infantry in the Civil War, by Lucien B. Crooker (Clinton, MA: 1887).
Morgan's Cavalry, by Basil W. Duke (New York: 1906).
The Orphan Brigade: The Kentucky Confederates Who Couldn't Go Home, by William C. Davis (New York: 1980).
One Year's Soldiering of the 14th Iowa Infantry, by W.W. Kiner (Lancaster: 1863).
"Co. Aytch," Maury Grays, 1st Tennessee Regiment, by Samuel R. Watkins, (Jackson, TN: 1952).
History of the Sixth Iowa Infantry, by Henry H. Wright (Iowa City, 1923).

Collections of eyewitness accounts of Shiloh and other Civil War battles can be found in the following anthologies:

The Blue and the Gray, edited by Henry Steele Commager (New York: 1950).
The American Iliad: The Epic Story of the Civil War as Narrated by Eyewitnesses and Contemporaries, edited by Otto Eisenchiml and Ralph Newman (New York: 1947).
Voices of the Civil War, edited by Richard Wheeler (New York: 1976).
Confederate Veteran Magazine, 40 volumes (Nashville: 1893-1932).

An excellent general summary of the arms and equipment carried by the soldiers in the Civil War is given in Jack Coggins' illustrated *Arms and Equipment of the Civil War* (Garden City, NY: 1962). More detailed information on the artillery can be found in *Artillery and Ammunition of the Civil War* by Warren Ripley (New York: 1970), and *Field Artillery Weapons of the Civil War* by James C. Hazlett, et al. (Newark, DE: 1983). Civil War tactics in general are discussed in *Attack and Die* by Grady McWhiney and Perry Jamieson (Alabama: 1982).

The life of the average soldier is perhaps best described in *Hardtack and Coffee* by John Billings (Boston, 1887). Also informative on this subject are two volumes by Bell I. Wiley, *The Life of Johnny Reb* (Indianapolis, 1943), and *The Life of Billy Yank* (Indianapolis, 1952).

The practice of medicine during the Civil War is discussed in Stewart Brook's *Civil War Medicine* (Springfield, IL: 1966), George W. Adams' *Doctors in Blue* (New York: 1962), and H.H. Cunningham's *Doctors in Gray* (Baton Rouge: 1958).

For brief biographies of all the generals in the war, see Ezra J. Warner's two volumes, *Generals in Blue* (Baton Rouge: 1984) and *Generals in Gray* (Baton Rouge: 1983). Other details about the Shiloh campaign and the Civil War in general are best gleaned from *The Civil War Dictionary* by Mark M. Boatner III (2nd edition, New York: 1979) or *Historical Times Illustrated Encyclopedia of the Civil War*, edited by Patricia Faust (New York: 1986).

One of the best Civil War novels on any battle is Shelby Foote's *Shiloh* (New York: 1952). This exciting work weaves together the experiences of seven fictional soldiers to create an excellent novel that is historically very accurate. The only other novel written specifically about the battle is by Joseph Altsheler.

Poetry and Drama

Johnny Clem and his fellow drummer boys were the inspiration for a popular play written in 1870 by Samuel J. Muscroft. The play "The Drummer Boy of Shiloh" remained popular until after the turn of the century. Novelist Herman Melville, author of Moby Dick, also wrote a famous poem about the battle. More recently, Dr. Maurice F. McCarthy has written a brief historical account of the battle in poetic form. The most popular Shiloh poem was Will S. Hay's song "The Drummer Boy of Shiloh."

The leading Civil War journals are *Civil War Times Illustrated*, *CWTI* (published ten times a year) and *Blue & Gray Magazine*, (published bimonthly). Both cover a wide variety of topics; *CWTI* occasionally has special issues devoted to one topic, while *B&G* regularly focuses each issue on one battle or campaign. Other more specialized Civil War era journals are *Military Images*, which covers photography and uniforms of the period; *Civil War History*, which places the war in its nineteenth century social and political context; *Civil War News*, which gives numerous book reviews and news of current releases; and *Strategy & Tactics*, which periodically includes major articles on the Civil

War and regularly carries news and reviews of Civil War simulation games.

Interest Groups

The most active Civil War study groups are the Civil War Round Tables, many of which were founded in the days of the Civil War centennial and are still going strong. Most feature excellent programs and discussions. For information on a Round Table in your area, contact Civil War Round Table Associates, PO Box 7388, Little Rock, AK 72217. For descendants of Civil War veterans, two groups, United Confederate Veterans and Sons of Union Veterans of the Civil War, are still active. Many descendents of veterans are not aware that detailed records of their ancestors' service are available at their state capitals or the National Archives in Washington. There are also a number of reenactment groups who dress in Civil War period uniforms to recreate battles and camp life. Many of these groups run ads in *Civil War Times Illustrated* or the *Civil War News*. For bibliophiles, the most complete regular catalogs of Civil War books in print are published by Morningside Bookshop, 260 Oak Street, Dayton, OH 45410.

Simulation Games and Videos

By far the most comprehensive war-game on the battle of Shiloh is *Bloody April*, published by Simulations Publications in 1980. It treats the entire battle at regimental level on two table-sized maps. The following games on the battle deal with it at brigade level on one map: *Shiloh* (with *Blue & Gray Quad Game*) by TSR Hobbies, 1984; *Fury in the West*, by Avalon Hill Game Company, 1983; and *The Battle of Shiloh*, by West End Games, 1984. One of the better videos on the campaign is *Shiloh: Surprise and Slaughter in Tennessee* by Classic Images (Columbia, Md: 1988).

Order of Battle

Union

Unit	Strength	Losses	(Killed/Wounded/Missing)
Army of the Tennessee Maj. Gen. U.S. Grant	47,721	10,944	(1513/6601/2830)
1st Division Maj. Gen. John A. McClernand	7028	1742	(285/1372/85)
1st Brigade Col. Abraham M. Hare (w)	2447	580	(104/467/9)
8 Ill	476	124	
18 Ill	400	87	
11 Iowa	750	194	
13 Iowa	717	162	
2nd Brigade Col. C. Carroll Marsh	1740	585	(80/475/30)
11 Ill	225	103	
20 Ill	526	136	
45 Ill	562	213	
48 Ill	427	133	
3rd Brigade Col. Julius Raith (k)	1902	535	(96/393/46)
17 Ill	400	138	
29 Ill	387	89	
43 Ill	500	197	
49 Ill		110	
Carmichael's Co. Ill Co. Cav.		1	
Attached	660		
1 Batn Ill Cav	247		
Stewart's Ill Cav	57	2	
Bat D, 1 Ill Art (McAllister)	62	3	
Bat E, 2 Ill Art (Nispel)	78	5	
14 Ohio Bat (Burrows)	108	30	
Bat D, 2 Ill Art (Timony)	108	13	
2nd Division Maj. Gen. W.H.L. Wallace (k)	8217	2749	(270/1173/1306)
1st Brigade Col. James M. Tuttle	1804	858	(39/143/676)
2 Iowa	490	72	
7 Iowa	383	34	
12 Iowa	489	479	
14 Iowa	442	273	

2nd Brigade	2296	580	(99/470/11)
Brig. Gen. John McArthur (w)			
9 Ill	600	366	
12 Ill	320	101	
81 Ohio	468	23	
13 Mo	450	81	
14 Mo	458	8	
3rd Brigade	3632	1247	(127/501/619)
Col. Thomas W. Sweeny (w)			
8 Iowa	689	481	
7 Ill	436	99	
50 Ill	530	84	
52 Ill	641	155	
57 Ill	613	138	
58 Ill	613	290	
Attached	485		
Bat A, 1 Ill Art (Wood)	110	30	
Bat D, 1 Mo Art (Richardson)		6	
Bat H, 1 Mo Art (Welker)		17	
Bat K, 1 Mo Art (Stone)		4	
2 Cos, *US Cav*		6	
2 Cox, *2 Ill Cav*	126		
3rd Division	7564	296	(41/251/4)
Maj. Gen. Lew Wallace			
1st Brigade	1998	132	(18/114/0)
Col. Morgan L. Smith			
11 Ind	631	62	
24 Ind	694	45	
8 Mo	673	19	
2nd Brigade	2236	122	(20/99/3)
Col. John M. Thayer			
23 Ind	633	43	
1 Neb	549	28	
58 Ohio	630	51	
68 Ohio	424	0	
3rd Brigade	2451	35	
Col. Charles Whittlesey			
20 Ohio	491	20	
56 Ohio	701	0	
76 Ohio	714	5	
78 Ohio	635	10	

Unit	Strength	Losses (Killed/Wounded/Missing)	
Attached	789		
Bat I, 1 Mo (Thurber)	118	1	
9 Ind Bat (Brown)	112	6	
5 Ohio Cav	283		
11 Ill Cav	267		
4th Division	7825	1869	(317/1441/111)
Maj. Gen. Stephen A. Hurlbut			
1st Brigade	2323	687	(112/532/43)
Col. Nelson G. Williams (w)			
28 Ill	558	245	
32 Ill	652	158	
41 Ill	553	97	
3 Iowa	560	187	
2nd Brigade	2583	630	(130/492/8)
Col. James C. Veatch			
14 Ill	722	165	
15 Ill	500	166	
46 Ill	710	160	
25 Ind	651	139	
3rd Brigade	1522	458	(70/384/4)
Brig. Gen. Jacob G. Lauman			
31 Ind	594	138	
44 Ind	478	198	
17 Ky	250	88	
25 Ky	200	34	
Attached	257	94	
2 Mich Bat (Ross)	84	61	
Bat C, 1 Mo Art (Brotzmann)		17	
13 Ohio Bat (Myers)	89	9	
5 Ohio Cav	84	7	
5th Division	7904	1901	(325/1277/299)
Brig. Gen. William T. Sherman (w)			
1st Brigade	1930	651	(137/444/70)
Col. John A. McDowell			
40 Ill	597	216	
6 Iowa	632	183	
46 Ohio	701	246	

2nd Brigade	1310	550	(80/380/90)
Col. David Stuart (w)			
55 Ill	400	275	
54 Ohio	400	166	
71 Ohio	510	109	
3rd Brigade	1833	356	(70/221/65)
Col. Jesse Hildebrand			
53 Ohio	646	44	
57 Ohio	542	94	
77 Ohio	645	218	
4th Brigade	2107	313	(36/203/74)
Col. Ralph P. Buckland			
48 Ohio	606	103	
70 Ohio	854	77	
72 Ohio	647	133	
Attached	609		
Bat B, 1 Ill Art (Barrett)	112	6	
Bat E, 1 Ill Art (Waterhouse)	103	18	
6 Ind Bat (Behr)	115	6	
4 Ill Cav	291	6	
Thielemann's Ill Cav	103		
6th Division	7460	2172	(236/928/1008)
Brig. Gen. Benjamin M. Prentiss (c)			
1st Brigade	2790	721	(113/372/236)
Col. Everett Peabody (k)			
12 Mich	832	190	
21 Mo	617	128	
25 Mo	514	149	
16 Wis	827	254	
2nd Brigade	2509	450	(44/228/178)
Col. Madison Miller			
61 Ill	437	75	
18 Mo	552	244	
18 Wis	735	280	
16 Iowa	785	131	
Attached	2161	1892	
11 Ill Cav	626	6	
5 Ohio Bat (Hickenlooper)	137	20	
23 Mo	490	496	
15 Iowa	782	185	
1 Minn Bat (Munch)	126	11	

Unit	Strength	Losses (Killed/Wounded/Missing)	
Unassigned Troops	2002	215	(39/159/17)
15 Mich	750	102	
14 Wis	750	93	
8 Ohio Bat (Markgraf)	112	3	
Bat H, 1 Ill Art (Silfversparre)	83	6	
Bat I, 1 Ill Art (Bouton)	83	2	
Bat B, 2 Ill Art (Madison)	112	0	
Bat F, 2 Ill Art (Powell)	112	9	
Army of the Ohio	17,918	2103	(241/1807/55)
Maj. Gen. Don Carlos Buell			
2nd Division	7552	918	(88/823/7)
Brig. Gen. Alexander McCook			
4th Brigade	2221	311	(28/280/3)
Brig. Gen. Lovell Rousseau			
6 Ind	660	42	
5 Ky	725	63	
15 US	331	63	
16 US	294	56	
19 US	206	37	
1 Ohio		50	
5th Brigade	2721	346	(34/310/2)
Col. Edward N. Kirk (w)			
34 Ill	726	127	
29 Ind	724	80	
30 Ind	767	129	
77 Pa	504	10	
6th Brigade	3074	247	(25/220/2)
Col. William Gibson			
32 Ind	812	96	
39 Ind	776	36	
15 Ohio	749	75	
49 Ohio	737	40	
Artillery			
Bat H, 5 US Art (Terrill)	116	14	

4th Division	4541	716	(93/603/20)
Brig. Gen. William Nelson			
10th Brigade	1528	130	(16/106/8)
Col. Jacob Ammen			
36 Ind	380	45	
6 Ohio	598	76	
24 Ohio	550	9	
19th Brigade	1424	406	(48/357/1)
Col. William B. Hazen			
9 Ind	569	170	
6 Ky	484	103	
41 Ohio	371	133	
22nd Brigade	1589	178	(29/603/11)
Col. Sanders D. Bruce			
1 Ky	522	71	
2 Ky	663	75	
20 Ky	404	32	
Attached			
2 Ind Cav		2	
5th Division	3825	465	(60/377/28)
Brig. Gen. Thomas L. Crittenden			
11th Brigade	2179	263	(33/212/18)
Brig. Gen. Jeremiah T. Boyle			
9 Ky	495	92	
13 Ky	529	59	
19 Ohio	695	55	
59 Ohio	460	57	
14th Brigade	1646	192	(25/157/10)
Col. William S. Smith			
11 Ky		55	
26 Ky		71	
13 Ohio		66	
Artillery			
Bat G, 1 Ohio Art (Bartlett)	118	2	
Bat HM, 4 US Art			
(Mendenhall)	66	8	

Unit	Strength	Losses (Killed/Wounded/Missing)	
6th Division Brig. Gen. Thomas Wood	2000	4	(0/4/0)
20th Brigade Brig. Gen. James Garfield *13 Mich* *64 Ohio* *65 Ohio*	not engaged		
21st Brigade Col. George Wagner *15 Ind* *50 Ind*	2000	4	(0/4/0)
57 Ind *24 Ky*		4	(0/4/0)
US Totals	65,639	13,047	(1754/8408/2885)

.

.

Confederate

Unit	Strength	Losses (Killed/Wounded/Missing)	
Army of the Mississippi	44,699	10,699	(1728/8012/959)
Gen A.S. Johnston (k)			
I Corps	9695	2357	(385/1953/19)
Maj. Gen. Leonidas Polk			
1st Division	4356		
Brig. Gen. Charles Clark (w)			
1st Brigade			
Col. R.M. Russell			
12 Tenn			
13 Tenn			
22 Tenn			
Bankhead's Tenn Bat	93	20	
11 La	550		
2nd Brigade			
Brig. Gen. Alexander P. Stewart			
13 Ark	306		
4 Tenn			
5 Tenn			
33 Tenn			
Stanford's Miss Bat	131	17	
2nd Division	3801		
Brig. Gen. Benjamin F. Cheatham			
1st Brigade			
Brig. Gen. B.R. Johnson (w)			
Blythe's Miss Regt			
2 Tenn			
15 Tenn			
154 Tenn (Sr.)	650		
Polk's Tenn Bat	102	24	
2nd Brigade			
Col. William H. Stephens			
7 Ky			
1 Tenn Batn			
6 Tenn			
9 Tenn			
Smith's Miss Bat	120	14	

Unit	Strength	Losses (Killed/Wounded/Missing)	
Attached	1538		
1 Miss Cav			
Brewer's Cav Batn	200		
II Corps	16,269	3628	(353/2441/634)
Maj. Gen. Braxton Bragg			
1st Division	6484		
Brig. Gen. Daniel Ruggles			
1st Brigade			
Col. R.L. Gibson			
1 Ark			
4 La	575		
13 La			
19 La	300		
2 cos. Ala Cav	109		
2nd Brigade	1634		
Brig. Gen. Patton			
Anderson			
1 Fla Batn	250		
17 La	326		
20 La	507		
9 Tex	226		
Confed. Guards			
Response Batn	169		
Hodgson's La Bat	155		
3rd Brigade			
Col. Preston Pond, Jr.			
16 La	330		
18 La	500		
Crescent La Regt			
Orleans Gd La Batn			
38 Tenn			
Ketchum's Ala Bat			

2nd Division   6482
Brig. Gen. Jones M. Withers

   1st Brigade
   Brig. Gen. A.H. Gladden (k)
   21 Ala
   22 Ala   435
   25 Ala   305
   26 Ala   440
   1 La
   Robertson's Fla Bat

   2nd Brigade   2039
   Brig. Gen. James R.
     Chalmers
   5 Miss
   7 Miss
   9 Miss
   10 Miss   360
   51 Tenn
   52 Tenn   400
   Gage's Ala Bat

   3rd Brigade   2208
   Brig. Gen. John R. Jack-
     son
   17 Ala
   18 Ala   413
   19 Ala
   2 Tex
   Girardey's Ga Bat
   47 Tenn (7 April)   731
   1 Corps Cavalry,
   Clanton's Ala Regt

Unit	Strength	Losses (Killed/Wounded/Missing)	
III Corps	6758	2481	(404/1936/141)
Maj. Gen. William J. Hardee (w)			
1st Brigade	2360		
Brig. Gen. Thomas C.			
Hindman (w)			
2 Ark	600		
6 Ark			
7 Ark			
3 Confed			
Swett's Miss Bat			
Miller's Tenn Bat			
2nd Brigade	2750		
Brig. Gen. Patrick R.			
Cleburne			
15 Ark			
6 Miss	425		
2 Tenn	365		
5 Tenn	369		
23 Tenn	570		
24 Tenn			
Trigg's Ark Bat			
Calvert's Ark Bat			
Hubbard's Ark Bat			
3rd Brigade	2508		
Brig. Gen. Sterling A.M.			
Wood (k)			
16 Ala	300		
8 Ark	280		
9 Ark	140		
3 Miss Batn	280		
27 Tenn	350		
44 Tenn	250		
55 Tenn	280		
Harper's Miss Bat	70		
Ga Dragoons	40		
7 Ala	518		

Reserve Corps	7211	2233	(386/1682/165)
Brig. Gen. John C. Breckinridge			

1st ("Orphan") Brigade 2400
Col. Robert P. Trabue
31 Ala
3 Ky
4 Ky 431
5 Ky
6 Ky
Crew's Tenn Batn
Cobb's Ky Bat
Byrne's Miss Bat
Morgan's Ky Cav

2nd Brigade 1100
Brig. Gen. John G.
 Bowen (w)
9 Ark
10 Ark
2 Confed
1 Mo
Hudson's Miss Bat
Beltzhoover's La Bat
Thompson's Ky Cav

3rd Brigade 3727
Col. Winfield S. Statham
15 Miss
22 Miss
19 Tenn
20 Tenn
28 Tenn
45 Tenn
Rutledge's Tenn Bat
Forrest's Tenn Cav 785

Unassigned Troops 1375
Wharton's Tex Cav Regt
Adams' Miss Regt
McClung's Tenn Bat
Roberts' Ark Bat
Clanton's 1st Ala Cav 670

Index